NAPOLEON AFTER WATERLOO

NAPOLEON AFTER WATERLOO

England and the St. Helena Decision

❧

MICHAEL JOHN THORNTON

1968
Stanford University Press
Stanford, California

STANFORD UNIVERSITY PRESS
Stanford, California
© 1968 by Michael John Thornton
Printed in the United States of America
L.C. 68-26782

To my wife

Preface

AMONG the hundreds of books about Napoleon, none has treated in complete detail the story of his detention on British warships, shortly after the battle of Waterloo, while he awaited his fate at the hands of the British government. The days in July and August of 1815 that he spent on board the *Bellerophon* and the *Northumberland* off the south coast of England are accorded a few summarizing sentences in many books, a paragraph or a page in others, a chapter or two in fewer still; but no book has fully examined them. Captain Frederick Maitland, in his *Narrative of the Surrender of Buonaparte*, recounted at book length the events of Napoleon's stay on board his vessel; but he dealt only with matters pertinent to his role in the affair, a role that was of considerably reduced importance once the *Bellerophon* had reached England. A detailed account of what occurred not only on the *Bellerophon*, but also in the ministries of His Majesty's government has never been related; nor has anyone adequately described the military and civilian personnel who served the ministries, or the English public who were avidly curious about England's most famous prisoner.

This gap in the chronicles of Napoleon's career surprises us for several reasons. First, the incident is unique—one finds no denouement quite like it in accounts of the lives of other great men. Second, the drama of the few days during which Napoleon and the world waited for the announcement of what would be done with him can be felt even today. Finally, Napoleon's surrender to the English, his detention aboard the *Bellerophon*, and the eventual decision of the British government to confine him on St. Helena led to countless debates—few of which have been unbiased—concerning the justice or magnanimity of the British government.

This book relates, as fully as possible, the confrontation between Napoleon and his captors. I have used as my primary sources of information official British government records and correspondence, contemporary newspaper accounts, and the writings of persons who played important parts in the drama: Captain Maitland's *Narrative of the Surrender of Buonaparte*, *The Keith Papers* (ed. Christopher Lloyd), *Correspondence, Despatches, and Other Papers of Viscount Castlereagh* (ed. the Marquess of Londonderry), *Napoleon and His Fellow Travellers* (ed. Clement Shorter), Count Las Cases' *Mémorial de Sainte-Hélène*, and the published memoirs of General Montholon, Count Bertrand, and Dr. O'Meara. I have quoted, at times, extensively from these and other sources with the hope that by letting the writers speak for themselves, I might create a sense of immediacy. Where analysis and interpretation have been unavoidable, I have sought to make them impartial.

For convenience I have cited French documents from published translations; some of them are not of the highest quality. In quoting from these translations I have occasionally come across peculiarities of wording, orthography, and the like that, if perpetuated, would serve only to distract the reader. In such cases, rather than burdening the text with ellipses, brackets, *sic*, and other apparatus, I have simply made a silent correction: for example, in a passage on page 15 that in the original reads "The success of our negotiations depends principally upon the certitude with which the Allied Powers wish to have of his embarkation," I have deleted "with." I have made no change more momentous than this, none that could possibly affect content or interpretation, and none where the oddity could not, in my opinion, lead a reader astray. Quotations from English sources have for the most part been reproduced exactly; I have not corrected or modernized punctuation, grammar, capitalization, or spelling. A very few errors in spelling that might seem to be errors in transcription or typesetting have been silently corrected.

Transcripts of Crown-copyright records in the Public Record Office appear by permission of the Controller of H.M. Stationery Office.

I wish to express my gratitude to the Marquess of Lansdowne and Constable Publishers for permission to quote from the Earl of Kerry's *The First Napoleon*; to the Marquess of Lansdowne and The Council of the Navy Records Society, London, for permission to quote from *The Keith Papers*, Volume III; and to Mr. H. W. Woollcombe and Mr. J. Stevens for permission to quote from Mr. Stevens's *A Summary Account of the Journals of Henry Woollcombe*.

I also wish to express my appreciation of the courtesies shown me by the following publishers in granting permission to quote from the books indicated: Hutchinson Publishing Group, *Napoleon in Exile*, by Norwood Young; J. B. Lippincott Company, *St. Helena* and *Napoleon: Soldier and Emperor* by Octave Aubry; Harper & Row, *Napoleon from the Tuileries to St. Helena* by Louis Etienne St. Denis; and Charles Scribner's Sons, *Famous Women of the French Court: Marie Louise* by Imbert de Saint-Amand.

The staffs of the British Museum Manuscript Department and Newspaper Library were most helpful. My warm thanks go to the staff of the Belmont Branch of the San Mateo County Library for their unstinting help in obtaining necessary and hard-to-locate books for me over a period of several years. Above all, I affectionately acknowledge the deep debt of gratitude that I owe to my wife, whose contributions as critic of and commentator on the manuscript of this book proved both indispensable and inspiring to me.

M. J. T.

Contents

NAPOLEON AFTER WATERLOO

No man who has won universal fame has had an end equal to that of Napoleon. He cannot be called, as he was after his first downfall, the autocrat of certain iron and marble quarries, of which these might furnish him a statue and those a sword. An eagle, they gave him a rock, on whose point he stood, sunbeaten, until his death, and from whence he was seen by all the earth.

—CHATEAUBRIAND

Prologue

SHORTLY before eight o'clock on the evening of July 23, 1815, the 74-gun English frigate H.M.S. *Bellerophon* sailed steadily before moderate breezes on an east-northeast course that would see her into Tor Bay early the next morning. She had made her landfall an hour earlier, raising the high land of Dartmoor off her larboard bow; and for some time now two men had been standing on the quarterdeck looking at the land. One, an angular six-footer wearing the uniform of a captain in the British navy, was Frederick Maitland, the *Bellerophon*'s commanding officer. The other, reaching only to Maitland's shoulder and clad in a flannel dressing gown over which he had thrown a greatcoat, was Napoleon Bonaparte.

As Napoleon studied the high contours of Devonshire through his field glass, he may well have mused on the irony of his thus approaching England. Twelve years before, he had planned an arrival far different from this one. Then, the military master of Europe, he had poised an army of 100,000 men and a flotilla of over 1,500 barges at Boulogne, Dunkirk, and Calais, awaiting a propitious time to mount a cross-Channel invasion. He had not doubted his success once he and his armies gained a foothold on England's beaches. One major battle, he had calculated, would have delivered London—and so the country—into his hands, and eradicated the threats that England's stubborn enmity posed to his ambitions. He had envisioned the mass of Englishmen as welcoming his contemplated remolding of the nation's political structure. But fate had never allowed him to test his calculations. At Trafalgar, the English navy had smashed his fleet and ended his plan for invasion and conquest.

The intervening years had seen him forge an empire and lose it, make kings and break them, win and lose great battles, and be exiled to Elba, only to return in triumph. Barely over a month earlier, he had mustered more than 135,000 soldiers in a supreme effort to hold the throne of France. Now—defeated in battle, his political life ended, little more than a fugitive, and heading a meager retinue of fifty persons—he sought asylum in England.

What circumstances had brought him to this moment off the coast of Devon?

I

Prelude to a Passage

THE Hundred Days were ending, their climax the three-day crescendo of artillery and musketry fire at Quatrebras, Ligny, and finally Waterloo. At Waterloo, on June 18, Napoleon had seen his army shattered as it drove time and again against the unyielding squares of the British—had witnessed even the Old Guard reeling in panic retreat from the infantry its charge had been unable to break.

"All is lost." Napoleon's words acknowledged what his career had demonstrated: the dynasty he had hoped to found could not survive a military disaster. For all his ability, he had never been successful in achieving a satisfactory political rapprochement with the Continental powers. To them he had remained always an adventurer, an upstart whose presence in Europe constituted a mortal threat to what they held that God and a thousand years of history had decreed as the ideal political condition under which men should live. Inexorable in their enmity, they had rejected him and fought him. For years his genius in handling armies and artillery had held them at bay or driven them back, but even that skill had not proved sufficient in 1814. He had learned then the political disasters that followed military defeat. And, as he hastened from Waterloo toward Paris, he could harbor few illusions concerning the political results of this catastrophic debacle.

Waterloo marked the setting of Napoleon's star—marked, also, the loss of something fundamental in him. The Napoleon who sped back toward the capital he had left just over a week before would never again be the Napoleon whose paramount characteristic was to *act*, to initiate the events that moved men and nations. Henceforth, he would only react to what others did, and at times so tardily that his response would prove ineffective.

This new lassitude displayed itself from the time he reached the Elysée Palace early in the evening of June 20. Desperate though his situation was, time remained for him to attempt to muster sufficient military and political support to confront the Allies and perhaps gain a respectable bargaining position. Instead of making such an attempt, however, he let the opportunity be snatched from him by men who were bent on dissociating themselves from him and his cause.

He found the Chambers overtly hostile to him. Panicked by the news of Waterloo, despairing of victory over the Allies, they sought a peace whose conditions would not be prohibitively harsh in terms of France's future—and their own. But peace, they knew, would not be possible so long as Napoleon led the nation. The Allied Powers had declared war expressly against him and would continue the conflict until they had disposed of him. And by this time most members of the Chambers were only too willing to be rid of him. Since his resumption of power and the promulgation of the Additional Act to the Constitution, many of them had distrusted and feared his motives. Others, whose sympathies lay with the Royalists, hated him. Still others, like his Minister of Police, Joseph Fouché, had served him solely to further their own ends; they were ready to desert him now with as few qualms as they had displayed when deserting Louis XVIII in March. In the Chamber of Deputies, voices rose to assert that Napoleon's abdication was the sine qua non of the country's quest for peace.

In answer to such formidable opposition, Napoleon's most practical course would have been to dissolve the Chambers, assume dictatorial powers, and declare martial law throughout France. With his will once more supreme, he might regroup his armies and repel or stall the Allied invasion. His brother Lucien strongly advised this course; but although Napoleon approved the plan, he did not act on it. To face the Chambers and forcibly take all their powers into his own hands was a step he could not bring himself to take. "I lacked courage," he said later; "I am only a man, after all. My memories of the Nineteenth Brumaire terrified me."

Even then, as it happened, it would have been too late for him. At a Cabinet meeting at the Elysée on the morning of June 21, the discussions were interrupted by the arrival of a message informing Napoleon and his ministers that the Chamber of Deputies had just passed resolutions proclaiming the state to be in danger and declaring itself to be in permanent session, with any attempt to dissolve it a crime of high treason. To move now could precipitate a civil war.

Napoleon did not act. Nor did he do anything when, later in the day, the Chamber boldly voted to itself his prerogative of negotiating directly with the Allies. Hesitant and apathetic, he watched everything he had seized on his return from Elba plucked from his slack fingers. Muttered recriminations against the Chambers, doleful political prognostications for France, were all that he offered in retaliation. The cries calling for his abdication increased; and indeed, by this time, he appeared resigned to the necessity of abdicating. "The smoke of Mont-Saint-Jean has gone to his head," lamented Lucien. "He is a ruined man."

The end came early on the morning of June 22. The Chambers sent a delegation to the Elysée to inform Napoleon that if he did not abdicate, they would depose him. Fatalistically, he acceded to their demand and dictated a declaration, not to the Chambers, but to "the French people": "In opening war to support national independence, I counted on a union of all efforts and all wills. Circumstances seem to me to have changed. I offer myself in sacrifice to the hatred of the enemies of France. May they prove sincere in their declaration that they aim at my person only. . . . My political life is over and I proclaim my son, under the title of Napoleon II, Emperor of the French."

Circumstances had indeed changed. The preceding two days had

demonstrated how superficial and ephemeral the union of efforts
and wills had been. But the most notable change had been that in
Napoleon. In earlier days what had mattered primarily was not
the desires and debates of ministers or assemblies, but his will and
efforts. In this crisis, both of the latter had been displayed in-
significantly as well as ineffectively: he had carried Waterloo with
him to Paris.

A delegation from the Chamber of Deputies called on Napoleon to express gratitude for what they termed his personal sacrifice in the interests of the nation. But they made it clear that the
Chamber had no intention of heeding his proclamation concerning his son. Instead of establishing a regency, the Chamber appointed five Directors to form a provisional government, with
Fouché its president.

Fouché's first order of business was to get Napoleon out of
Paris; his remaining in the city could constitute a potential danger to the provisional government. During the past two days
crowds had gathered round the Elysée, cheering Napoleon, calling on him to save France, and denouncing the Chambers as
traitors. The regular soldiery in the capital were also stirring
restlessly, moved by General Charles de Labédoyère's invectives
in the Chamber of Deputies against those who refused to recognize Napoleon II. On June 24, an obscure deputy named
Duchesne demanded in the Chamber that, in the name of the
country, Napoleon be invited to quit Paris, where his continued
presence could lead only to trouble and public danger. The Chamber so voted; and Louis Davout, the Minister of War, brought
its request to Napoleon.

Napoleon agreed to leave. But where would he seek refuge?
His stepdaughter Hortense, who had hurried to his side on
learning of his arrival in Paris, urged him to decide on a destination. Why not write to Emperor Alexander of Russia? He and
Alexander had once been friends, and the Russian was noted for
his generosity. Or Napoleon might request asylum from his father-in-law, the Emperor Francis of Austria.

Napoleon rejected both suggestions. He would never write to Francis: "I have too much to complain about for his having kept my wife and child from me." As for Alexander, he was like other men, not to be trusted. In addition, Napoleon said, he did not wish to give himself up to a single man. It would be preferable to address himself to a people—to England, say. Hortense was appalled. The English! "It would be giving them too much glory," she protested. "They would shut you up in the Tower of London."

Another possibility remained—the United States, with which his relations had always been amicable. There he would be granted land, or he could purchase an estate and till it, living on the produce of his fields and his herds. There he could live with dignity and, though an ocean removed from Europe, perhaps still cause his enemies to tremble. To America, therefore, he would go. He requested that the provisional government issue him passports to the United States and place at his disposal the frigates *Saale* and *Méduse*, which were in harbor at Rochefort. Denis Decrès, the Minister of Marine, promised to attend promptly to these requests.

Thus, about noon on June 25, Napoleon, accompanied by the Grand Marshal of the Palace, Henri-Gratien Bertrand, left the Elysée, slipped through a garden gate and into an inconspicuous carriage in the Champs-Elysées, and began the nine-mile trip to Hortense's villa at Malmaison. The carriage rattled along the hot streets, came at length to the edge of Paris, and left behind the city whose history Napoleon had done so much to shape. Few in the capital knew that he was departing. He left almost as meekly as had Louis XVIII three months before. But, unlike Louis, he would never again enter Paris alive.

Napoleon erred if he thought that the pressures on him would ease once he was out of Paris. That same evening Lieutenant-General Nicolas Beker arrived at Malmaison at the head of a 340-man military contingent assigned by the provisional government nominally to serve as Napoleon's bodyguard, but actually to keep him under surveillance—an embarrassing duty for Beker, who

had long been loyal to Napoleon. So long as Napoleon remained
in France, Fouché and his associates would rest uneasy, suspicious
of his movements and his motives. Add to this that some members of the government had no real intention of abetting Napoleon's flight to the United States. Indeed, Fouché had applied
to the Duke of Wellington for Napoleon's passports, thereby
alerting the British to his intentions. If, while escaping the onus
of having betrayed Napoleon to the enemy, Fouché and his fellows could place impediments in the way of his departure and
so assure his falling into Allied hands, their political future in the
new France would rest on a firmer foundation.

While at Malmaison, Napoleon received a steady stream of
visitors: his brothers Joseph and Jérôme, his mother, the banker
Jacques Laffitte, loyal members of the Chambers, and numerous
army officers. But no one brought the passports he had requested.
Anxious, he sent General Beker to Paris to inquire about them
and about the availability of the frigates.

The orders that Beker received from the government did not
prove reassuring. True, the frigates were now to be considered at
Napoleon's disposal; but they were forbidden to sail from Rochefort before the passports requested from Wellington arrived.
Thus Napoleon's fate depended on the British. In the circumstances, Napoleon declined to leave Malmaison. "On my arrival
at Rochefort," he stated, "I should consider myself in the position of a prisoner, my departure for America being dependent
upon the arrival of passports which will doubtless be refused. I
am determined to await my arrest here."

Meanwhile, the reports reaching him grew more alarming.
Wellington and General Blücher were marching on Paris, Blücher in the van. The Prussian, rumors said, had received intelligence that Napoleon was at Malmaison and had ordered a
regiment of hussars and two battalions of infantry to seize him
there. Napoleon knew that, once in the hands of the implacable
Blücher, he might well face a firing squad. Escape by sea, therefore, beckoned even more imperatively. On June 28 he posted his

aide-de-camp, General Flahaut, to Paris to inform the government that he refused to leave Malmaison unless the restriction
delaying the departure of the frigates was lifted immediately. A
fiery scene ensued between the young general and Davout—but
the restriction remained in force.

At Malmaison, the inhabitants of the villa could distinctly
hear cannon fire from the direction of Gonesse. Napoleon, among
whose visitors that day had been Baron Jean Corvisart, his favorite doctor, handed his valet, Louis Marchand, a small vial containing a reddish liquid. "See that I have that with me," he said,
"either in my coat or in some other part of my clothing, in such a
place that I can get it quickly." If the Prussians did succeed in cutting him off, they would not take him alive.

Then came the news Napoleon was awaiting. At dawn on June
29, Decrès arrived at Malmaison and announced that the government had lifted its restriction on the sailing of the frigates.
Napoleon was free to proceed without delay to the United States.
He told Decrès he would set out for Rochefort that day. But
neither Decrès nor Napoleon knew how problematical a speedy
and safe departure from France had now become. Fouché, who
was being pressed by the Chamber of Peers to hasten arrangements for Napoleon's escape, had received word from the maritime prefect at Rochefort that English cruisers were blockading
the straits, making escape by sea nearly impossible. Once in Rochefort, Napoleon would be forced to choose between surrender to
the English, arrest by the Bourbons, and capture by the Prussians.
Fouché could well afford to appear generous; for no matter what
happened now, not even barring the unlikely event of Napoleon's escape, he and his fellow Directors could present themselves both to the Allies and to the French people as above re-
proach.

But now, on the threshold of his final departure, Napoleon
manifested a sudden surge of energy. Scanning his maps that
morning, he noted the gap that had grown between Wellington's
and Blücher's armies as they marched on Paris. Here was an

opportunity for a man with the troops and the daring to grasp it. Forces, Napoleon knew, did exist: Marshal Grouchy and General Vandamme had just reached Paris with a considerable body of troops. As for the daring—he straightened up, his eyes shining. "France must not submit to a handful of Prussians!" he exclaimed. "I can still crush the enemy and give the government the opportunity to negotiate with the Allies."

Summoning Beker, he sent him to Paris with an offer to the provisional government. He stood ready, Napoleon stated, to take command of the army—and as a general only. His presence at the head of the troops would again mold them into a formidable force. When he had repulsed the enemy, he would at once relinquish his command and sail for America. He was so certain his offer would be accepted that, while awaiting Beker's return, he donned the uniform of a colonel of the Chasseurs of the Guard, pulled on riding boots, belted on a sword, and ordered his horses saddled and all made ready for his return to the army. But when Beker returned that afternoon, he was somber-faced. The provisional government, he reported, had categorically rejected Napoleon's offer. Furthermore, it had stated that Napoleon would be well advised to leave immediately for Rochefort. If he remained at Malmaison, he ran the risk of being captured by the Prussians.

After a moment of bitterness, Napoleon quietly gave orders for his departure and changed into civilian clothes. When all was ready, he bade farewell to those he was leaving behind—his brother Joseph, Cardinal Fesch, the tragedian Talma, Hortense, and, last of all, his mother. At five in the afternoon, he left Malmaison in a coach-and-four, accompanied by Beker, Bertrand, and General René Savary. The remainder of his suite followed shortly thereafter—48 persons in all, including his aides-de-camp Generals Lallemand and Montholon, General Gourgaud, the Count de Las Cases and his young son, the wives and children of Bertrand and Montholon, and assorted officers and servants.

The men inside the carriage rode without speaking, more than the oppressive heat weighing upon their minds. They reached Rambouillet after dark, spent the night in the castle there, delayed departure until nearly noon of the next day, and then resumed their journey, speeding southwestward toward the coast. Through Châteaudun, Vendôme, Tours, and Poitiers they rolled, pausing only to change horses or to dine. Finally, after nearly 36 hours of constant traveling, they entered Niort at ten o'clock on the night of July 1. There they dismounted and slept at an inn.

Word of Napoleon's arrival spread quickly, and next morning the prefect of the department called on Napoleon and invited him to stay at the prefecture. While he was there, his brother Joseph visited him and revealed that he was bound for Bordeaux, from whence he expected to sail to the United States. Later in the day, a delegation of officers from two regiments of hussars stationed in the city presented themselves and urged him to lead their troops to join the army of the Loire. Although touched by their loyalty, Napoleon declined: to accept their proposal, he told them, would lead to civil war, and he wanted no blood spilled that way.

At this point a letter from Captain Bonnefux, the maritime prefect of Rochefort, informed Napoleon of the English ships blockading the coast. Clearly, unless the passports that he had requested were forthcoming, he would have to run a gauntlet of guns to reach the open waters of the Atlantic—a perilous venture, to judge from past engagements between French and English men-of-war. To remain in France, however, presented an even darker prospect. The provisional government, Napoleon knew, would not scruple to use him as a pawn in its dealings with the Allied Powers and the Bourbons; and neither side could be expected to treat him well.

At his bidding, Beker addressed a letter to the provisional government, asking it to grant Napoleon permission to communicate with the commander of the English squadron "if extraordinary events should make that course necessary, both for the personal safety of His Majesty and to spare France the sorrow and the

shame of seeing him taken from his last refuge, to be delivered
to the mercies of his enemies. If in this situation the English
cruiser prevents the frigates from leaving, you may dispose of
the services of the Emperor as a General having no other thought
than to be of service to his country." It seems likely that Napoleon's renewed offer to head the army was made less in the hope
that the government might reverse its refusal of his first proposal than in the hope of worrying it into greater cooperation
with his plans for escape.

Little remained but to push on to Rochefort. Napoleon left
Niort at dawn on July 2 and arrived in Rochefort early the same
morning. As he stepped out of the carriage, an enthusiastic crowd
welcomed him. Rochefort, situated about halfway down the west
coast of France on the Charente River, had enjoyed better days.
The naval school that had been established there had since been
moved; and the city's fleet, which had served the republic well,
had shrunk to a fraction of its former size. In 1809, the destruction
of a French fleet by the English in the roadstead of the Ile d'Aix
had ended the city's era of prosperity.

Now, Rochefort again turned its attention seaward, where English vessels patrolled the Basque Roads, keeping vigilant watch
on the channels and on the French frigates *Saale* and *Méduse,*
which were anchored a few miles offshore in the Aix Roads.
Would the guns of French and English ships of war clash once
more in the roadstead? Or would Napoleon, who had evaded
English ships when returning to France from both Egypt and
Elba, be able to do so a third time?

A chart of the Basque Roads reveals that at this juncture Napoleon's chances of success were not negligible. The French frigates
lay just south of the small Ile d'Aix, about six miles out from the
mouth of the Charente. Once on board one of them, Napoleon
could elect one of three exits to the sea. The first was a northwest
route through the Pertuis Breton, which separates the mainland
from the long, narrow Ile de Ré that parallels it. The second
was a dash straight west through the Pertuis d'Antioche, which

runs between the Ile de Ré and its longer, broader neighbor to the southeast, the Ile d'Oléron. The third was a risky passage southward through the shoal water between the east coast of the Ile d'Oléron and the mainland, down to a point opposite the mouth of the Seudre River, and from thence westward through the Pertuis de Maumusson.

The *Saale* and the *Méduse* had already taken stores and powder on board and were ready to put to sea. They had only two English ships opposing them: the brig *Myrmidon* and the *Bellerophon*, an old, slow 74-gun frigate. The *Saale*, by contrast, was one of the newest and fastest ships in the French navy. Now, if ever, was the time for Napoleon to be away, before additional English vessels arrived to seal off all the escape routes.

Napoleon, however, procrastinated, a fact that his devotees have lamented ever since. On the day of his arrival in Rochefort, he met with naval and military officers to discuss the possibility of sailing without being challenged by the English. Their decision was unanimous: if he sailed, the English ships would beyond question move to intercept him. And British naval gunnery was so formidable that, even granting a successful breakthrough to the Atlantic, it would exact a toll in blood and lives. It would not be improper for Napoleon to ask that the officers and men of his suite brave the hazards of such an attempt, but what of the others who would be accompanying him? Broadsides—perhaps even boarding parties—were no respecters of persons. Who could guarantee that the women, children, and servants would remain unscathed?

Napoleon could have suggested that the married men in the party leave their wives and children behind for the present, to be sent for later if they reached the United States safely. One can credit him, however, with feeling his own separation from his wife and son sharply enough to make him reluctant to ask such a sacrifice of others. Besides, what surety could he give these men that France and the Allied Powers would consent to their families' rejoining them? He chose, therefore, to wait and hope for the arrival of the passports. Once he had them in hand, the threat from the English ships would vanish.

Three days passed: still no word from Paris on the passports, no reply to Beker's letter of July 2. The *Saale* and the *Méduse* rode at short anchor in the Aix Roads, ready to weigh the moment Napoleon came on board. To the west, within short sailing distance, the *Bellerophon* and the *Myrmidon* continued their vigil. At any hour the sails of other English ships of war might appear on the horizon.

Other possibilities of slipping through the blockade were raised during these days. Captain Besson, a Frenchman commanding the Danish sloop *Magdaline*, offered his vessel to Napoleon. The English, with their attention focused on the French frigates, might allow the sloop to pass; in the event they should halt and search her, Napoleon could be concealed in a cask stowed in the ballast, with special tubes constructed for him to breathe through. Napoleon showed little taste for this plan. If the sloop were stopped and detained for a day or two, he would perforce have to reveal himself and so not only fall prisoner to the English but also forfeit any claim to preferential treatment. In addition, he considered such a means of escape unworthy of a man who had been Emperor. When he left, he would go not like a fugitive, but openly and in company with his suite.

If worse came to worst, he could give himself up voluntarily to the English, trusting to their well-known hospitality. England had in the past opened her doors to others harried by fortune— ex-King Theodore of Corsica, Napoleon's boyhood idol General Pasquale Paoli, and even Napoleon's brother Lucien. Napoleon himself had previously toyed with the idea of residence in England. During the negotiations at Fontainebleau the previous year, Lord Castlereagh, England's foreign minister, had communicated such a suggestion to him through the Duke of Vicenza. If Napoleon were to go to England rather than to Elba, Castlereagh had said, he would be received there with the greatest consideration and would experience a treatment infinitely preferable to exile in the Mediterranean. Let him but retire to England without conditions or negotiations, and he would find that English honor was more to be trusted than any treaty he could negotiate. While at Elba, Napoleon had often mentioned this suggestion.

For the present, however, he would consider other possibilities of escape. He could join Joseph at Bordeaux and sail with him for America. He could go to Royan at the mouth of the Gironde and there embark on the French ship *Bayadère,* whose commander, Lieutenant Commander Baudin, was his staunch adherent. He acted on neither of these alternatives, however. A certain apathy, Beker noted, had again possessed him, and decisive action seemed beyond his concern. He sat stoically, unmoved by the sense of urgency revealed in the faces of those around him, waiting for the next blows to fall.

They were not long in coming. On July 7 H.M.S. *Slaney* sailed in to join the two English ships already on station. And that evening Beker received a dispatch from Paris, signed by all five members of the provisional government. "Napoleon must embark without delay," they wrote. "The success of our negotiations depends principally upon the certitude which the Allied Powers wish to have of his embarkation, and you do not know to what extent the safety and tranquillity of the State are imperilled by these delays." They rejected again Napoleon's offer of military service, and they concluded by saying that "the Commission sees some inconvenience in Napoleon's communicating with the English squadron. It cannot accord the desired permission on that head." Not a word referred to the passports that Napoleon had requested.

So much for any hopes he might have retained of cooperation from the provisional government. So much for any illusions he might have nursed about the freedom of choice and movement yet left him. To board the *Saale* or the *Méduse* but not to sail, to refrain from communicating with the English squadron, to wait— what were these instructions but the prelude to his being delivered as prisoner either to the Bourbons or to the Allies? He could, of course, ignore the directives of the government; but doing so would place him in direct conflict with Beker, and he did not wish to force such a situation on the general.

Napoleon did not attempt to evade or delay the embarkation called for by the provisional government. The next afternoon he and his suite boarded small boats at Fouras Point and were rowed out to the French frigates. Napoleon boarded the *Saale*, from whose deck he may have watched the *Slaney* weigh and sail off out of sight to the south. The departure of the English ship could have given him no great sense of respite, since her presence in the Basque Roads would hardly have been required had the British government intended to grant the passports he desired. Still, she had gone, thus reducing the risks of his making a dash for the sea. At a word from him, the attempt would begin. But Napoleon let the opportunity pass. On the following day, a Sunday, he left the *Saale* to visit the Ile d'Aix, where he spent hours inspecting the fortifications, meeting the officers in charge of the island's defense works, and reviewing a regiment of marines. The interlude was a pleasant one; everywhere, enthusiastic crowds of islanders acclaimed him.

When he returned to the *Saale* that evening, ominous news greeted him. Bonnefux had come on board, bearing fresh orders from Paris. The government, he informed Napoleon, insisted that he and his suite sail at once. Failing that, they might board one of the British ships if they so desired. But on no account was Napoleon to set foot anywhere on French soil again. If the commander of the vessel he was on violated this order, he would be guilty of high treason.

Napoleon could defer a decision no longer. And, choose as he might, his position would remain perilous. If he sailed, he would have to fight his way to the open sea. If he waited (assuming that he could prevail upon Bonnefux, Beker, and Captain Philibert of the *Saale* to disregard their orders), the arrival of additional English ships would preclude all reasonable hope of escape by sea. Waiting would also increase another growing danger—that of arrest by the Bourbons or the Allies. If he should abandon the idea of escaping by ship and try to return to the mainland contrary to the wishes of Bonnefux, Beker, and Philibert, he would have to force his way ashore, a course he was ill-equipped to undertake and would in any event be unlikely to benefit from. City after city in the area was replacing the tricolor with the white flag of the Bourbons; and once on the mainland again, he would be in imminent danger of capture by Bourbon adherents. Nor could he now expect to reach another port farther down the coast in time to sail before Royalists had alerted the English to his movements.

He had another alternative: to board one of the English ships, place himself in British custody, and ask for asylum in England. Such a move would have uncertain results, but it would be clearly preferable to falling into Bourbon or Prussian or Austrian hands. This last fate he would never suffer; the vial of poison he carried on his person would guarantee that.

After a conference with Beker and Bertrand, Napoleon decided to send the Count de Las Cases and General Savary to the *Bellerophon* to sound out Britain's intentions at first hand. He did not select these emissaries haphazardly. Savary would greet Captain Maitland of the *Bellerophon* as no stranger, having met and conversed often with him years before in the Middle East at the Convention of El Arish. Las Cases understood English well, having lived in England for ten years as an émigré. By pretending ignorance of the language, he might glean valuable information from the unguarded conversations of the ship's officers.

At daybreak, then, on July 10, the two men set out for the *Bellerophon* on board the schooner *Mouche*. They bore a letter signed by Bertrand but actually dictated by Napoleon, addressed to the admiral commanding the British cruisers before the port of Rochefort:

9 July, 1815

Sir,

The Emperor Napoleon having abdicated the throne of France, and chosen the United States of America as a retreat, is, with his suite, at present embarked on board the two frigates which are in this port, for the purpose of proceeding to his destination. He expects a passport from the British Government, which has been promised to him, and which induces me to send the present flag of truce, to demand of you, Sir, if you have any knowledge of the above-mentioned passport, or if you think it is the intention of the British Government to throw any impediment in the way of our voyage to the United States. I shall feel much obliged by your giving me any information you may possess on the subject.

I have directed the bearers of the letter to present to you my thanks, and to apologize for the trouble it may cause.

The letter appears straightforward if one overlooks the statement "He expects a passport from the British Government, *which has been promised to him.*" When Napoleon had first requested his passports, Decrès had promised that he would apply for them immediately. But at no time did Napoleon receive a promise from anyone—least of all from the British government—that the passports would be granted him. The phrase, therefore, seems intended to deceive the commander of the British squadron—in which case Napoleon might better have omitted the subsequent "or if you think it is the intention of the British Government to throw any impediment in the way of our voyage to the United States," a statement that is hard to reconcile with the previous assertion.

As the *Mouche* neared the *Bellerophon*, which was patrolling in the Pertuis d'Antioche about two or three miles off the Ile d'Oléron, the schooner hoisted a flag of truce; and shortly after seven o'clock Savary and Las Cases boarded the English frigate. On deck to receive them they found her commander, Captain Frederick Maitland, who from that day on would have his name linked with Napoleon's.

Tall and thin, with deep-set eyes and a shock of unruly hair, Maitland had followed in his father's footsteps by going to sea in His Majesty's service at an early age. Despite his years aboard English men-of-war in many waters—the Mediterranean, the Atlantic off the French and Spanish coasts, and the Halifax and West India stations—he had not lost the strong Scottish burr in his speech. Now, at 38, he was a prime specimen of the British naval officer—brave, intelligent, efficient, selflessly committed to his duties. In addition, he possessed two qualities that many naval officers of his time seldom if ever displayed—consideration for subordinates and compassion for the unfortunate.*

The *Bellerophon* had been off Rochefort since May 31, having been ordered there by Rear Admiral Sir Henry Hotham to prevent a French corvette from putting to sea and to report on the number and strength of the French ships lying in the roadstead. Throughout most of June Maitland had kept the corvette, plus a brig and the frigates *Saale* and *Méduse*, from sailing, and had detained and sunk or sent to Hotham several other French vessels. On June 28 the crew of a captured French vessel gave him the news of Waterloo; and on June 30 a boat from Bordeaux brought him a letter asserting that Napoleon had fled from Paris and was en route to Bordeaux to escape. Maitland responded by sending the *Myrmidon* to Bordeaux and the *Cephalus* farther down the coast to Arcachon. He himself remained off Rochefort, considering it the port Napoleon would be most likely to choose.

His opinion was confirmed on July 1, when a ship from Rochefort brought information that the *Saale* and the *Méduse* were ready to sail and that a number of ladies and gentlemen believed to form part of Napoleon's suite had arrived at the Ile d'Aix. Maitland increased his vigilance, bringing the *Bellerophon* in to anchor as close to the French squadron as the batteries on the Ile d'Aix permitted, keeping guard boats rowing throughout the night, drilling the sailors and marines of the ship's company to meet any contingencies that might arise, and immediately recalling the *Myrmidon*.

But despite these precautions and the added presence of the *Slaney* in the area, Maitland was a worried man when Savary and

---

* Maitland's account of the rescue of two youths who had been adrift for 36 hours in a punt off Rochefort reads: "I kept the boys on board two or three days, for the purpose of recruiting their strength, and then landed them with the punt, close to their village, to the great joy and wonder of their parents and countrymen."

Las Cases boarded his ship on July 10. Three days earlier, orders from Admiral Hotham had directed him to prevent Napoleon from escaping in the French frigates; however, in an accompanying letter Hotham had confessed that he had no frigate available in the Baie de Quiberon to send to reinforce Maitland. And in another letter on July 8 the admiral had stated that he still had no frigate to send. Thus, if the *Saale* and the *Méduse* separated when running for the sea, Maitland could hardly hope to stop them both. Taking one, he might discover that Napoleon was on the other—and by then that other might have smashed its way past the smaller, lightly armed *Myrmidon*. Hotham might enjoin an increased vigilance, but he knew as well as Maitland that vigilance alone could not substitute for increased forces.

Hotham's letter of the 8th, however, contained information that proved invaluable to Maitland, namely that the British government had received and rejected an application for a passport for Napoleon. Hotham also conjectured that Napoleon would await the British government's answer before embarking. On July 10, then, Maitland knew that no passport would be forthcoming, and he learned from Bertrand's letter that Napoleon had not yet been so informed. This knowledge, plus the request for Maitland's opinion of the British government's intentions toward Napoleon, raised Maitland's hopes. As Hotham had surmised, the Frenchmen evidently did not contemplate embarking until word on the passports arrived. If Maitland could induce them to remain in Rochefort, he might yet gain the reinforcements he so urgently needed to prevent Napoleon's flight.

In his talk with Savary and Las Cases in the *Bellerophon*'s after-cabin, Maitland played for time. The emissaries asked if he would permit the French frigates to sail. Maitland replied that since France and England were at war with each other, he naturally could not. Would he object, then, to Napoleon's sailing in a neutral vessel? Maitland stated that he would have to refer the question to his commanding officer; pending the arrival of an answer, he would be obliged to halt any vessel, no matter what its flag might be, that carried a person of such consequence. He assured Savary and Las Cases that he would immediately forward Bertrand's letter, together with a report of the emissaries' visit to the *Bellerophon*, to Hotham. They might expect the admiral's answer in a few days.

While the three were talking, they were joined by Captain Knight of H.M.S. *Falmouth*, which had just come up. Knight brought Maitland a letter and secret orders from Hotham, plus several recent French newspapers. The letter summarized the newspapers' accounts of French plans for Napoleon's escape, urged Maitland to do the utmost to intercept him, and again expressed regret that no frigate could be dispatched to the Basque Roads. The secret orders had been communicated to Hotham from the Admiralty, via the commander of the Channel Fleet, Admiral Lord Keith. They informed Maitland that he was

required and directed . . . to keep the most vigilant look-out for the purpose of intercepting him [Napoleon]; and to make the strictest search of any vessel you may fall in with; and if you should be so fortunate as to intercept him, you are to transfer him and his family to the ship you command, and there keeping him in careful custody, return to the nearest port in England (going into Torbay in preference to Plymouth) with all possible expedition; and on your arrival you are not to permit any communication whatever with the shore, except as herein after directed; and you will be held responsible for keeping the whole transaction a profound secret, until you receive their Lordships' further orders.

Maitland said nothing about the contents of the letter and the orders to Savary and Las Cases. While the two stood by, he sat down and penned his reply to Bertrand's letter:

> H.M.S. *Bellerophon*,
> off Rochefort, July 10th, 1815
>
> SIR,
> I have to acknowledge the receipt of your letter of yesterday's date, addressed to the Admiral commanding the English cruisers before Rochefort, acquainting me that the Emperor, having abdicated the

throne of France, and chosen the United States of America as an asylum, is now embarked on board the frigates, to proceed for that destination, and awaits a passport from the English Government; and requesting to know if I have any knowledge of such passport; or if I think it is the intention of the English Government to prevent the Emperor's voyage.

In reply, I have to acquaint you, that I cannot say what the intentions of my Government may be; but, the two countries being at present in a state of war, it is impossible for me to permit any ship of war to put to sea from the port of Rochefort.

As to the proposal made by the Duc de Rovigo [Savary] and Count Las Cases, of allowing the Emperor to proceed in a merchant vessel; it is out of my power,—without the sanction of my commanding officer, Sir Henry Hotham, who is at present in Quiberon Bay, and to whom I have forwarded your despatch,—to allow any vessel, under whatever flag she may be, to pass with a personage of such consequence.

As he later confessed, Maitland wrote this letter in the hope that it might induce Napoleon to remain in Rochefort until Hotham had been heard from, thus giving the English time to strengthen the blockade. The letter was well calculated to achieve this purpose. Maitland did not lie about the passport, as some have accused him of doing. He simply did not mention it. Let the Frenchmen assume, if they would, that he had no knowledge of it. Further, his statement that "I cannot say what the intentions of my Government may be" is, in its way, a masterpiece of Delphic phrasing. If the Frenchmen interpreted the words as indicating Maitland's ignorance of Britain's intentions, rather than his having been forbidden to mention them, that also was their mistake.*

Savary and Las Cases tarried on the *Bellerophon* between two and three hours, waiting for the turn of the tide that would facilitate their return to the *Saale*. They spent most of this time

---

* Some writers have assailed Maitland's veracity and have both excoriated and exaggerated his cunning in this situation. The ambiguous wording of his letter aside, however, he hardly deserves to be criticized for not divulging his secret orders to men who were still officially his country's enemies.

attempting to persuade Maitland that Napoleon's situation in France was not desperate. The Emperor, they said, was moved primarily by motives of humanity in his decision to quit Europe; he was unwilling to see further bloodshed on his account. They stated that his party was still strong in central and southern France, so that if he chose to prolong the war he could still cause a great deal of trouble. Though it was improbable that he could ultimately succeed against the Allied Powers, it was nevertheless possible that fortune would favor him one more time; and therefore it would be in the interest of England to permit him to proceed to America.

Maitland was not deceived by their protestations. The presence of the two men on his ship, plus Bertrand's letter on the table, had convinced him that Napoleon was anything but confident about his present situation. In response he dangled the lure of the hoped-for passport before his visitors. "Supposing that the British Government should be induced to grant a passport for Bonaparte's going to America," he asked, "what pledge could he give that he would not return to put England, as well as all Europe, to the same expense of blood and treasure that had just been incurred?"

Savary replied that circumstances had changed. Napoleon's first abdication had been the work of a faction headed by Talleyrand, he said; the nation had not been consulted. This time, however, Napoleon had voluntarily resigned his power; his influence over the French people was gone and could never be regained. "Therefore," Savary concluded, "he would prefer retiring into obscurity, where he might end his days in peace and tranquillity; and were he solicited to ascend the throne again, he would decline it."

"If that is the case," said Maitland, "why not seek an asylum in England?"

"There are many reasons for his not wishing to reside in England," Savary replied. "The climate is too damp and cold. It is too near France. He would be, as it were, in the center of every change and revolution that might take place there, and would be subject to suspicion. He has been accustomed to consider the English as his most inveterate enemies, and they have been induced to look upon him as a monster, without one of the virtues of a human being." No more was said on the point. Nevertheless, the question of asylum in England had been raised again—and this time by a British officer.

Soon after, Savary and Las Cases left the *Bellerophon* with Maitland's reply to Bertrand's letter. Captain Knight also departed on the *Falmouth*, bearing Bertrand's letter and Maitland's dispatches to Admiral Hotham in the Baie de Quiberon. As Maitland watched the *Mouche* make her way back to the French squadron, he may have reflected that the visit of the Frenchmen had gained nothing tangible for Napoleon, while he had gained valuable information and, possibly, time. But he could not relax vigilance; the visit might have been a stratagem designed to lull him off guard and so facilitate Napoleon's escape.

Back on the *Saale*, Maitland's letter was being examined and discussed. The single definite pronouncement in it—that, in the present state of affairs, Maitland would undertake to prevent Napoleon's sailing in any vessel whatever—was discouraging, as was Maitland's failure to supply any information about the sought-for passports. Nor did Maitland's suggestion that Napoleon seek asylum in England encourage any sanguine expectations about Napoleon's position if he were to give himself up. Only as a last resort would he commit himself to that action. Besides, it was premature to consider acting on Maitland's suggestion; too many developments favorable to Napoleon's plans might occur in the next day or two. The passports might yet arrive, or Admiral Hotham might agree to Napoleon's leaving the country on a neutral vessel. If Hotham refused this, a successful escape attempt might still be mounted—and not necessarily from Rochefort. To explore this possibility, Napoleon sent General Lallemand to Royan to confer with Captain Baudin of the *Bayadère* about carrying Napoleon to the United States.

But July 11 brought bitter and alarming news to the fugitives.

The Paris newspapers of July 5 reached them, carrying stories of the city's capitulation to the Allied Powers and of Louis XVIII's return. Napoleon raged at this information, but some of his followers responded more in fear than in anger. With the King back in power, any hour might bring orders for their arrest. Bertrand, Savary, Lallemand, Montholon, and Gourgaud in particular had reason to dread the King's vengeance, it being almost inevitable that their names would appear on any list of traitors. If they should be arrested and tried, their lives would undoubtedly be forfeit.

But what lay before their eyes soon drew their thoughts away from Paris. Shortly after midday, the *Myrmidon* and the *Bellerophon* weighed anchor and beat out of the Pertuis d'Antioche against the flood tide, the former to turn south toward the Pertuis de Maumusson, the latter to assume a position between the lighthouses on the western tips of the Ile de Ré and the Ile d'Oléron. The *Bellerophon* was joined that evening by the *Slaney*. This redeployment could indicate that the British ships expected reinforcements any moment. If that were so, Napoleon could hope no longer that Admiral Hotham's answer to Bertrand's letter might hold good news. To escape the vise inexorably tightening on him, he must act at once.

He did not lack men eager to help him. Captain Ponée of the *Méduse* came forward with a daring escape plan. That night he would sail his frigate out ahead of the *Saale*, surprise the *Bellerophon*, and, grappling with her, prevent her from pursuing the speedy *Saale*. Ponée maintained that he could hold out for two hours against the *Bellerophon*, by which time the *Saale* would be freely at sea and on her way to America. Neither the *Myrmidon* nor the *Slaney* could hope to halt or overtake her. Napoleon rejected the offer—and the next day saw H.M.S. *Cyrus* join the *Slaney* and the *Bellerophon* and take up her station off the Pointe des Baleines lighthouse on the Ile de Ré. Henceforth, no matter which of the three possible escape routes Napoleon chose, the balance of ships, men, and guns would weigh heavily against him.

As if to acknowledge these odds, he once again left the *Saale* for the Ile d'Aix. There, word reached him that the white flag of the Bourbons had appeared on the towers of La Rochelle, on the mainland coast north of the Ile de Ré. True, it was struck and replaced by the tricolor before sunset; but on July 13 the Bourbon standard again flew over La Rochelle—and over parts of the Ile d'Oléron as well—adding to the fugitives' fear of imminent encirclement by Bourbon supporters. At sea, on the mainland, and now even on the islands, their enemies were pushing them into a more impossible position.

And still Napoleon failed to act. He received the proposal of a number of young marine officers to man two chasse-marées (small decked vessels fitted with sails), try to reach the high seas, and, once there, persuade or force the first merchant vessel they met to carry them to the United States. He ordered the boats purchased, armed, and loaded with some of his effects, but he declined to go aboard. On the same day, July 13, Joseph arrived from Bordeaux. He announced that he had chartered an American ship, which was waiting for him in the estuary of the Gironde, and urged Napoleon to join him. Napoleon refused. Neither would he bestir himself when Lallemand returned from Royan later in the day to report that Captain Baudin still held himself and the *Bayadère* at Napoleon's service and that Baudin had pledged to take Napoleon to the ends of the earth if necessary. Nor did he accept the offer of Mr. Lee, the United States consul at Bordeaux, who was holding at Napoleon's disposal the American ship *Pike*, destined for New York and capable of outrunning any warship.

Numerous explanations have been advanced for Napoleon's enigmatic refusal to try any of these escape plans. It has been argued that he did not choose to escape as a private individual, that he was too ill to act promptly, that he knew any attempt to escape by sea would fail, and that he was moved by an overriding concern for the welfare of his companions and so did not seize the nearest, if the most dangerous, way. To some degree, each of the explanations is plausible, but none can claim to be completely convincing; and perhaps a fully satisfactory answer will never be given. It is noteworthy, however, that from the time Napoleon quit Paris he constantly insisted that his departure from France have the sanction of those against whom he had contended. All evidence indicates that the issuance of the passports he had requested vitally concerned him. Fear of the British naval blockade of Rochefort initially played no part in his concern because he knew nothing of it until Bonnefux's letter reached him in Niort on July 2. Moreover, as we have seen, the primary purpose of Bertrand's letter to Maitland on July 10 was to ascertain if any information concerning the passports had reached Maitland.

Why did Napoleon attach such importance to the passports? The answer may lie deep within his essential character. He had reached a position beyond which his pride would not allow him to descend. He had been defeated at Waterloo, abandoned by France and forced to abdicate, officially requested to leave Paris, and reduced to the necessity of seeking refuge abroad—humiliations that would have agonized lesser men. Now, he faced a final humiliation, the choice between fleeing for his life and being taken prisoner. Even a successful escape would be humiliating, for his enemies would unquestionably accuse him of having fled in abject fear for his life. His whole soldier's being must have shrunk from choosing any course that might invite that charge. When he returned from Elba, he had bared his breast to the muskets of the troops sent to apprehend him; and he would not now court the imputation that he had showed his back to danger. To flee without the passports would be to act like the outlaw that the Congress of Vienna had pronounced him to be following his return from Elba. So undignified an exodus was beneath his consideration: he was Napoleon. Thus, on the night of July 13, he canceled the preparations being made for boarding the chasse-marées and the Danish schooner.

Napoleon knew, however, that by waiting and gambling on the arrival of the passports he risked capture by the Bourbons or the

Allied Powers. The contents of the little vial he carried would
spare him that fate, but his suicide would delight his enemies.
Only one course consistent with his sense of honor and dignity
seemed left to him: he could surrender to the British. Then the
onus of the end he made would be transferred to them. Let the
British and their allies do what they would—shelter and honor
him, imprison him, or shoot him—they could not ultimately
triumph over him.

The matter was settled late that night at a council to which
Napoleon summoned the principal members of his suite. There,
he put the question to them: should he attempt to escape by sea,
with all the dangers attendant on that course, or should he seek
asylum in England? The accounts of the discussion vary, but evidence indicates that a majority—the Bertrands, Savary, Lallemand, and Las Cases—advocated that Napoleon go on board the
Bellerophon. Napoleon agreed with them. To Bertrand, he said,
"There is always some danger in trusting to one's enemies, but it is
better to risk reliance on their sense of honor than be in their hands
as a prisoner by law." Napoleon knew that he would in reality be
a prisoner, and that he could not depend on England's sense of
honor to overcome her desire for vengeance. But he had never
shirked risk; indeed, his imagination had always been drawn to
the dramatic possibilities of the unexpected.

Before retiring, he dictated the following letter to the Prince
Regent of England:

Your Royal Highness,
    A victim to the factions which distract my country, and to the
enmity of the greatest powers of Europe, I have terminated my political career, and I come, like Themistocles, to throw myself upon the
hospitality of the British people. I put myself under the protection of
their laws; which I claim from your Royal Highness, as the most
powerful, the most constant, and the most generous of my enemies.

                                    Rochefort, 13 July, 1815,
                                    Napoleon.

Its literary merits aside, the letter reveals the measure of the man with whom England had to contend. Its every verb asserts Napoleon's absolute freedom of action. There is not even a tacit admission of guilt for the events following his return from Elba— not a word of supplication, not a hint of humility. The subtle flattery of the Prince Regent is counterbalanced by the proud assertion that his enemy cannot but grant what he claims as his right.

This was no letter of conciliation, as some historians have claimed; it was one of confrontation. Whether it would serve Napoleon well or ill was perhaps secondary to him. What mattered was that the letter gave him the first word in this affair. That gained, let England and her allies act as they chose—they would be fortunate ever to have the last word.

The letter was not immediately dispatched to Maitland for forwarding. Prudence dictated making a last inquiry concerning the passport. At daybreak, therefore, on July 14, the *Mouche* sailed once more to the *Bellerophon* under a flag of truce. As on her first trip, she carried the Count de Las Cases; but this time he was accompanied by General Lallemand. The latter, like Savary, knew Maitland, having been Maitland's prisoner for three weeks on board the *Camelion* in Egypt. Once on the quarter-deck, Las Cases asked Maitland if he had received Hotham's reply to Bertrand's letter. Maitland answered that he had not, but that as a result of his dispatch to the admiral he hourly expected Hotham in person. He added, "If that was the only reason you had for sending off a flag of truce, it was quite unnecessary, as I informed you, when last here, that the Admiral's answer, when it arrived, should be forwarded to the frigates by one of the *Bellerophon*'s boats; and I do not approve of frequent communications with an enemy by means of flags of truce."

This testy reply, quite uncharacteristic of Maitland, betrays the tension under which he had been operating during the preceding fortnight and especially since July 10. Following his dispatch of

Bertrand's letter to Hotham, he had not heard from the admiral. In addition, he suspected that, Bertrand's letter notwithstanding, Napoleon might still attempt to escape—and his suspicions had been reinforced by a report from the mainland that an escape was indeed being planned. The preparations of the French frigates for putting to sea did not ease his mind either. Finally, despite the arrival of the *Cyrus* on July 12, he had the gravest doubts that he could stop the frigates, or any small vessels that Napoleon might use, if they should try to break through his blockade. One can understand why this latest overture of his enemy should find him disinclined to observe the amenities of polite conversation. Having expressed his disapproval of the envoys' action, Maitland went into the cabin and ordered breakfast for himself and them. He wanted no further discussion until Captain Sartorius of the *Slaney*, for whom he had signaled, arrived on board.

Breakfast ended, the four men repaired to the after-cabin, where Las Cases again stressed the motives underlying Napoleon's desire to sail to the United States. "The Emperor is so anxious to spare the further effusion of human blood that he will proceed to America in any way the British Government chooses to sanction, either in a French ship of war, a vessel armed *en flûte*, or even in a British ship of war."

Maitland answered, "I have no authority to agree to any arrangement of that sort, nor do I believe my Government would consent to it; but I think I may venture to receive him into this ship and convey him to England. If, however, he adopts that plan, I cannot enter into any promise as to the reception he may meet with, as, even in the case I have mentioned, I shall be acting on my own responsibility and cannot be sure that it would meet with the approbation of the British Government."

Much more conversation followed, during which Lucien Bonaparte's residence in England was mentioned. Las Cases asked Maitland if he thought Napoleon would be well received in England, to which Maitland replied that he did not at all know the intention of his government, but that he had no reason to suppose Napoleon would not be well received. He emphasized, however, that this was only his private opinion, repeating to Las Cases that he had no authority to make conditions of any kind.* At one point Lallemand asked if there would be any risk that any of Napoleon's suite who accompanied him might be given up to the French government. "Certainly not," Maitland assured him. "The British Government never could think of doing so under the circumstances contemplated in the present arrangement." The two Frenchmen left the *Bellerophon* about nine o'clock. Before boarding the *Mouche*, Las Cases confided to Maitland, "Under all circumstances, I have little doubt that you will see the Emperor on board the *Bellerophon*."

Despite this assurance, Maitland still could not relax. Later that morning he was rejoined by the *Myrmidon*, sent up from the Pertuis de Maumusson with a letter received there by the *Daphne*. It revealed Napoleon's supposed intention to escape from Rochefort in the Danish ship, concealed in a cask in the ballast. Maitland at once directed the *Myrmidon* to take up a position northeast of the *Bellerophon* and the *Slaney*, thus tightening the blockade of the Ile d'Aix.

On the Ile d'Aix, meanwhile, the discussion centered on Maitland's statement that he would convey Napoleon to England. Encouraging though this may have seemed, it revealed nothing about the intentions of the Cabinet of St. James. But what else could Napoleon do now except throw himself upon England's generosity? His one chance was to walk into the open jaws of the British lion and hope that they would not snap shut.

Late that afternoon the *Bellerophon*'s lookouts reported a barge rowing off from the French frigates toward their ship, with a flag of truce showing. Maitland immediately recalled Captain Sartorius and Captain Gambier, of the *Myrmidon*, to his ship to

---

* In view of the historical controversy about this conversation, it is worth emphasizing that Maitland had received no instructions specifying what to do should Napoleon voluntarily surrender. Indeed the conversation centered on a hypothetical instance. Maitland did not know of the decision Napoleon had reached the previous night or of Napoleon's letter to the Prince Regent.

act as witnesses. The barge reached the *Bellerophon* about seven in the evening, bearing, as usual, Count de Las Cases, accompanied this time by General Gourgaud. Las Cases bore the following letter from Bertrand to Maitland:

14 July, 1815

Sɪʀ,

Count Las Cases has reported to the Emperor the conversation which he had with you this morning. His Majesty will proceed on board your ship with the ebb tide tomorrow morning, between four and five o'clock.

I send the Count Las Cases, Counsellor of State, doing the duty of Maréchal de Logis, with the list of persons composing His Majesty's suite.*

If the Admiral, in consequence of the despatch you forwarded to him, should send the passport for the United States therein demanded, His Majesty will be happy to repair to America; but should the passport be withheld, he will willingly proceed to England, as a private individual, there to enjoy the protection of the laws of your country.

His Majesty has despatched Major-General Baron Gourgaud to the Prince Regent with a letter, a copy of which I have the honour to enclose, requesting that you will forward it to such one of the ministers as you may think it necessary to send that general officer, that he may have the honour of delivering the letter with which he is charged to the Prince Regent.

After Maitland had read the letters, he informed Las Cases that he would receive Napoleon on board and would at once send General Gourgaud to England on the *Slaney*, together with his own dispatches to the Admiralty. He added that Gourgaud would not be allowed to land until permission was received from London or until his landing was sanctioned by the admiral of the port to which the *Slaney* put in; but he assured Las Cases that the copy of Napoleon's letter would be forwarded without delay and presented by the ministers to the Prince Regent. But Maitland again repeated one point: "Monsieur Las Cases, you will recollect that

* See Appendix I.

I am not authorized to stipulate as to the reception of Bonaparte in England, but that he must consider himself entirely at the disposal of his Royal Highness the Prince Regent." "I am perfectly aware of that," Las Cases replied, "and have already acquainted the Emperor with what you said on the subject."

Soon after, the French barge carried a letter from Las Cases to Bertrand, notifying him of Maitland's willingness to take Napoleon on board and convey him to England. Las Cases remained behind on the *Bellerophon*, helping Maitland see to the arrangements for receiving Napoleon. General Gourgaud accompanied Captain Sartorius to the *Slaney*, which sailed immediately for England. Sartorius bore a letter from Maitland to the Secretary of the Admiralty, of which the following is an extract:

For the information of the Lords Commissioners of the Admiralty, I have to acquaint you that the Count Las Cases and General Lallemand this day came on board His Majesty's ship under my command, with a proposal from Count Bertrand for me to receive on board Napoleon Buonaparte, for the purpose of throwing himself on the generosity of the Prince Regent. Conceiving myself authorized by their Lordships' secret orders, I have acceded to the proposal, and he is to embark on board this ship tomorrow morning. That no misunderstanding might arise, I have explicitly and clearly explained to Count Las Cases, that I have no authority whatever for granting terms of any sort, but that all I can do is carry him and his suite to England, to be received in such manner as his Royal Highness may deem expedient.

Maitland had little time in which to exult over this development. He spent a busy night arranging for the reception of Napoleon and his suite the next day. The *Bellerophon* had been cleared for action, with all her bulkheads down; now the cabins had to be reconstructed and the supply of stores checked. Added to these concerns were two worrisome pieces of information. About ten o'clock a boat from shore put aboard a man who stated that Napoleon had that morning passed La Rochelle in one of the chassemarées and intended to escape to sea via the Pertuis Breton during the night. Extremely anxious, Maitland confronted Las Cases with this revelation, only to be assured that Napoleon could not have been on either of the two vessels, since Las Cases had left him on the Ile d'Aix at half past five that same evening. But at three o'clock in the morning, another boat from shore brought the same report as the first. Although he took no action in consequence of these reports, having decided to trust Las Cases' word of honor that Napoleon fully intended to board the *Bellerophon*, Maitland's thoughts and feelings concerning the possible end of the affair and his role in it must have made the hours before dawn seem interminable. "The anxiety of my situation may be easily conceived," he wrote years later, "when it is recollected that I sent off a ship to England with despatches announcing the intention of Buonaparte to embark the following morning in the *Bellerophon*."

One surmises that Napoleon's suite spent the hours before their departure from France somewhat more serenely than Maitland did. The indecision and inactivity of the past fortnight were ended, and a course of action acceptable to nearly all of them had been adopted. The danger of arrest by the Bourbons or the Allies had faded. The English ships, which until that day had posed a threat, now offered what seemed a sanctuary. True, they would be putting themselves in the hands of the enemy, but at least they would be temporarily safe on the ship; and they had Maitland's personal opinion that he saw no reason to think they would not be well received in his country. They had seen the *Slaney* sail that evening and knew that Gourgaud was aboard her, bound for the Prince Regent with Napoleon's letter. Further, their hopes for the future had been raised by the portraits of the English people and of English life drawn for them by Las Cases and Madame Bertrand, both of whom had lived in England. Governing everything, however, was the certainty that their claim to English protection and hospitality would be honored.

One cannot know to what degree Napoleon shared these sentiments of his followers. Certainly his abdication statement, his letter to the Prince Regent, and his statement to Bertrand on the night of July 13 indicate his cognizance of the deep-seated animosities of the English and their allies. He could scarcely have forgotten that the ministers of the Allied Powers, on March 13, 1815, at Vienna, had declared him to be an enemy and disturber of the world and an outlaw deserving of public vengeance. Whatever rights Napoleon might claim from the English, he knew now that the protection of their laws had been officially denied him. Still, he had always been enough of a romantic to gamble on the grand gesture and trust it to dazzle his opponents into withdrawing from their position. If this gamble succeeded, his exit from Europe's political scene would be as memorable as his entrance upon it had been.

He had learned, too, that the safest step now left him was to board the *Bellerophon*. That night Beker brought Napoleon news he had received from Captain Philibert of the *Saale*. Bonnefux had shown Philibert a letter from the Count de Jaucourt, the new Minister of Marine appointed by Louis XVIII. It ordered Bonnefux to keep Napoleon on the *Saale*, and to prevent him both from landing on French soil and from communicating with the British ships. Out of sympathy for Napoleon and a desire to help him, Bonnefux had delayed executing the orders; but he could not safely delay much longer. If Napoleon did not go on board the *Bellerophon* quickly, Bonnefux would have to arrest him.

In the chill hours before dawn on July 15, Napoleon rose and dressed for his departure from France. He donned a white waistcoat and breeches, military boots, a plain gold-hilted sword, and the green coat, with scarlet cape and cuffs and scarlet-edged lapels, of a colonel of the Chasseurs of the Guard. Pinned on the coat were the Grand Cross and the small cross of the Legion of Honor, the Iron Crown, and the Union. Last came his olive-colored greatcoat and the famous cocked hat with the tricolor cockade. He was rowed out to the brig of war *Epervier*, which was to carry him and his suite to the *Bellerophon*. The brig weighed, made sail, and, flying a flag of truce, stood out with the ebbing tide toward the English frigate. Day broke as she put distance between herself and the two French frigates near which she had been anchored. But by five-thirty the ebb tide had failed, and the wind was beating in against them, holding up their progress. The *Bellerophon* and the *Myrmidon* lay near each other at the eastern entrance to the Pertuis d'Antioche, less than a mile away; and in the offing the sails of another English vessel were visible—those of Admiral Henry Hotham's flagship, the *Superb*.

Maitland noted those sails, too, and their appearance quickened the nervous pace with which he had been walking the quarterdeck since the *Epervier* had left the Aix Roads. He wanted Napoleon on board his ship before Hotham arrived, perhaps to deprive him at the last minute of the custody of the most sought-after man in the world. He ordered his First Lieutenant, Andrew Mott, to take the ship's barge to the *Epervier* and bring Napoleon back with him.

When the barge pulled alongside the brig, Mott explained his mission and received word that Napoleon would join him. Beker, who was aboard the *Epervier* in order to see Napoleon off, offered to accompany him in the barge, but Napoleon protested. "Don't accompany me on board," he said. "I don't know what the English intend doing with me; and should they not respond to my confidence, it might be said that you have sold me to England." With Bertrand, Napoleon boarded the English barge and took his seat. At Mott's word, the crew shoved off and gave way for the *Bellerophon*. Looking up, Mott noticed tears in the eyes of most of the officers and men lining the rails of the brig. At the same time, the sailors crowding its rigging began to wave their hats and cheer Napoleon. As long as the barge remained in earshot, the men in it heard the cheering continue.

The barge approached the *Bellerophon*, then ranged alongside her. Silence fell over the decks of the frigate as the men on board her strained their eyes to see the beginning of what they sensed to be the most important historical event in which they would ever participate. Then, Bertrand ascended the gangway and stepped on board. He bowed to Maitland, who stood on the quarterdeck, announced, "The Emperor is in the boat," and stepped aside.

The boatswain's whistle shrilled out the honor of the side. Before its final notes had sounded, Napoleon had come up the gangway and onto the deck. Buttoned to the chin in his greatcoat, he paused a moment, then walked past a guard of marines drawn up on the break of the poop. They stood stiffly at attention as he strode past their ranks, but did not present arms. Napoleon advanced to the quarterdeck. He pulled off his hat and, addressing Maitland, said firmly, "I am come to throw myself on the protection of your Prince and laws."

The confrontation had begun.

II

A Halcyon Handful of Days

IF ANY English ship of the line other than the *Bellerophon* had directed the blockade of Rochefort, Napoleon might not have vetoed the plans to escape by sea. For his knowledge of that vessel may have disinclined him to test the French frigates against her. Launched in 1786, the *Bellerophon* had joined England's naval battle line first against the Revolution, then against Napoleon. In 1798 she had distinguished herself in the Battle of the Nile, pitting her 74 guns against the 120 of Admiral Brueys's flagship, the *Orient,* and fighting magnificently and victoriously despite the loss of her mizzenmast and mainmast, fires in three places, and 197 casualties out of a complement of 570 men— nearly one-quarter of the entire English squadron's losses. She alone had received special mention in Nelson's dispatches after the victory, and Nelson himself had boarded her three days after the battle to personally thank her captain and crew for the gallant manner in which they had fought her. Trafalgar, too, had seen the *Bellerophon* in action against the French: she had fired the first shot of that supreme English naval triumph, and at one time during the fighting had been engaged with no fewer than five of the enemy's squadron—three Spanish and two French ships. Old and slow though she now was, the "Billy Ruffian" (so nicknamed by her crew) was a ship to fear; and there is little doubt that Napoleon was reluctant to brave her fire.

From the moment that the Frenchmen boarded the *Bellero-phon,* they must have been alert to any indications of their future treatment. It would have been natural for them to conclude that their treatment on the ship foreshadowed their reception in England. And, from the beginning the signs were auspicious. True, when coming on board, Napoleon had not been received with manned yards and given the salute, the usual honors accorded persons of high rank, but more than compensatory measures had been taken by Maitland to ensure Napoleon's comfort and defer to his dignity. The whole of the after-cabin, which had been Maitland's, was now given over to Napoleon's use, Maitland having removed his cot to the wardroom. The anteroom served as a dining room as well as a waiting room for those attending on Napoleon. To its right and left, two small cabins had been constructed, one to serve as Napoleon's dressing room, the other as a sleeping room for his valet. At the entrance to the anteroom, Maitland had stationed two sentinels as a guard of honor. The deck, between the mainmast and the mizzenmast, had been covered with a tent for the comfort of the ladies; and the gun ports had been netted over to prevent the children from falling overboard.

The consideration for their well-being that these preparations revealed fostered optimism among Napoleon's followers. And Maitland's words to Napoleon, when the latter admired the appearance of the after-cabin, did not diminish it. "Such as it is, Sir," he said, "it is at your service while you remain on board the ship I command." Royal prerogatives were accorded Napoleon without his insisting on them. When he appeared on deck, the men in his vicinity removed their hats. Whenever spoken to, he was addressed as "Sire." After only a few hours on board, it was apparent that, within the bounds of prudence, whatever he requested would be his.

Never hesitant to impress people who could further his purposes, Napoleon immediately set out to ingratiate himself. Few persons have shown a greater talent for this than he. His method was simple but effective: by his manner and his questions, he displayed an intense interest in the other person, drew him to talk about himself and his life, and subtly flattered him. Napoleon knew his stature, and knew that few men can ignore the attentions paid them by the eminent. Within minutes after boarding the *Bellerophon*, therefore, he had Maitland talking about his wife and children, about England, and about the service he had seen. He spoke with each of the ship's officers, whom he asked to meet, and while Maitland led him on a tour of the ship, he put numerous questions about her and commented favorably on English ships and seamen. Afterward, at breakfast, he inquired about English customs. "I must now learn to conform myself to them," he told Maitland, "as I shall probably pass the remainder of my life in England."

Ever since Napoleon had come on board, the *Superb* had been steadily approaching. As she drew nearer Napoleon showed signs of uneasiness; two or three times he asked Maitland how soon the flagship would anchor. He appeared most anxious to discover if Hotham would approve of Maitland's having received him, and he voiced a strong desire to see the admiral. Maitland, also, was anxious. The exigencies of the past several days had forced him to assume an initiative that had not been specifically granted him, and he could not be certain that his action would win approval. When the *Superb* dropped anchor at ten-thirty, therefore, he immediately went aboard her. But after hearing Maitland's report, Admiral Hotham reassured him. "Getting hold of him [Napoleon] on any terms would have been of the greatest consequence," he said. "But as you have entered into no conditions whatever, there cannot be a doubt that you will obtain the approbation of His Majesty's Government." He acceded to Maitland's strong desire to carry Napoleon to England on the *Bellerophon*; and, in response to Napoleon's request to see him, said that he would be pleased to wait on Napoleon that afternoon.

The meeting was amicable. Hotham invited Napoleon, the ladies, and the principal officers of the suite to breakfast the next morning on the *Superb*, and he joined them at dinner that eve-

ning. At the meal, Napoleon conducted himself as a royal personage, leading the way into the dining room, seating himself at the
center of the table at one side, and specifying where the others
should take their places. Neither Hotham nor Maitland in any
way indicated that he considered this conduct presumptuous.
Napoleon was voluble, cheerful, and even playful at times; and
after dinner he took the group into the after-cabin to show them
his famous little green camp bed. When he retired about seven-
thirty, he may have reflected that although the day had been
long and tiring, it had exceeded his most sanguine expectations.
Both the admiral and the captain had treated him with deference;
and although neither of them had admitted to any knowledge of
how he was likely to be treated by their government, they had not
challenged his claims to English hospitality and the protection of
English laws.

Nevertheless Napoleon may have been troubled by disquieting
thoughts. He had received no passports for America, nor any
message that they might be forthcoming; if he had not boarded
the *Bellerophon* that morning, the blockade of Rochefort would
have continued, tighter than ever now that the *Superb* had arrived. Obviously the British government was not content merely
to be rid of him—it wanted him in its power. His appeal to its
generosity might well prove futile. History had taught him that
many a defeated man, in throwing himself on the mercy of his
enemies, had only thrown himself under the headsman's sword.

But such thoughts perhaps seemed excessively somber the next
morning. When he came on deck around ten o'clock, to be rowed
to the *Superb* for breakfast, he found a captain's guard of marines
turned out in full-dress uniform to see him over the side. He
delayed his departure long enough to inspect them and put them
through part of their exercise, expressing his pleasure with them.
On getting into the *Bellerophon*'s barge, he saw that the *Superb*
had the tompions out of her guns and her yards manned, which
indicated that Hotham officially recognized his guest's importance. In addition, when Hotham received him on the quarter-

deck, Napoleon found another captain's guard turned out for him and the ship's company drawn up in divisions. The officers of the *Superb* were presented to him, and, as on the *Bellerophon*, he was escorted on a tour of the ship. In sunny spirits over this reception, he delighted the company with his conversation at breakfast. That morning he elicited from Hotham a promise that a French vessel would be permitted to transport to England the 45 horses and six carriages left behind at Rochefort.

At noon Napoleon, the members of his suite who had gone with him to the *Superb*, Maitland, and one of the *Superb*'s officers returned to the *Bellerophon*. At their approach, the yards were manned. Once the group was on board and the barge had been hoisted in, Maitland gave orders to get under weigh. His ship carried, besides Napoleon, 33 members of Napoleon's suite, 17 others having boarded the *Myrmidon* the preceding day in accordance with orders from Hotham, which read:

You are hereby required and directed to take the *Myrmidon* under your orders, and, putting on board her such persons composing a part of the suite of Napoleon Buonaparte as cannot be conveyed in the *Bellerophon*, you are to put to sea in His Majesty's ship under your command, in company with the *Myrmidon*, and make the best of your way with Napoleon Buonaparte and his suite to Torbay, and there landing the officer of the ship bearing my flag, whom I have charged with a despatch addressed to the Secretary of the Admiralty, as well as an officer of the ship you command, for the purpose of proceeding express to Plymouth with the despatch you will herewith receive, addressed to Admiral Lord Keith, and a copy of these instructions . . . , await orders from the Lords Commissioners of the Admiralty, or his Lordship, for your further proceedings.

Standing with Maitland on the break of the poop, Napoleon watched the crewmen heave up and secure the anchor and shake out the sails. As her canvas took the light breeze, the old frigate answered her helm, coming around to point her bowsprit west. "What I admire most in your ship," Napoleon remarked to Maitland, "is the extreme silence and orderly conduct of your men.

On board a French ship, everyone calls and gives orders, and they gabble like so many geese."

The *Bellerophon* began beating out of the long, shoal stretch of the Pertuis d'Antioche, passing within a cable's length of the anchored *Superb,* whose crew crowded along the bulwarks and waved and shouted as she slid past; heaving to briefly when, soon after, the *Mouche* joined her to put aboard some sheep, vegetables, and other foodstuffs that the French commander at Rochefort had sent as gifts to Napoleon; then working out between the Ile de Ré and the Ile d'Oléron, the *Myrmidon* following her; and finally, around six o'clock, clearing the Chassiron shoal and making the open waters of the Bay of Biscay.

They were at sea. Ahead lay England—and exile. Those who accompanied Napoleon knew that while he lived and they served him they would not return to France.

Who were Napoleon's companions, and what motivated them to follow the man they persisted in calling "the Emperor"? Devotion, self-interest, a habit of complete obedience to Napoleon's directives, fear of Bourbon or Allied reprisals—any of these, or any mixture of them, may have prompted them to couple their destinies with his. But whatever their reasons, by following him from France and sharing his fate, they assured themselves of a place in history.

Most prominent among the group was Lieutenant General Count Henri-Gratien Bertrand, Grand Marshal of the Palace and the only Grand Officer of the Court to accompany Napoleon. He had long known and served Napoleon, and was a friend and confidant as well as an officer. The two had been together since the expedition to Egypt in 1798, where Bertrand—whose skills as an engineer exceeded his skills as a soldier—had directed the fortification of Alexandria. In 1805, following the battle of Austerlitz, Bertrand had been appointed aide-de-camp to Napoleon. In 1809 he had been made a count and appointed governor of Illyria for having directed the construction of the bridges by which the

French army crossed the Danube at Wagram. He had become Grand Marshal of the Palace in 1813, had accompanied Napoleon to Elba in 1814, and had helped him to return to France. Bertrand was 42 years old, tall and thin, balding, and quiet-mannered; he compensated for his lack of brilliance with fidelity, honesty, and a sense of duty that Napoleon valued.

His wife, Fanny, was the daughter of Arthur Dillon, an Irishman in the French service who had been guillotined during the Revolution. She spoke English well, having lived in England for a number of years, and was familiar with English customs and manners. A protégée of Josephine's, she had had her marriage arranged by Napoleon, who settled a handsome dowry on her. She was twelve years younger than her husband, as tall as he, blond and pretty. Her whimsical nature and unpredictable outbursts caused Bertrand many an uneasy hour; nonetheless, she was an honest and loyal wife and a good mother to their three children. During the deliberations at Rochefort, hers had been one of the voices most frequently raised in favor of Napoleon's seeking asylum in England.

Another member was Lieutenant General Anne Jean Marie René Savary, Duke of Rovigo, the mere mention of whose name in those days aroused feelings of hatred in the breasts of countless Bourbon and Allied supporters. For Savary had been intimately associated with Napoleon in two incidents that had hardened Europe against any compromise with Napoleon. In 1804, as Minister of Police, he had played a prominent and decisive role in the clandestine trial and execution of the young and gallant Duke of Enghien. In 1808 he had persuaded the weak-witted Ferdinand of Spain to quit Madrid and speed to Bayonne for a meeting with Napoleon, and he had there informed that unfortunate prince that the Bourbon dynasty had ended in Spain and that Ferdinand's life was in Napoleon's hands. The universal condemnation that Napoleon's enemies had heaped upon Savary for his participation in those sensational affairs had tended to obscure his otherwise distinguished military career; so now, at 41, this tall, handsome man lived with the alarming knowledge that his accusers far outnumbered his advocates and that Bourbon France would hold no mercy for him.

Brigadier General Count Charles-Tristan de Montholon was a man whose rise in the world owed as much to his connections as to his capabilities. Born in 1783 into a family that numbered chancellors of France among its ancestors, Montholon claimed to have made the acquaintance of the Bonapartes at 19, alleging that when on shore leave in Ajaccio he had lodged at their house and had studied mathematics under Napoleon (then a lieutenant home on furlough) and Latin under Lucien. Later, his association with persons highly placed in the Consular Court—he became Josephine's chamberlain in 1809—had resulted in his promotion to a colonelcy when only 26. But then he took a step that nearly ruined his career. Without Napoleon's knowledge or consent, he secretly married his mistress, Albine-Hélène de Vassal, a fashionable woman whose reputation had provided Parisian gossips with many hours of eyebrow-raising conversation. When Napoleon, then in Russia, heard of the marriage, he angrily dismissed Montholon and banished him to the provinces, where the young man lived not only in disgrace but also in deep debt. Eventually a shortage of generals worked to his advantage, bringing him the command of the Department of the Loire in 1814. Following Napoleon's first abdication, Montholon's stepfather, Semonville, prevailed upon Louis XVIII to appoint Montholon a brigadier general. But Montholon promptly relinquished his responsibility when Napoleon returned from Elba, waiting for him in the Forest of Fontainebleau and following him to Paris. Although he played no significant role in the Hundred Days, Montholon had again attached himself to Napoleon after Waterloo.

Madame de Montholon was several years her husband's senior. Although no longer beautiful, she had kept a slender figure that, together with striking blue eyes and lovely brown hair, made her still attractive. Because of her gentle, tactful manner, she became one of the more popular members of the suite. With the Montholons was their young son.

Baron Charles François Antoine Lallemand, a thick-set, powerfully built, 42-year-old lieutenant general, had served with Napoleon since the Egyptian campaign, and for several years had been one of his aides-de-camp. Like Savary, he was certain to be on any Bourbon list of traitors, for he and his troops had broken allegiance to Louis and gone over to Napoleon on his return from Elba. In addition, Lallemand had been one of the organizers of an unsuccessful plan to seize the roads between Paris and the Belgian frontier and so prevent Louis from fleeing the country. He had fought at Waterloo and acquitted himself well there. But, following that defeat and Napoleon's abdication, he knew that if he remained in France the scaffold awaited him.

At 49, Emmanuel Auguste Dieudonne Marius Joseph, Count de Las Cases, was the oldest of the suite. This short, slightly built man with a wrinkled face and graying hair was the cosmopolitan of the group. Born into a prominent family in Languedoc, Las Cases had traveled widely, experienced poverty as well as affluence, met people from many different social strata, and acquired a breadth of experience unmatched by any of his companions. He had begun his career as a navy man, but after the massacre of the Royalists at Quiberon had fled to London, where he lived for a number of years. While there he wrote a historical atlas that proved a notable success, and so fared better financially than many of his fellow émigrés. He returned to France after the Treaty of Amiens and thereafter espoused Napoleon's cause; but aside from being made count in 1814, he did not reap very outstanding social or remunerative rewards for his services. Under the Restoration he became a councillor of state and, he later claimed, a captain in the navy. He rejoined Napoleon's household after the return from Elba, and was acting as chamberlain at the Elysée, along with Montholon, when Napoleon returned there from Waterloo.

From that time, the intimacy between Napoleon and him grew —to such an extent that he left behind his wife and family, with the exception of his 15-year-old son Emmanuel, to accompany Napoleon. Napoleon himself later explained Las Cases' importance to him. "Las Cases," he said, "is the only one of the French who can speak English well or explain it to my satisfaction. I cannot now read an English newspaper. Madame Bertrand understands English perfectly; but you know one cannot trouble a lady. Las Cases was necessary to me." At Rochefort, during the discussions concerning asylum in England, Las Cases' eulogies of the country and its people had reinforced those of Madame Bertrand. They, along with Las Cases' reports of his conversations with Maitland on the *Bellerophon*, may have influenced Napoleon's decision.

The last principal member of Napoleon's entourage was 32-year-old Major General Baron Gaspard Gourgaud, who was preceding the others to England on the *Slaney* with Napoleon's letter to the Prince Regent. From the age of 18, Gourgaud had led a strictly military life. An artilleryman like Napoleon himself at the beginning of his career, Gourgaud had risen rapidly in that branch of the army; and after the Spanish and Austrian campaigns of 1811, he had become Napoleon's orderly. He had fought in Russia, where he was the first to enter the Kremlin. For discovering a mine planted there by the Russians he was made a Baron of the Empire. Impetuous, ambitious, and impatient for action, he had been wounded in battle several times; and in January 1814, at Brienne, he had earned a colonelcy and become a commander in the Legion of Honor for saving Napoleon's life by killing a Cossack who was charging the Emperor. After the first abdication, he had retained his commission under Louis; but, like so many of the military, he had defected to Napoleon after the return from Elba. He had accompanied Napoleon to Belgium and fought at Waterloo, where he saw his hopes of becoming a marshal of France destroyed by that defeat.

These six men formed Napoleon's small court. Before leaving Paris they had determined the function each would officially fulfill. Bertrand kept his post as Grand Marshal; Gourgaud, Lallemand, Montholon, and Savary served as aides-de-camp, and Las

Cases as Councillor of State. In carrying out their duties, they did
their utmost to foster and maintain an aura of royalty that pre-
served for Napoleon some measure of the imperial prerogatives
that he still claimed and that he wished to impress upon others.
It also clothed them with a dignity that they would not have enjoyed otherwise.

Now, the five of them on board the *Bellerophon*, along with
Mmes. Bertrand and Montholon, set about creating a courtly
atmosphere within the areas of the ship allotted to them. In the
after-cabin and the anteroom, the protocol of the court obtained.
No one was allowed to enter the after-cabin except on the express
invitation of Napoleon, whose wishes were usually made known
through Bertrand. If an audience with him was granted, one was
formally announced and ushered into his presence. When Napoleon dined, only those invited by him ate at his table, and they
took their seats as he indicated. This applied to the Englishmen as
well as to the French. Dinner was prepared by his maître d'hôtel
and was served in the French fashion on his silver plate. Each
night after Napoleon retired, his valet or one of his aides slept
on a mattress stretched across the doorway of his cabin.

When Napoleon was on deck, the same atmosphere prevailed.
Excepting those he bade walk with him, the members of his suite
followed him at a respectful distance, the men remaining bare-
headed. No one spoke unless first addressed by Napoleon. Before
long the English also adopted these manners in his presence; one
cannot find among their writings any disapproval of what might
have been regarded as a usurpation of privilege. They took their
cue from Maitland, who saw that Napoleon still considered himself a royal personage but who did not dispute the point, considering that to do so would be both ungracious and uncalled-
for under the circumstances. Maitland had Admiral Hotham's
courteous treatment of Napoleon as an example; and, even more
to the point, he did not know how his government intended to
deal with his passenger. Since the comportment of the suite in no
way interfered with the efficient administration of his ship, Maitland did nothing to discountenance it. Furthermore, the affability,

gentlemanliness, dignity of manner, and interest in things English that Napoleon constantly displayed during the voyage would have demeaned any effort to impose a more austere regimen.

Another prevalent sentiment conquered any uneasiness that the crew may naturally have felt in Napoleon's presence. From the officers on down to the humblest seaman, they all were consumed by curiosity about him. For years he had been a dominant figure in their lives—the principal cause of their serving in the Royal Navy. Their actions had been directed to effecting his defeat and overthrow, and some had even shed their blood in battles against his forces. They had heard and read much about him, talked about him among themselves, judged him on the basis of imperfect knowledge heavily tinged with the prejudices fed by propaganda. Now they could scrutinize the "Corsican ogre" at first hand. And their avidity for any revelation about him was made more acute by their awareness that they were the first of the English commons to be in such close proximity to him. Not a man among them but knew, in his own way, that fate had assigned him a part in one of history's singular episodes.

They eagerly gathered every possible personal detail about Napoleon, storing them against the days when—gathered around their hearths or in the crowded public-rooms of inns, in barracks or in the fo'c'sles of other ships—they would regale rapt audiences with stories of the days when they had rubbed elbows with Napoleon. They closely observed his appearance:

Napoleon Bonaparte is about five feet seven inches high, rather corpulent, remarkably well-made. His hair is very black, cut close, whiskers shaved off; large eyebrows, grey eyes, the most piercing I ever saw; rather full face, dark but peculiar complexion, his nose and mouth proportionate, broad shoulders, and apparently strongly built. Upon the whole he is a good-looking man, and when young must have been handsome. He appears about forty-five or forty-six, his real age—greatly resembles the different prints I have seen of him in London.

His teeth were finely set, and as white as ivory, and his mouth had a charm about it that I have never seen in any other human countenance.

His limbs particularly well-formed, with a fine ancle* and very small foot, of which he seemed rather vain. . . . His hands were also very small, and had the plumpness of a woman's rather than the robustness of a man's. . . . His hair was of a very dark brown, nearly approaching to black, and, though a little thin on the top and front, had not a grey hair amongst it.

Even his clothes elicited their attention. After the *Bellerophon* put to sea, he no longer wore the uniform of the Chasseurs of the Guard, but dressed in white breeches and waistcoat, white silk stockings and gold-buckled shoes, and a green, single-breasted coat adorned always with the Grand Cross of the Legion of Honor. But the small cocked hat displaying the tricolor cockade remained part of his apparel.

His habits especially interested the English observers: "Bonaparte was whilst with us an early riser, and most of his time was employed in reading. . . . With whomsoever he conversed he always appeared affable and polite, and I must acknowledge that his manners struck me as very engaging." When dinner was served, "Nothing was carved upon the table, the servants removed each dish for the purpose. . . . On the removal of the dishes a cup of very strong coffee was served to each. It was poured out by a servant of Napoleon's." "Seldom more than half an hour passed from the time of his going to dinner until he was again on the quarter-deck. He wore his hat always but when at meals, and even then he sat down to table with it on, when it was removed by his valet, and handed to him again before he rose."

They studied him closely when he appeared on deck for one of his frequent strolls:

We were always sure of a sight of the Emperor and the chief part of his suite immediately after dinner, when he generally remained on deck for about half an hour. Lady Bertrand, Captain Maitland, Bertrand, Savary, L'Allemande, Las Cases, and his aide-de-camp Montholon, formed the principal figures of the group ranged round the Emperor,

---

* English letters, orders, entries from diaries, etc., have been reproduced exactly as they were written. Errors in spelling, punctuation, and grammar have not been corrected.

while us young gentlemen took up our station on the poop to feast our eyes with a sight of the great man whose name had been sounded in our ears since we drew our first breath, and become, like a second nature to us, a name of fear. He generally kept his gold snuff-box in his hand while in conversation in these family groups, taking a pinch quite in a homely way; but I never saw him offer it to anyone else, neither did I ever observe him use it while walking the deck himself or when in earnest conversation with any of his suite individually.

Notwithstanding that we have him invariably drawn and busted with his arms folded across his breast, I never saw him in that attitude but once during the whole three weeks we had him on board. . . . His more common posture was his right hand stuck into the breast of his waistcoat, or thrust into his breeches pocket, while he held the snuff-box in the other.

His walk is a march, or (as far as a sailor may be allowed to judge) very like one; and to complete the portrait I must add that in walking he generally carries his hands in the pockets of his pantaloons or folded behind his back.

From quarterdeck to orlop deck, the interest and conversation of the *Bellerophon*'s crew centered on what Napoleon and his companions had looked like, said, and done during the day. Among the watch on deck, down in the boatswain's and carpenter's rooms, and outside the slop room and sail rooms, the men gathered to exchange their impressions of "Boney" and his company and to wager on their destiny. As the foregoing quotations illustrate, some of the ship's company were aware of the historic importance of the event in which they were participating, and they put down in writing what they witnessed and how they felt about it—filling the pages of their journals, diaries, and letters, and linking their names familiarly with the name of the man whose threat to England had drawn them from their homes and into uniform.

For the Frenchmen, these days of voyaging were a pleasant respite from the pressures of flight and from danger. Pleased and flattered by the attention and the courteous treatment accorded them by the *Bellerophon*'s company, they assumed they might expect the same in the future. Many of their thoughts must have fixed on Gourgaud, preceding them on the *Slaney*. He would, they knew, reach England two days before them, and they envisaged him immediately posting to London to present Napoleon's letter to the Prince Regent. Perhaps, when they arrived at Tor Bay, they would find him already returned, accompanied by an august delegation waiting to greet them and escort them to London. Friendly and respectful crowds would line the streets of villages and towns as they progressed toward the capital; and, once arrived there, they would be warmly welcomed by the Prince Regent and shown a hospitality that could not be provided on the *Bellerophon*. Honors would be bestowed upon Napoleon—and them. It was not inconceivable that the Prince Regent would confer the Order of the Garter upon the Emperor!

Once they were granted asylum and settled in England, the pattern of their lives would depend on how Napoleon chose to spend his. In conversations at Rochefort and on the *Bellerophon*, he had divulged his intentions to them. After the tremendous turmoil of the past twenty years he wished, he confessed, to end his days in peace and tranquillity. He knew that what he had done and what he represented would influence history, but he disclaimed any desire to play a further role in making it. He resolved to live in England as a private person, assuming the name of Colonel Meuron (who had been killed at his side while shielding him from enemy gunfire at Arcole). He would purchase a small estate in the country, far removed from London. There he would live in retirement, receiving very few visitors and never speaking on political subjects, forming a friendship with some savants and occasionally enjoying their society, riding out every day, then returning to read or to finish his history, and devoting himself to the education of his son. If and when he did diverge from this routine, one thing above all else would give him the greatest pleasure:

To be able to go about incognito in London and other parts of England to the restaurants with a friend, to dine in public at the expense of half a guinea or a guinea, and listen to the conversation of the company; to go through them all, changing almost daily, and in this manner, with my own ears, to hear the people express their sentiments, in their unguarded moments, freely and without restraint; to hear their real opinion of myself and of the surprising occurrences of the last twenty years.

One wonders if these dreams were voiced for others' contemplation rather than for his own—if he really believed that England would grant him the opportunity of realizing them. Did he truly think that he could long endure a mode of life so alien to his character and experiences?

So this halcyon handful of days passed. After a brief bout of seasickness, the Frenchmen had settled into an easy existence. After breakfast all of them would join Napoleon at cards, playing *vingt-et-un.* They laughed good humoredly at Maitland when, on being invited once by Napoleon to join the game, he confessed that he had no money: he always left it at home with his wife when he went to sea. On deck they took the sun and breathed of the benign sea air. With lazy interest they watched the barefoot sailors in their white trousers go about their duties, or amused themselves in watching the children form military lines and squares on the deck and engage in noisy maneuvers. And on one occasion they were entertained by a play that the midshipmen performed especially for them. Napoleon, with Madame Bertrand interpreting for him, remained until the end of the third act, "appeared much amused, and laughed very heartily at our ladies, who were personated by great strapping fellows dressed in women's clothes, and not in the most tidy fashion."

On July 17 and 18, the *Bellerophon* raised several English vessels, and on July 21 and 22 she exchanged signals with two or three others. To inquiries about them, Maitland replied that England had had several frigates patrolling those waters for the purpose of intercepting Napoleon if he had eluded the ships stationed off Rochefort. It seemed to him that by this time the Frenchmen were convinced that they could not have escaped the dragnet that had been spread for them.

On Sunday, July 23, the *Bellerophon* neared the end of her voyage. The day was fine, and Napoleon spent a great part of the morning on deck. While he was there, the ship, making for the English Channel, passed quite close to the Ile d'Ouessant, off the northwest coast of France. For a long time, Napoleon gazed at it, lines of grief etching his face. That evening England lifted into view on the northern horizon. And, as the ship beat through the choppy waters of the Channel, Napoleon and his companions had to face the fact that they knew absolutely nothing of what lay in store for them.

III

"What Is to Become of Buonaparte?"

THE magnitude of the gamble Napoleon took in surrendering to the British is revealed by two documents that the Allies had published following his return from Elba. The first was the decree of outlawry, pronounced from Vienna on March 13, 1815:

The powers in congress at Vienna who have signed the Treaty of Paris, being informed of the escape of Napoleon Bonaparte and of his forcible entry into France, owe to their own dignity and to social order a declaration of the sentiments which this event has made them experience.

In thus breaking the convention which had established him in the island of Elba, Bonaparte destroys the only legal title on which his existence depended; and, by appearing again in France with projects of confusion and disorders, he has deprived himself of the protection of the law and has manifested before the world that there can be neither peace nor truce with him.

The powers consequently declare that Napoleon Bonaparte has placed himself beyond the pale of civil and social relations, and that as an enemy and disturber of the world, he has delivered himself up to public vengeance. They declare at the same time that, firmly resolved to maintain entire the Treaty of Paris of the 30th of May, 1814 [which excluded Napoleon from the French throne], ... they will employ all their means, and will unite all their efforts, that the general peace, the object of the wishes of Europe, and the constant purpose of their labors, may not again be troubled.

The second document was the Treaty of Vienna, signed on June 9. In Article I of this treaty, the Allies had reaffirmed their intention of enforcing the Treaty of Paris and the decree of outlawry. And in Article III they had agreed that they would never lay down their arms, except by common consent, until Napoleon had been disposed of and the peace of Europe made secure.

Subsequent events did little or nothing to mitigate the hatred and fear that Napoleon's reappearance had occasioned. Waterloo had ended in an Allied victory, but its cost had been tremendous —over half a million troops mustered against the French, more than 60,000 Allied soldiers killed and wounded in the fighting, a financial expenditure of hundreds of millions—not to mention the dark sense of fatalism that had pervaded Europe during the Hundred Days. Napoleon's second abdication did not satisfy his enemies. His appetite for power unappeased, he had broken faith and come back within a year after his first abdication to threaten them with a ruin of apocalyptic proportions. Given the chance, they judged, he would do so again; they must make sure that he could not. But first they had to apprehend him. Where exactly was he bound and what did he really intend to do? One rumor had him en route to join the army of the Loire. Not until the early days of July were the Powers assured that Napoleon intended to leave the country, and as late as July 7 they remained uncertain of the port from which he would embark. He was reported to be in Cherbourg, in Poitiers, in Bordeaux, in other cities from the Channel to Cape Finisterre. The wearisome work of watching, checking, searching for him continued. But cost what it might, they would have him.

In the quest to find and capture Napoleon, none of the other Powers exceeded the efforts and expenditures of England. Exclusive of ships patrolling the English Channel, she had dispatched thousands of men in at least twenty ships to stations off the west coast of France, all of them operating under one order: if Napoleon tries to pass, intercept him and take him. Should he outwit, outshoot, or outrun the English navy, England's pride would suffer a major blow and her position at the conference table in Paris would be appreciably weakened. The ministry did not intend that either should happen. England had fought Napoleon too long on too many fronts—from Egypt to the Spanish Peninsula to the Indies, at times almost unaided—for her to spare any pains to lay hands on him now.

No one in the Liverpool administration could rival Napoleon in brilliance and dynamism. Lord Castlereagh, the Secretary of State for Foreign Affairs; Henry, Earl Bathurst, Secretary of State for War and the Colonies; Lord Melville, First Lord of the Admiralty; and the Earl of Liverpool himself had relied instead on a singleminded and tenacious opposition in order to effect Napoleon's defeat. In this endeavor, they had nearly drained Britain of her resources, spending men and ships and money in a conflict whose duration seemed to lengthen interminably and whose outcome always remained doubtful. But they had prevailed; and now that Napoleon had been overcome, they meant to see that he would never again endanger the peace. The extent to which his whereabouts and fate claimed their attention is made evident by a letter from Liverpool to Castlereagh in Paris.

Fife House, July 7, 1815

... What is to become of Buonaparte? What course is to be adopted with respect to those who assisted him in resuming his authority? ... I conclude the Emperors and King will come to Paris, as soon as they hear of the capitulation. By that time we shall be able to form some judgment of the probable fate of Buonaparte. If he sails from either Rochefort or Cherbourg, we have a good chance of laying hold of him. If we take him, we shall keep him on board of ship till the opinion of the Allies has been taken. The most easy course would be to deliver him up to the King of France, but then we must be quite certain that he would be tried and have no chance of escape. I have had some conversation with the civilians, and they are of opinion that this would be, in all respects, the least objectionable course. We should have a right to consider him as a French prisoner, and as such to give him up to the French Government.

If it is asked why so much importance is attached to one man, it is because I am thoroughly convinced that no other man can play the same part that he has done, and is likely to play again, if he should be allowed the opportunity. Independent of his personal qualities, he has the advantage of fourteen years' enjoyment of supreme power. This has given him a title which belongs to no other man, and which it would be very difficult for any one to acquire.

Napoleon proved the subject of Castlereagh's thoughts, too. On the night of July 8, he wrote to Liverpool: "I understand from the King, this evening, that he had given orders to Fouché to use every exertion to arrest Buonaparte. I apprized both his Majesty and Talleyrand that I conceived the policy of Europe towards France must be materially influenced by Buonaparte's being left at liberty to return again to the charge, when a new complot could be arranged."

A week passed—the momentous week culminating in Napoleon's boarding the *Bellerophon*. But the developments of those days were unknown at the time to the men in power in London and Paris. Their latest reports told them that although Napoleon remained at large he had not yet succeeded in escaping. Their anxiety persisted, but their confidence that he would eventually be captured increased. Time and circumstances were now in their favor. Daily the Bourbon flag was being raised over more French cities and towns; daily additional French army units that had been clinging stubbornly to resistance declared their allegiance to Louis; daily the English blockade of the coast grew more impenetrable. The net was drawing tighter around their archenemy, and soon it would close.

But once having taken him, what should they do? Three possibilities presented themselves to Liverpool and his Cabinet. They could send Napoleon back to France to be tried and executed as the rebel that Louis XVIII had declared him to be. They could try him in the name of the Allies as an outlaw whose crimes demanded the severest retribution. Or they could confine him somewhere—in England, on the Continent, or far from Europe. Two points qualified their choice. One was that if Louis were to insist that Napoleon be turned over to him, they must honor his request if at all possible. It was doubtful that Louis would do so, however, for he faced the difficult tasks of welding into an operable government factions that were inimical to each other and in some cases to him, of treating with the Allies for terms that would not leave France prostrate, humiliated, and ripe for further political eruptions, and of winning recalcitrant army units to allegiance. To bring Napoleon to summary justice could only compound his difficulties. The second point was that the capture of Napoleon by British forces would not confer on England the privilege of unilaterally deciding his fate. Her allies must be consulted and must consent to any action she might propose to take.

In their discussions the English ministers in London reduced to two the possibilities they preferred, regardless of who apprehended Napoleon. On July 15, Liverpool communicated them to Castlereagh.

I am desirous of apprizing you of our sentiments respecting Bonaparte. If you should succeed in getting possession of his person, and the King of France does not feel sufficiently strong to bring him to justice as a rebel, we are ready to take upon ourselves the custody of his person on the part of the Allied Powers; and, indeed, we should think it better that he should be assigned to us than to any other member of the Confederacy. In this case, however, we should prefer that there were not Commissioners appointed on the part of the other Powers, but that the discretion should be vested entirely in ourselves, and that we should be at liberty to fix the place of his confinement, either in Great Britain, or at Gibraltar, Malta, St. Helena, the Cape of Good Hope, or any other colony we might think most secure.

We incline at present strongly to the opinion that the best place of custody would be at a distance from Europe, and that the Cape of Good Hope or St. Helena would be the most proper stations for the purpose. If, however, we are to have the severe responsibility of such a charge, it is but just that we should have the choice of the place of confinement, and a complete discretion as to the means necessary to render that confinement effectual.

While this letter was on its way to Paris, a more important one reached there on July 17. Written by Bonnefux to Fouché, it narrated the circumstances of Napoleon's surrender to the British. Fouché at once notified Castlereagh: "I have the honour to acquaint your Lordship, that Napoleon Bonaparte, not being able to escape from the English cruisers, or from the guards kept upon the coasts, has taken the resolution of going on board the English ship *Bellerophon*, Captain Maitland."

They had him at last then; and Castlereagh, who had closed his dispatches to London for that day, reopened them to include this momentous news. But England had not captured Napoleon; and that fact circumscribed her freedom of action in dealing with him, even though no convention or understanding had preceded the surrender. The London *Courier* for July 21 accurately summed up the state of affairs:

The situation in which we are placed is somewhat embarrassing. Louis the 18th, by his Proclamation of the 6th of March last, declared him [Napoleon] a traitor and rebel, and ordered him to be arrested and brought to trial as such. The usage, we believe, is between Governments in a state of amity and friendly relations with each other, to give up mutually, to be tried by their own laws, persons accused of treasonable practices. Shall we do this in the present instance? We shall not if Buonaparte surrendered himself upon an understanding that his life should be spared, or even if he gave himself up unconditionally to us.

The Courier clarified this point of embarrassment in its next issue:

Buonaparte voluntarily surrenders himself a prisoner of war into the hands of the Prince Regent of Great Britain, and the law of nations prescribes that "as soon as your enemy has laid down his arms and surrendered his person, you have no longer any right over his life." If it be said that he paid no regard to the Law of Nations, and has no right to their protection, it may be answered, that his former violation of them would afford us no justification in violating them ourselves, especially when he is no longer in any condition to repeat that violation. . . . He must have surrendered himself under the conviction that he should receive an asylum, which conviction we confirmed by the act of receiving him—or Captain Maitland would have refused receiving him. It seems, therefore, that we cannot give him up—that we shall afford him an asylum—that his life will be spared—but that we shall have him in such safe custody, that he shall not be able to disturb again the repose or the security of the world.

What circumstances prevented England from doing in this matter her allies could not well do without compounding England's embarrassment. The technically voluntary nature of Napoleon's surrender precluded them, too, from trying and executing him as an outlaw. Thus, confining him remained the only feasible action. All the governments were anxious that it be quickly arranged.

In the interim before Liverpool learned of the surrender and replied to Castlereagh's letter, Castlereagh committed a serious diplomatic blunder. Apparently assured by his Allied colleagues that England could assume charge of Napoleon's custody, he acted precipitously, suggesting that the other Powers appoint commissioners to keep Napoleon under surveillance during his detention. His suggestion was accepted, but he must have regretted his hastiness when he received Liverpool's letter of July 15, with its explicitly stated preference that if Napoleon became England's prisoner there be no Commissioners appointed on the part of the other Powers. It was too late, however, for Castlereagh to retract. On July 18 Metternich had written to Marie Louise: "According to an arrangement that has been agreed upon between the Powers, he [Napoleon] will be established as a prisoner in Fort St. George, in Scotland, and placed under the surveillance of Austrian, Russian, French, and Prussian Commissioners."

In London, meanwhile, the Cabinet, still unaware of Napoleon's surrender and of Castlereagh's gratuitous concession to the Allies, continued its discussions. We know few of the details, since Cabinet deliberations and proceedings are secret, and no official record of them is kept, but it appears that they were concentrated primarily on the contingency that would most involve

England, i.e. her being granted custody of Napoleon. The sentiments concerning him and his fate contained in Liverpool's letter
of July 15 were transformed into clearly outlined plans. The
Admiralty, to whose charge prisoners of war are committed, had
exerted considerable influence. Poring over its maps, charts, and
lists of prison sites, it weighed the effectiveness of each suggested
place of detention and, through its First Lord, Viscount Melville,
passed on its recommendations to Liverpool and his Cabinet.
Therefore when, on July 21, Castlereagh's dispatch announced
the surrender of Napoleon, the Government had nearly determined its course, and Liverpool could answer his foreign minister
immediately:

Fife House, July 21, 1815

My dear Castlereagh—

I have this moment received your letters of the 17th instant, with
the intelligence of the surrender of Bonaparte, of which I wish you joy.
When your letter was written, you had evidently not received mine
of the 15th, which will explain to you the sentiments of Government
on the subject of his detention.

We are all decidedly of opinion that it would not answer to confine
him in this country. Very nice legal questions might arise upon the
subject, which would be particularly embarrassing. But, independent
of these considerations, you know enough of the feelings of people in
this country not to doubt he would become an object of curiosity immediately, and possibly of compassion, in the course of a few months:
and the circumstance of his being here, or indeed anywhere in Europe,
would contribute to keep up a certain degree of ferment in France.

Since I wrote to you last, Lord Melville and myself have conversed
with Mr. Barrow* on the subject, and he decidedly recommends
St. Helena as the place in the world the best calculated for the confinement of such a person. There is a very fine citadel there, in which he
might reside. The situation is particularly healthy. There is only one
place in the circuit of the island where ships can anchor, and we have
the power of excluding neutral vessels altogether, if we should think it
necessary. At such a distance and in such a place, all intrigue would

---

* John Barrow, Second Secretary of the Admiralty.

be impossible; and, being withdrawn so far from the European world, he would very soon be forgotten.

We are very much disinclined to the appointment of Commissaries on the part of the other Powers: such an arrangement might be un-objectionable for a few months, but when several persons of this description got together in a place in which they had nothing to do, they would very soon be tired; they would be very likely to quarrel amongst themselves; and the existence of any disputes amongst them might seriously embarrass the safe custody of the prisoner.

St. Helena was the most satisfactory place for Napoleon's de-tention for a more important reason than any Liverpool specif-ically mentioned. The island was not only remote, but also im-pregnable. The Foreign Office's "Memorandum on St. Helena," written during this time, and probably studied by Liverpool, Melville, and Barrow, stressed this point:

There are undoubtedly several local circumstances peculiar to the island of St. Helena, which seem to render it pre-eminently suitable to the purpose of confining a State Prisoner. Its remote Situation from all other parts of the Globe,—its compact form and size—the small number of its inhabitants, amongst whom no stranger can introduce Himself without immediate Detection, together with the extraordinary formation of the Island itself, being encompassed on all sides by stu-pendous and almost perpendicular cliffs, rising to the Height of from six to more than twelve hundred feet, and through which formidable Barrier there are but few Inlets to the Interior, are collectively, such a variety of *natural* advantages for the purpose in question, that perhaps they are not to be equalled nor surpassed in any other part of the British Dominions.

The only accessible landing Places are James' Town, Ruperts' Bay, and Lemmon Valley on the North—and Sandy Bay on the South. All these points are well fortified and powerfully protected by *Fleur d'eau* Batteries, furnished (excepting Sandy Bay) with Furnices for heating Shot:—and as Cannon are also placed upon the Cliffs in their vicinity, far above the reach of ships, it may be readily imagined that if a Martello Tower with one gun, could beat off a seventy-four gun ship in the Mediterranean, how much more efficacious would be those prep-arations on the Island of St. Helena. In short, it appeared to be the decision of several experienced Naval officers, who have recently visited that Island, that no ships could possibly stand the fire of the Defences which protect the Anchorage and the whole of the Northern coast; and in regard to the Southern landing Place, Sandy Bay, it is equally secure against a naval attack.

Besides the principal landing places . . . there are several small Paths from the Interior leading down the Precipices to the Sea, which are frequented by Fishermen, but they are so very difficult of Access that Persons unaccustomed to such frightful Roads would find it extremely difficult, if not impracticable, and particularly in the Night, to ascend them. All these Paths should of course be attended to, and guarded, and they might very easily be defended by rolling stones from the Heights.

In addition to this natural strength of the place, and its numerous Batteries, it may be proper to mention that a great acquisition has lately resulted from an admirable establishment of Telegraphs. These are placed upon the most commanding Heights, some of which are two thousand feet above the level of the sea, and are so connected one with another, and so spread all over the Island, that no vessel can approach without being descried at the distance of sixty miles. The vast ability of such an Establishment may be easily imagined. Nothing can pass in any part or even in sight of the Island without being instantly known to the Governor and equally can he convey his orders whenever they may be necessary either during the Day or Night. . . .

This concise view of the *nature* of the Island and its Defences, together with the recent topographical survey, will be sufficient for determining how far a State Prisoner would be secured against all external attempts for effecting his release. . . .

St. Helena belonged to the East India Company and served its vessels as a port of call on their voyages to and from India. Jurisdiction over the island would have to be temporarily transferred from the company to the Crown; Bathurst, as Colonial Secretary, would arrange this. Castlereagh, of course, would handle the pertinent details of the detention with the Allied representatives in Paris. But the essential arrangements and the bulk of the work would devolve upon the Cabinet ministers in London. The conditions governing Napoleon's activities on St. Helena had to be formulated and their practical details worked out. Arrangements for transporting him to the island and keeping him in safe custody there needed to be undertaken. The most pressing task, however, was to ensure that he would be secure while in port in England. Lord Melville, in a letter dated July 21, notified Admiral Keith in Plymouth that Napoleon was to be afforded no latitude that might encourage him to cast about for means to escape. If Maitland should come to Plymouth, Melville wrote,

he should remain in the Sound in a line-of-battle ship and the most positive orders should be given to prevent any person whatever, except the officers and men who form the complement of that ship, from going on board. No person, whether in His Majesty's service or not, who does not belong to the ship, should be suffered to go on board, either for the purpose of visiting the officers, or on any pretence whatever, without permission from the Admiralty. I do not wish of course to put any restraint upon your Lordship or on Sir John Duckworth* in case either of you should think it necessary to go on board, but you will probably agree with me in opinion that any such visit had better if possible be avoided. It would be uncomfortable to you to have requests made in a personal communication with which in all probability we should feel ourselves obliged to refuse compliance.

Events quickened now, increasing the urgency for swift and effective governmental action. Late at night on July 22, the *Slaney* anchored in Plymouth Sound and Captain Sartorius hastened to Admiral Keith, aboard his flagship, *Ville de Paris*, in Hamoaze. The dispatches that Sartorius bore and the information that he verbally supplied to Keith induced Keith to order him to London without delay. He carried a letter from Keith to John Wilson Croker, First Secretary of the Admiralty:

July 22

SIR,

Captain Sartorious of His Majesty's ship *Slaney* has this moment landed with the enclosed despatch from Captain Maitland of the *Bellerophon* by which it appears that Bonaparte proposed on the 14th

* Naval commander in chief at Plymouth Station.

instant to embark on board the *Bellerophon* and throw himself on the generosity of His Royal Highness the Prince Regent, and that he [Maitland] had acceded thereto.

There is a General Gourgaud on board the *Slaney* who is charged with a letter to the Prince Regent, of which a copy is enclosed, and as I understand from the captain of the *Slaney* that he refuses to deliver that letter to any other person than His Royal Highness I have directed that he is to remain on board the *Slaney* and ordered her to Torbay there to await their Lordships' commands. That their Lordships may be in possession of every circumstance that has occurred on this important occasion, I have ordered Captain Sartorius to convey this despatch as he was present with Captain Maitland through the whole transaction.

I shall send directions to Torbay to-morrow to meet Captain Maitland, enforcing the orders contained in your letter of the 1st instant, and if my presence should be considered useful there I shall hold myself in readiness to set off upon the receipt of a telegraph message to meet any instructions their Lordships may address to me there.

The stage was set. But as Sartorius sped toward London, as the *Slaney* and the schooner *Express* made for Tor Bay to await the arrival of the *Bellerophon*, and as Englishmen devoured the newspaper accounts of Napoleon's surrender and speculated about his probable fate, Napoleon had still to make his appearance.

On July 24, he did.

IV

A Mixed Reception

DAWN promised a lovely day. A light breeze blew; sunlight sparkled on the Channel and on the foaming bow waves of the *Bellerophon* and the *Myrmidon* as they sailed close alongshore off Dartmouth. Napoleon had been up and out on the poop deck at four-thirty, looking at the green hills that undulated northward from the clean, cliff-lined coast. The boldness of the coast drew his admiration. "You have in that respect a great advantage over France, which is surrounded by rocks and other hazards," he told Maitland.

The *Bellerophon*, running freely with her fore-topmast studding sail set, stood on her way east-northeastward—past Scabbacombe Head, past Long Sands and the Cod Rocks, past Crabrock Point, and toward Sharkham Point. The eyes of all on deck were directed ahead to where the long, gray, two-hundred-foot-high cliffs of Berry Head jutted eastward into the Channel. Once around its point, the ship would be in Tor Bay, her voyage completed. When the *Bellerophon* opened the bay, shortly after six, Napoleon was struck by the scene. "What a beautiful country!" he exclaimed. "It very much resembles the bay of Porto Ferrajo in Elba."

The nearly semicircular bay, about three and a half miles long by about four miles wide at its entrance, presented a panorama of blue waters tilting up tawny pebble beaches and washing against low red sandstone bluffs. Brightly painted, red-sailed trawlers dotted the bay. Sloping gently down to the water were rounded hills patterned with green pastures, golden grainfields, red-soiled fallow fields, tufted rows of apple orchards, wooded parks, and long lines of tall elms that ran down to the water's edge. Towns and villages fringed the coves. This area of England was far different from the only other part of the country that Napoleon had seen—the sheer chalk cliffs of Dover, which he had scanned from Boulogne twelve years earlier. But more important to the Frenchmen than the scenery was the sight of the *Slaney* lying at anchor, which meant that Gourgaud had arrived.

While the *Bellerophon* tacked in toward an anchorage, Maitland ordered her gig lowered, and Andrew Mott, his first lieutenant, and Lieutenant Fletcher of the *Superb* went ashore with letters to Admiral Keith in Plymouth and John Wilson Croker, First Secretary of the Admiralty, in London. Maitland's alacrity in communicating with his superiors is explained by his uncertainty about the official judgment of his conduct. Admiral Hotham had approved it, but Hotham was not the Lords Commissioners of the Admiralty or the Commander in Chief of the Channel Fleet. Although Maitland might reasonably expect congratulations for his initiative in securing Napoleon, he could not simply assume that they would be forthcoming. Thus, Lieutenant Fletcher, bound for London with Hotham's dispatches for the Admiralty, also bore Maitland's report of his arrival in Tor Bay, the list of Napoleon's suite, and—most important of all—a copy of a letter that Lieutenant Mott was carrying, along with a report of Maitland's arrival, to Admiral Keith. The letter, which Maitland had written on July 18, supplemented the brief dispatch of July 14 that he had sent ahead on the *Slaney*. It was primarily a statement of extenuation, meant to "explain the circumstances" in which he was placed "when induced to receive Napoleon Buonaparte" on board his ship.

After the first communication was made to me by Count Bertrand . . . that Buonaparte was at Isle d'Aix, and actually embarked on board the frigates for the purpose of proceeding to the United States of America, my duty became peculiarly harassing and anxious, owing to the numerous reports, that were daily brought from all quarters, of his intention to escape in vessels of various descriptions, and from different situations on the coast, of which the limited means I possessed, together with the length of time requisite to communicate with Sir Henry Hotham at Quiberon Bay, rendered the success at least possible, and even probable. Thus situated, the enemy having two frigates and a brig, while the force under my command consisted of the *Bellerophon* and *Slaney,* (having detached the *Myrmidon* to reinforce the *Daphne* off the Mamusson passage, where the force was considerably superior to her, and whence one of the reports stated Buonaparte meant to sail,) another flag of truce was sent out, for the ostensible reason of enquiring whether I had received an answer to the former [i.e. Bertrand's letter, forwarded by Maitland to Hotham], but I soon ascertained the real one to be a proposal from Buonaparte to embark for England in this ship.

Taking into consideration all the circumstances of the probability of the escape being effected, if the trial was made either in the frigates, or clandestinely in a small vessel—as, had this ship been disabled in action, there was no other with me that could produce any effect on a frigate, and from the experience I have had in blockading the ports of the bay, knowing the impossibility of preventing small vessels from getting to sea—and looking upon it as of the greatest importance to get possession of the person of Buonaparte, I was induced, without hesitation, to accede to the proposal, as far as taking him on board, and proceeding with him to England: but, at the same time, stating in the most clear and positive terms, that I had no authority to make any sort of stipulation as to the reception he was to meet with.

I am happy to say, that the measures I have adopted have met with the approbation of Sir Henry Hotham, and will, I trust and hope, receive that of your Lordship, as well as of his Majesty's Government.

At seven o'clock the *Bellerophon* shortened sail and anchored less than a mile from the quay of Brixham, a fishing village on the southern side of the bay. Hardly had the ship finished swinging round her cable when an officer from the schooner that Keith had sent the day before came on board. He delivered orders and a letter, both dated July 23, from the admiral to Maitland. The first, couched in the formal prose of official directives, informed Maitland that his dispatch of July 14 had been delivered by Captain Sartorius and had been forwarded by Keith to the Admiralty. It instructed Maitland to remain in Tor Bay until he received further orders, to prohibit any communication with the shore, to prevent anyone from coming on board for any purpose whatever, and to remove Gourgaud from the *Slaney* to the *Bellerophon*.

The letter had a more personal tone. "You will perceive from the newspapers," he wrote,

that the intelligence had reached London before Captain Sartorius. . . . I have a letter from Lord Melville to-day, enforcing in the strongest manner the former orders,—even that no person, myself or Sir John Duckworth excepted, shall be suffered to come on board the ship, till orders are sent from Government; which you will be so good as strictly to comply with. Let him and his want for nothing; and send to me for any thing Brixham cannot furnish; I will send it to you by a small vessel. You may say to Napoleon, that I am under the greatest personal obligations to him for his attention to my nephew,* who was taken and brought before him at Belle Alliance, and who must have died, if he had not ordered a surgeon to dress him immediately, and sent him to a hut. I am glad it [the taking of Napoleon] fell into your hands at this time. . . .

The letter contained little to allay Maitland's apprehensions. The last sentence intimated Keith's approval, but it was far from being completely reassuring. Maitland informed Napoleon of Keith's message to him, and Napoleon, who remembered the incident referred to, was much gratified—surely the warm sentiments of this first communication from a high-ranking officer ashore augured well for the future.

But the situation looked less auspicious when Gourgaud returned from the *Slaney* during the morning: surprise at his unexpected appearance was replaced by consternation when he reported that he had not been permitted to land and so still retained

---

* James Drummond Elphinstone, a captain in the 7th Hussars, who was gravely wounded and taken prisoner by the French during the fighting on June 17, 1815.

Napoleon's letter to the Prince Regent. It was true that Captain Sartorius had taken a copy of it ashore—but why had Gourgaud not been allowed to land and go to London? In what light were Napoleon and his suite to be considered? Were they prisoners of war? What was to be done with them? Maitland, when asked, could only tell them that all unauthorized communication to and from the ship had been forbidden and that he was waiting for further orders.

The English newspapers that were brought on board that day increased their alarm. While celebrating the glory and triumph accruing to England because of Napoleon's surrender, the press almost without exception referred to Napoleon in vituperative terms. Most outspokenly hostile were *The Courier* and *The Times*. The first called him "the disturber and scourge of the human race" and referred to his "enormous crimes." The other characterized him as "the ex-rebel," and "a man who has committed every species of crime in one country"; it spoke of his "guilty career," and stated that "his propensity to mischief will continue as long as his life." *The Courier* termed his surrender an advantage whose importance could not

be duly appreciated, without contemplating the possible, nay probable, consequences of his having been able to secrete himself or to escape. Had he got to America, who would have treated it as a chimerical speculation that he might have obtained great sway in the United States, or that he might have procured vast influence in those provinces of South America which are now in arms against Spain.— Would Turkey, had he escaped thither, have opened no field for the mind of a man possessed of such military talents as Buonaparte? Might not the Turks have been eager to have revenged themselves upon Russia? Had he been able to secrete himself for a time, might not even France herself have again opened him the road to pre-eminence and power? All these chances are at an end—all these apprehensions are now idle. But it is by weighing these things, by considering the danger that might have occurred had he escaped that we are able to feel and appreciate the full value of his having surrendered himself to us.

Neither newspaper was reticent about recommending what the government should do with Napoleon. *The Times* flatly stated:

Deliver him up to the justice of an injured Sovereign, and of a country which he has involved in every species of ruin. We confess, indeed, that we are not content with M. Bonnefoux, for not following him on board the British ship, and demanding his person in the name of his most Christian Majesty, the Ally of Great Britain. However, as he is to come here, we should propose before his surrender, that a commission be appointed to interrogate him as to the murder of Captain Wright:* and his answers upon this subject, and others of a similar nature, will, no doubt, in addition to the imperfect retributions which his wretched body owes France, give us the power of demanding satisfaction upon the delinquent, from the Sovereign of that country. The blood of the murdered Palm,† of Nuremberg, must also cry out for justice against him.

The Courier averred that "though we may not give him up to the condign punishment he has so amply and so often deserved, we are responsible in the eyes of the world for his being kept in such safe custody that though his life may be spared, he shall be as dead to all political purposes, to all the business and designs of this world as if he were no longer in existence." It reported a rumor that he was likely to be sent "to Dumbarton Castle, situated on a projecting rock between two deep vallies, on the river Clyde, between Glasgow and Greenock, a spot extremely beautiful in its situation, as it overlooks a delightful country, but from which it is next to impossible that anyone should escape." But it also said, "This report, we understand, is incorrect, and we have heard that he is to be sent to St. Helena, where an English regiment will be stationed to watch him." Other rumors

---

* An English naval officer, captured and accused of disembarking in France several conspirators bent on assassinating Napoleon. He died in a Paris prison—his throat cut. The French government stated that he had committed suicide, but the English believed that he had been murdered.

† Palm, who published an anonymous pamphlet attacking Napoleon and the conduct of the French army in Germany, was arrested by order of Napoleon, tried by a military court, and shot.

named the Tower of London and Sheerness as possible places of detention.

These articles both worried and incensed Napoleon's followers. If the views expressed in them reflected the views of the British government, Napoleon and they were in dire trouble. They sought out Maitland and crowded around him, protesting the arbitrariness and injustice of the government's contemplated action—"talking to me," Maitland wrote, "as if I had been one of his Majesty's Ministers, and had influence in determining their future destination." Though he pleaded that he knew nothing of the government's policy regarding Napoleon and was, in any case, unable to influence it, he could not prevent them from frequently seeking him out and inveighing against the Ministry. Napoleon, however, for whom Las Cases read and interpreted the papers, appeared unruffled, and he attempted to soothe the fears and doubts of his suite. The fulminations of newspapers that had always been inimical to him were to be expected. It would be foolish to give credence to their reports and surmises and to equate them with what the Ministry might be discussing and deciding about him. The government had as yet announced nothing respecting its position or intentions—witness Maitland's statement that he had received no orders that clarified these points. The government must be waiting to hear Napoleon out before determining how to treat with him, and Downing Street should receive at any moment the copy of his letter to the Prince Regent. All would yet be well.

Napoleon could point out more obvious signs that showed he would be well received. Already, though it was still early morning, boatloads of people were swarming out from the shore toward the *Bellerophon*, drawn there by the knowledge that he was on board. For these Devon folk this was the greatest day in the history of Tor Bay since William of Orange had first set foot in England at Brixham in 1648. "Happy was the possessor of a boat," one of them wrote. "Every sort of craft that could be pulled by oars or propelled by sail was brought into requisition."

Packed to capacity, they crowded around the *Bellerophon*, approaching as close as the frigate's sentries permitted; the passengers chanted insistently, "Bonaparte! Bonaparte!"

Napoleon did not ignore their shouts. He appeared on deck often and showed himself at the gangways and stern windows, taking off his hat and bowing to the people in the boats. At the sight of him, the crowd was moved to further demonstrations. The men removed their hats, the women waved handkerchiefs and shawls in salute, and the massed voices rose repeatedly in shouts of "Hooray!" Napoleon inspected the crowd through his pocket-glass, frequently exclaiming, "What charming girls! What beautiful women!" He removed his hat time and again and bowed to them, evoking renewed cheers of appreciation. "What curious people these English are," he remarked to Maitland. But beyond question he was pleased by their display of interest in himself. The holiday humor of the throng, the sight of still more boats rounding Berry Head, a gift of wall fruit in season from the owner of Torre Abbey—all these betokened the kind of welcome to England he had hoped to receive. The members of his suite, too, grew more sanguine concerning their fate. The spectacle on the water, Montholon wrote, "revived our hopes that the national feeling would open the gates of England for our reception, or at least force the ministers to allow us to proceed to America."

While the boats were clustering around the *Bellerophon* that noon, Maitland's first lieutenant, Andrew Mott, arrived in Plymouth and presented his captain's dispatches to Admiral Keith. The tall, gray-haired Admiral of the Channel Fleet read them through, his stern face unmoving. When he finished, he dictated his reply:

> *Ville de Paris*, Hamoaze
> July 24, 1815

SIR,

    The officer of the ship you command has just delivered to me your letter of this date, reporting your arrival in Torbay, with the *Bellerophon* and *Myrmidon*, having on board Napoleon Buonaparte and his suite. I have also received your other letter, explaining the circumstances under which you were placed, when you were induced to receive Napoleon on board; and I shall transmit the same to the Lords Commissioners of the Admiralty, in confident expectation, that his Majesty's Government will fully approve of your conduct.

Then, taking quill and paper, he sat down and wrote another letter to Maitland:

I take the opportunity of your officer's return, to congratulate you and the nation, and to thank you for the perfect manner in which you entered into my views on the subject, and for the management of the blockade, about which I was most anxious. It will not be long ere you are instructed by the Government: the first express would arrive about four o'clock this morning, and I attempt a telegraph message, but it is cloudy. I beg you will send for any thing you may want, to me, and it shall be sent instantly; and I beg to present my respects to Napoleon, and if I can render him any civility, I will consider it my duty, as well as in gratitude for Captain Elphinstone's report of the attention he received from him on the field of battle.

Obviously Keith had not missed the apprehensive tone of Maitland's letter of July 18; and he was not a man who let his rank prevent him from displaying a personal interest in the concerns of the men under his command. A long life in the navy had exposed him too intimately—and at times too dramatically—to them for him to ignore their existence or belittle their importance.

"The Right Honourable The Viscount Keith, G.C.B., Admiral of the Red, Channel Fleet," had gone to sea at fifteen as plain "George Keith Elphinstone, Midshipman"—sent there, he was fond of saying, with a five-pound note in his breeches pocket and an injunction to make his fortune. In that he had succeeded, accumulating in prize money won during his commands at the Cape of Good Hope, in the Mediterranean, and in the Channel a sum probably exceeding that earned by any other naval officer before or since his time. But the promotions leading to his present high rank and his elevation to the peerage were the results not of his wealth, but of his record. He had served with distinction throughout the American Revolution and during the long struggle against revolutionary France and Napoleon. Although he had never won fame in a battle at sea, he had spent his share of time afloat, in the North Sea, the Channel, the Atlantic, and the Mediterranean. It was as an administrator, however, that he excelled.

During his more than fifty years in service, Keith had become used to vital and challenging assignments. It was he whom, in June 1797, the Admiralty had sent to handle the great mutiny of the fleet at the Nore, and who had satisfactorily settled that dangerous and ugly affair. In 1801 Keith had played a leading part in the expedition to Egypt that drove the French from Cairo and Alexandria and inaugurated British occupation of the country. When Napoleon had threatened England with invasion in 1803, Keith had been appointed to the North Sea Station, which command carried the responsibility for the defense of England's shores. From 1812 to 1814, and again during the Hundred Days, he had served as Commander in Chief of the Channel Fleet. As such, he had directed the blockade of the French coast and the navy's efforts to prevent Napoleon's flight; and now, so long as Napoleon remained on board ship in England, Keith was directly responsible for his safe custody.

Nearing seventy and no longer in good health, the admiral was undertaking his last assignment before retirement. The task promised to be a difficult one—if only because unauthorized persons persisted in trying to involve themselves in it. "There has been the most ridiculous altercation between General Browne* and Duckworth about which was to keep Buonaparte," he wrote to his daughter Margaret. "The General sent Colonel Byres to me today to say he had ordered a guard to receive and conduct him to the Government House. To this I replied: 'He is in my care; I am responsible, and shall give neither of you any trouble till the Government send orders.' He, the General, is more absurd than ever." Maitland's modesty and deference must have been a relief from Browne's officiousness.

Maitland undoubtedly read Keith's letters with relish when

---

* The lieutenant governor of the garrison at Plymouth.

Mott returned to the *Bellerophon* that evening. For the first time since July 14, he was free from worries about his conduct and the future of his career; the tone of the admiral's letter gave good reason to picture his future as bright.

Napoleon's hopes, too, were raised by Keith's second friendly gesture. The warm tone of both messages, plus the unrestrained enthusiasm of the people who had flocked out in the boats to see him, more than offset the rancorous editorials in the newspapers. All in all this first day in England had not proved disappointing.

At dusk the boats that had hemmed the *Bellerophon* headed homeward, to Brixham, Elberry Cove, Roundham Head, Paignton, Torquay, and the villages fronting the coves and beaches. The next day promised to be another profitable one for the boatmen, for already the people of Dartmouth were arriving on foot and in carts and chaises; and that evening the first post chaise rolled into Brixham from Exeter, filled with gentlemen avidly seeking a glimpse of "Boney."

In London, the ministries had spent a busy day. Captain Sartorius, carrying Keith's and Maitland's dispatches, had arrived at Lord Melville's home in Wimbledon between three and four o'clock that morning. After reading the dispatches, Melville had informed Liverpool, who was at Combe Wood, of their contents; and the Prime Minister had at once ordered a Cabinet meeting to be held at noon at the Foreign Office. Melville then hastened to London for an hour's audience with the Prince Regent, at Carlton House, to inform him of the latest developments—which probably included the arrival of the copy of Napoleon's letter. When the audience ended, Melville proceeded to the Cabinet meeting, which lasted until nearly five o'clock. The ministers' decision to confine Napoleon on St. Helena was likely reached at this meeting.

In the meantime the Admiralty officers had been making plans. Napoleon was in their charge while he was in England—but what should they do with him, how should they treat him, once he reached Tor Bay? Melville had sent Sartorius, with Keith's and Maitland's dispatches, to John Barrow, second secretary of the Admiralty, and Barrow now wrote to Major General Sir Henry Bunbury in the War Department.

24 July

SIR—

I am commanded by my Lords Commissioners of the Admiralty to transmit to you for the information of Earl Bathurst Copies of a Letter and it's enclosures which I have received from Admiral Lord Keith relative to the embarkation of Napoleon Buonaparte on board His Majesty's Ship *Bellerophon*; and I am to request you will move his Lordship [Bathurst] to take the pleasure of His Royal Highness the Prince Regent, and to signify the same to my Lords relative to the disposal of Buonaparte and the officers and Suite embarked with him on the arrival of the *Bellerophon* in Torbay and also of General Gogaud who is on board the *Slaney*—

Their Lordships have ordered the *Bellerophon* and *Slaney* to proceed from Torbay to Plymouth Sound.

Orders from Barrow flowed out. To Sartorius: "Proceed immediately to rejoin the *Slaney* in Torbay, and proceeding from there with her to Plymouth Sound, report your arrival to Admiral Lord Keith," and, on Sartorius's return to Tor Bay, "deliver the accompanying Letter to Captain Maitland of HMS *Bellerophon*, whom you may expect to find there." To Maitland:

Proceed immediately with the ships under your command to Plymouth Sound, and reporting your arrival to Admiral Lord Keith follow such orders as you may receive from his Lordship with regard to the disposal of Napoleon Buonaparte, his officers and Suite, observing the regulations which his Lordship has been instructed to issue relative to the conduct to be pursued by the Captain of any of His Majesty's Ships having Buonaparte on board, during such time as he shall continue on board the *Bellerophon*.

To Keith:

Give the most positive orders to Captain Maitland to prevent all communication whatever with the shore, but through him, and by him through your Lordship, and on no account to permit any person whatsoever to go on board the ship without Your Lordship's permission given in writing for that purpose, which permission for obvious reasons, will only be granted in such cases as the public service may require; and proper measures are to be taken to prevent boats and small craft from crowding near the *Bellerophon*. . . . P.S. Your Lordship will restrict the Captains and Commanders of your Squadron from communicating until further orders with the *Bellerophon*.

And to Duckworth: "Give the most positive orders to the Captains and Commanders of His Majesty's Ships and Vessels under your command, not to communicate with the *Bellerophon* till further order."

The decisions that the Cabinet had reached at its meeting were quickly transformed into orders. From the War Department, Earl Bathurst replied to Barrow's resquest of that morning:

MY LORDS—

I have had the honour to submit to His Royal Highness the Prince Regent the substance of the communication which Your Lordships have caused to be made to me respecting the surrender of Napoleon Bonaparte to Captain Maitland of His Majesty's Ship *Bellerophon*;—and I am commanded by His Royal Highness to signify his Pleasure to the following effect.

Your Lordships will be pleased to give immediate Orders that upon the Arrival of His Majesty's Ship *Bellerophon*, Napoleon Bonaparte should remain untill the Prince Regent's further pleasure shall be signified, on board of that, or of such other Ship of War as may be appointed by their Lordships—and shall not be permitted upon any account to come ashore or to hold communication with the shore, or with other Vessels, either personally or by Writing. Not more than four or five Persons of His Suite (exclusive of Menial Servants) are to remain on board the same ship with Himself:—the remainder of his Suite are to be kept under similar restraint on board other Vessels of War.

Napoleon Buonaparte is to be considered and addressed as a General Officer.

With regard to General Gorgaud, I am to request your Lordships will give orders that the said General should be conveyed on board His Majesty's Ship *Bellerophon*, and be considered in the same light as the other French officers composing Buonaparte's Suite. General Gorgaud cannot be permitted to land in England with the view of delivering in person the letter with which he is charged;—but, if He shall think proper the said letter may be conveyed through the Medium of the Naval Commander in Chief in Plymouth,—and any additional communications He may be desirous to make, may be transmitted through the same Channel.

Bathurst sent another letter at the same time—this one to Major General Sir Hudson Lowe at Marseilles requesting him to surrender the command of the British troops there and to return to London with all possible speed to take charge of Napoleon —stopping in Paris only to ask the commands of Wellington and Castlereagh.

A private letter, from Melville to Keith, reveals additional details of Cabinet decisions reached that day:

Admiralty, 24th July, 1815

My DEAR LORD,

I am much obliged to you for remembering me in directing Captain Sartorius to come to Wimbledon; he arrived there between three and four this morning, and we have since had a Cabinet on the business. I am afraid that the result will not come in the shape of an official letter from Lord Bathurst in time to send off by this post; but I can state, for your private information, that in all probability the ex-Emperor will be sent to some foreign colony. In the mean time he will not be allowed to land, or to have any communication whatever with the shore, and we shall not apprize him immediately of his future destination. With a view to his personal accommodation, we must diminish the number of his suite in the *Bellerophon*; but they also must be kept in strict seclusion. Sir John Duckworth and you will be able to judge whether, if there is any influx of small boats getting round the boat from curiosity, it may not be necessary to have guard boats to keep everything at a distance, except boats approaching with official communications or other necessary business, and the ship's own business. I suppose he will usually walk on the quarter-deck only, where he will not be easily seen and gazed at from the water. We once thought of allowing him to remain in Torbay; but as he may be here some weeks, and that anchorage is not very eligible at all times, and as moreover the strict surveillance which we require may be under your own eye or Sir John Duckworth's . . . I thought it on the whole better and more secure to trust to Plymouth Sound, with all its inconveniences of greater publicity, than to leave the ship in Torbay, or send her to any other port, where connivance . . . could not be so effectually prevented. The Aide-de-Camp on the *Slaney* will be sent back to the *Bellerophon*, there to remain, and he will be told that he must send this [i.e. Napoleon's letter to the Prince Regent], and all other letters through you, as no others will be allowed to come on shore. I am afraid we shall find Buonaparte and his suite troublesome guests while they remain here; but we have no cause to grumble on the whole—very much the reverse.

In Paris, Castlereagh had been discussing the question of Napoleon's custody with the other Allied representatives; but he was hampered in his dealings with them because of slow communications with London. So on the 24th he wrote to Liverpool:

I am impatient to receive the notification of Buonaparte's arrival in England, and to be informed of the steps you have thought it advisable to adopt, both towards himself and his suite, which contains two very flagrant criminals, Savary and L'Allemand. . . .

I forgot to mention that I believe there will be no sort of difficulty in leaving the unrestricted custody of Buonaparte's person to the British Government, under perhaps some engagement with the other Powers not to turn him loose without their consent. The idea of Commissaries was a party suggestion of my own, which, upon reconsideration, appears to be open to much objection.

That evening a telegraph message from Plymouth brought the Government the news that the *Bellerophon* had arrived in Tor Bay. Ironically, on the same day, in Marseilles, Major General Sir Hudson Lowe wrote Earl Bathurst:

My Lord,

There being no longer any avowed Enemy existing in the South of France, I have consulted Admiral Lord Exmouth as to the best mode of Employing the Force under my Command, whose opinion is in perfect concurrence with mine, that it could not be more usefully Engaged, than in compelling the garrison of the Island of Elba, to strike the Tricolor Flag, which is the only Spot in the Mediterranean where it is at present displayed; and in Execution of this design, we have decided on Embarking forthwith the Force here, and proceeding for that Island. . . .

On July 25 the ministries took further steps to implement the Cabinet's decision. Bathurst proceeded to work out the terms of the agreement by which the Crown, acting under the King's military authority, would assume control of St. Helena from the East India Company. The Lords Commissioners of the Admiralty—Melville, Yorke, and Paulet—forwarded to Keith the orders they had received from Bathurst stating the Prince Regent's wishes. Barrow transmitted a copy to Duckworth, along with instructions that Duckworth should cooperate with Keith if Keith decided to remove some members of Napoleon's suite to another vessel in Plymouth Sound.

Two other decisions were made that day. Since Sir Hudson Lowe would need time to travel from Marseilles to London and to make arrangements for assuming the command at St. Helena, and since it was desirable that Napoleon be settled on the island as soon as possible, someone would have to be put in charge of conveying him to St. Helena and keeping him in safe custody until Lowe arrived. Admiral Sir George Cockburn was given this assignment, which was made acceptable to him by carrying with it a higher command. Next, a replacement had to be found for the *Bellerophon,* whose recent tour of duty had left her in no condition to undertake a lengthy voyage. Fortunately, Cockburn's flagship, the 74-gun frigate *Northumberland,* was in the Medway River at Long Reach, still fully manned and ready to sail. Orders for reducing her had been sent out only the day before; now, they were hastily canceled and new orders directed her to proceed without delay to Spithead.

Early on the 25th, Melville's suspicion that Napoleon would prove a troublesome guest was confirmed. Lieutenant Fletcher, who had arrived from Tor Bay with Hotham's and Maitland's dispatches to the Admiralty, reported to Melville on Napoleon's visit to Hotham's flagship in the Basque Roads and on the treatment accorded Napoleon on board the *Bellerophon* during the voyage to England. Melville was very much perturbed by these reports. The efficacy of his ministry's strict orders to isolate Napoleon and his suite and so minimize their opportunities to plot mischief or escape was threatened by the preferential treatment that they had been and probably still were enjoying on board the ship that should be his temporary prison. He had made fools of the commissioners on Elba and stunned the world by his escape; he must not be given the opportunity to do the same thing again on the very doorstep of England. Melville wrote immediately to Keith:

Admiralty. 25th July, 1815

Confidential.

MY DEAR LORD,

It would appear that the yards were manned when Bonaparte visited the *Superb* (which was an unnecessary visit), that he insists upon being treated with royal respect, that he invites Captain Maitland and other officers to dine with him, and in short, that if we do not interfere, the same follies in this respect are likely to be committed as were exhibited last year by some officers in the Mediterranean. I have written the inclosed which may assist you in putting a stop to any thing of that kind, and which you can shew where it may be necessary.

I think we shall send Bonaparte to St. Helena, and that Sir George Cockburn's appointment as Commander-in-Chief on the Cape Station, which was suspended, will now go forward, and that he will convey the Prisoner to St. Helena and remain there for some time. We must take it under the King's Military authority, to which the Court of Directors, I believe, will not object.

If Bonaparte or his suite are desirous of writing letters, they must be sent through you open, or addressed to some member of the Government. You had better transmit them all to the Admiralty, unless there is anything very confidential which you may prefer sending direct to me.

[Enclosure]

Admiralty, 25th July, 1815

My dear Lord,

On conversing with the Officer who came to England in the *Bellerophon* with the dispatches from Sir Henry Hotham and Captain Maitland, I think it would appear that Bonaparte had been allowed to assume a great deal more state, and even authority, and had been treated with more submissiveness, than belongs to his station as a prisoner of war, or to his rank as a General Officer, which is all that can be allowed to him in this country. No British officer would treat his prisoner with inhumanity, and the recollection of the station which Bonaparte has so long held in Europe would naturally, and almost involuntarily, lead an officer to abstain from any line of conduct that could be construed into insult, and therefore to go rather beyond than to fall short of due respect; but such indulgent feelings must be restrained within proper bounds, and I will be obliged to your Lordship to give such hint on this subject as may appear to you necessary.

On the *Bellerophon* another seemingly interminable day of waiting passed for Napoleon and his suite—no orders arrived for Maitland, no official recognition of Napoleon's arrival, no statement of the government's intentions concerning him. In the face of this silence and apparent indifference to their peace of mind, the Frenchmen began to despair; their foreboding increased as they perused the newspapers, which continued to assert that their destination would be St. Helena. Were the *Bellerophon* and the *Myrmidon*, then, merely awaiting orders to convey them there? Were Napoleon and they prisoners? Were they to be denied the right to speak in their own defense?

As on the day before, however, the boats that gathered around the ship somewhat diverted their distressful thoughts and served to keep their hopes alive. At daybreak large numbers of craft were already on their way toward the *Bellerophon*, their occupants intent on being among the first arrivals, and obtaining positions close to the ship. A Brixham resident described the scene:

Boats! There never was before or since such an assembly of craft in Torbay. . . . Torquay was little but a fisherman's village . . . but the population, such as it was, seemed to have turned out altogether and crossed the bay. From Exmouth, Teignmouth, Plymouth, the boats and yachts continued to arrive all day . . . and on that day all the country seemed to come in. Gentlemen and ladies came on horseback and in carriages; other people in carts and waggons; and to judge by the number of people, all the world inland was flocking to see Bonaparte. The Brixham boatmen had a busy time of it, and must have taken more money in two days than in an ordinary month. It seemed a gala day as the boats thronged round the *Bellerophon*, and Tuesday found Brixham in a whirl of excitement. Every inn was full; there was not room for the visitors, nor stabling for the horses.

Gunwale to gunwale, the boats jostled each other for favorable positions, their passengers straining for a glimpse of Napoleon. What was he like? Was he really human? Was his voice like thunder? Would they let him be seen? Or was he locked up? They waited for him to appear, meanwhile satisfying themselves by watching the members of his suite and speculating about who they were. At last, that afternoon Napoleon showed himself on deck, walking it for over an hour and frequently standing at the gangway or opposite the quarterdeck ports so that the people could see him better. The tightly packed boats rocked and creaked as their occupants craned to see him. The tones of their voices, excited and not abusive, came across the water to him. Pleased, he pulled off his hat again and again and bowed to them, at which the spectators in the nearest boats removed their hats in turn and cheered. Bonaparte! How little he looked, how stout—how human after all. And they were seeing him! "I recall a feeling of triumph mixed with a natural satisfaction at seeing a wonderful sight," one of them later reminisced. "Now we had the Emperor —the conqueror, the tyrant, the villain—a safe prisoner in an English ship."

It is impossible to know if Napoleon interpreted all this attention as a personal tribute. At dinner that evening, however, he ate with relish and talked amiably to his table companions, remarking several times on the local boatmen: "They are generally smugglers as well as fishermen," he said. "At one time a great many of them were in my pay, for the purpose of obtaining intelligence, bringing money over to France, and assisting prisoners of war to escape. They even offered, for a large sum of money, to seize the person of Louis and deliver him into my hands; but as they could not guarantee the preservation of his life, I would not give my consent to the measure."

Casual remarks only? Or a veiled hint that he expected England to be as considerate of his well-being as he had been of Louis's? Or an insinuation that he was not isolated from aid should he need and desire it?

At three o'clock the next morning, July 26, a boat did approach the *Bellerophon*; but it brought no smugglers' rescue party for Napoleon. Captain Sartorius, just returned from London, had come on board to deliver the Admiralty's sailing orders to Maitland. The watch was roused, and at four o'clock the ship got under weigh. The sounds from the deck as the men heaved up the anchor and made sail awakened some members of the suite. Las Cases came on deck as the anchor was raised. He sought out Maitland, who informed him that the ship, together with the *Myrmidon* and the *Slaney*, was ordered to Plymouth. The east had already lightened as the ships worked out of the bay and rounded Berry Head before a moderate southeast breeze. Then the weather turned squally, and they were forced to take in their royals and studding sails and haul to the wind.

Soon after the *Bellerophon* was at sea, Maitland faced a different kind of squall: Madame Bertrand came on deck. She attacked Maitland for what she considered his unmannerly neglect in not having acquainted Napoleon with the orders he had received. Napoleon, she said, was extremely indignant. Maitland, having had to contend with her tongue and temper once or twice before this, got rid of her as best he could; and, when she had returned to her cabin, he sought out Las Cases. Her visit had left him angry. Her warm language, flung at him as if he were a mere midshipman, had ruffled his usually even temper; but more important if what she had asserted were true, his authority on his ship was being challenged. "Though I was inclined to treat him [Napoleon] with every proper consideration," he wrote later, "it never was my intention to be looked upon as responsible to him for my movements." He informed Las Cases of what Madame Bertrand had told him and asked if he would discover whether Napoleon really was displeased. Las Cases went at once to the after-cabin. When he returned a few minutes later, he informed Maitland that there must have been some mistake. Nothing of the kind described by Madame Bertrand, he assured the captain, had occurred.

Throughout the day the three ships stood to the west, beating up along the coast for Plymouth Sound through a choppy sea and into squalls blown at them by a strong north wind. Tacking occasionally, they left astern the long, forbidding promontory of Start Point, with its barren, storm-blasted western rocks and pinnacles over which thousands of gulls and kestrels wheeled; they edged past Prawle Point, past the cliffs between Bolt Head and Bolt Tail, and past Bigbury Bay and Wembury Bay.

Napoleon remained on deck the greater part of the trip. He walked the quarterdeck, silently watching the coastline as it slid past. To the members of his suite, their being sent westward could signify only one thing: the British government was not going to allow Napoleon to land. His bid for asylum had failed. Why else was he being removed farther from London? Was Plymouth to be their last port of call before they were sent to St. Helena? A few of them tried to inject a more optimistic note into their muted conversations. Perhaps they were being carried to Plymouth to pick up the passports to the United States that Napoleon had requested originally. Perhaps they were even to be put ashore there, since that city offered better accommodations and better transportation to London than Brixham did. But these conjectures did not win many converts.

By midafternoon the ships had come within sight of Plymouth Sound. At 3:50 the *Bellerophon* shortened sail and came to with her best bower in the Sound, just inside the breakwater. As soon as she had anchored, Maitland informed Napoleon that he was going ashore to call on Keith and asked if Napoleon had any message for the admiral. Napoleon told the captain to convey his thanks to Lord Keith for the kind words the admiral had expressed in his letters to Maitland. He added that he was extremely anxious to see Keith, if the visit was at all possible.

The Frenchmen, standing at the rail and by the ports on the quarterdeck, watched as Maitland was rowed ashore, noted the firing of signal guns from the decks of two frigates—the *Liffey* and the *Eurotas*—that were moored in the Sound, and a short time later observed boats carrying officers put out from the city toward the frigates. The officers and boat crews boarded the ships, then the ships slipped their moorings and slowly approached the breakwater. When the *Liffey* came abeam of the *Bellerophon* on the latter's larboard side, she dropped anchor and came to. The *Eurotas* did the same astern of the *Bellerophon*. From each ship a lieutenant and armed seamen descended into boats, which the frigates had towed alongside as they came out, and began to row around the *Bellerophon*. The members of the suite looked at one another without speaking. They knew now that they were being held prisoner.

V

Civility and Security

THE *Liffey* and the *Eurotas* had flanked the *Bellerophon* on orders from Keith to their captains, Hancock and Lillicrap, who only a few days before had brought their vessels into Plymouth after completing patrol assignments off the French coast.

Ville de Paris in Hamoaze
26th July 1815

The *Liffey* and *Eurotas* are to take up an anchorage on each side of the *Bellerophon* at a convenient distance, and observe the following directions, as well for the purpose of preventing the escape of Buonaparte or any of his suite from that Ship, as for restraining shore Boats and others from approaching too close to her either from curiosity or from any other motive.

A constant watch of an Officer, a Quarter Watch, and double sentinels are to be kept by day, as well as a Boat manned and armed alongside in constant readiness as a Guard Boat.

The same precaution is to be observed all night, with the exception that one of the Boats in charge of a Lieutenant is to row guard and to be relieved every hour.

Neither Shore Boats nor others are to be suffered either by night or by day to approach nearer to the *Bellerophon* than one Cable's length; and no boats are to be permitted to loiter about the Ship even at that distance either from curiosity or any other motive.

Keith had learned from Melville's letter of the 24th that Napoleon would be kept in custody. He had also been told about the crush of people that had surrounded the *Bellerophon* at Tor Bay, and he had already refused many applications to visit the ship. He knew that only very rigorous measures would ensure the security of his prisoner and discourage the boats of townspeople and visitors from gathering too close to the *Bellerophon*.

When Maitland called on Keith on the afternoon of July 26, he conveyed Napoleon's thanks for the admiral's friendly messages and informed Keith of Napoleon's desire to see him.

"I would wait upon him with much pleasure," Keith answered, "but, to tell you the truth, I have as yet received no instructions as to the manner in which he is to be treated; and until I do receive these, I cannot well visit him."

The old admiral was as curious as anyone else to see Napoleon, and despite Melville's suggestion that his visiting Napoleon might embarrass the government, he was awaiting an opportunity to call on him. Keith had attained an age, rank, and reputation that enabled him to interpret and act on the suggestions of his superiors with an independence that would have frightened a lesser man. He would scrupulously attend to his duty of keeping Napoleon in safe custody; but once he had learned how Napoleon was to be addressed, Keith would not insult him by refusing to see him. As he wrote to Melville that day, "As long as the keeping of Napoleon Buonapare is entrusted to me I will venture to say it shall be done in a secure and civil manner, and the same attention shall be paid which has heretofore been done to prevent any kind of insult, or his suffering from excess of idle curiosity, notwithstanding the situation in which the ship must be placed, which is certainly inconvenient."

Maitland very likely elaborated on his first description of the events and discussions that had preceded Napoleon's surrender, and summarized Napoleon's conduct on the *Bellerophon*. Keith reported to Melville that when Maitland returned from Sir Henry Hotham's ship in the Basque Roads, "he found the table covered with the plate of Bonaparte. He [Napoleon] assumes the company and invites officers to dine with him. No one sits down covered in his presence. Captain Maitland sups in the master's cabin. In Torbay he looked over the side and took off his hat to the people and seemed pleased. He has walked over the ship and attempted to converse with the people." Maitland probably also assured Keith that Napoleon had neither tried to interfere with his management of the ship nor proved demanding, but rather had made every effort to be a model passenger. Before Maitland left, Keith handed him copies of his orders to the captains of the *Liffey* and the *Eurotas*, the Admiralty's orders of July 24, which directed Maitland to prevent communication with the shore and to permit no unauthorized persons on the *Bellerophon*, and a General Order sent by Keith that day to the captains and crews of the ships under his command, forbidding them to communicate with the *Bellerophon*.

On Maitland's return to the ship his gig had to maneuver through the considerable number of shore boats that had already assembled around the *Bellerophon*. Plymouth had been waiting for Napoleon to arrive. During the day the city had been filling with people who had journeyed to Tor Bay to see him, only to discover that he had been sent to Plymouth. Speeding toward that city in post chaises, in carriages, and on horseback, many of them had arrived before the *Bellerophon* and had spread the word that the ship and her illustrious passenger were to be expected that day. The news set the city ablaze with a curiosity as intense as its indignation two years before, when its citizens had burned an effigy of "the Scourge of Mankind" on the Hoe overlooking Plymouth Sound. Therefore, when the *Bellerophon* anchored that afternoon, scores of people rushed into their boats and off toward her. The day was finishing with fine weather; and, undeterred by the lengthening shadows, many of those in the boats lingered, crowding in upon the guard boats, hoping for a look at Napoleon. The guardsmen, finding it difficult to maintain the stipulated cable's length of open water between the *Bellerophon* and the shore boats, had earlier taken to firing their muskets periodically into the air in an attempt to hold the intruders at a safe distance.

When Maitland boarded the ship, he reported to Napoleon what Keith had said concerning a meeting. "I am extremely anxious to see the admiral," Napoleon answered, "and therefore beg he will not stand on ceremony. I shall be satisfied to be treated as a private person until the British Government has determined in what light I am to be considered." That he would concede this indicates how uneasy the past two days had made him. His outward imperturbability at Gourgaud's return, at being held incommunicado, and at being transferred to Plymouth Sound only masked his tension. A man of action, he was thwarted by the official silence and secrecy that had greeted his arrival. A soldier, he felt defenseless without knowledge of his adversary's plans. He had to communicate with someone in England and attempt to discover what to expect from the government.

He also showed his first signs of bitterness and anger at the manner in which he was being treated. He complained to Maitland of the stationing of the *Liffey* and the *Eurotas* as guard ships. "As if I were not perfectly secure on board a British line-of-battle ship," he said scornfully. Pointing to the guard boats, he added, "The guard-ships' boats have been firing musketry all the evening to keep the shore-boats at a distance. It disturbs and distresses me, and I shall be obliged to you to prevent it, if it lies in your power." Maitland at once sent a request to Captains Hancock and Lillicrap to put a stop to the firing; and it ceased.

Night came, clear, warm, and calm. The ships rode at anchor, their riding lights palely reflecting in the water. Less than two miles north across the Sound, lights shone from the homes of the 20,000 inhabitants of Plymouth, Stonehouse, and Plymouth Dock; in the northwest rose the dark, wooded eminence of Mt. Edgcumbe, and to the east lay the high, open fields of Staddon Heights.

It is doubtful whether the peacefulness of the midsummer night had a very salutary effect on the Frenchmen aboard the *Bellerophon*. Through the open cabin windows or from their stations on the quarterdeck, they could hear the guard boat's oars and could make out the shadowy forms of the boat and crew as they circled the ship. Their eyes were drawn to the formidable outlines of the *Liffey* and the *Eurotas* nearby, and from them to the other warships that lay in the Sound: the *Slaney*, the *Myrmidon*, the *Tonnant*, the *Havannah*, and the *Menelaus*. And always, to the southwest, lay the Atlantic, whose waters rolled against the precipitous rocks of St. Helena, over two thousand miles distant.

The hopes for asylum they had indulged in during the passage from France had proved fruitless. "It was no longer possible to be under any illusion respecting our fate," wrote Montholon, "and we would have deemed ourselves fortunate in being able to hope that the Castle of Dumbarton in Scotland, or the Tower of London, might be assigned as the Emperor's prison. St. Helena appeared nothing less than a burning tomb in the midst of the Atlantic." Some among them must have reexamined the motives that had led them to follow Napoleon to England, must have asked themselves if they had been truly wise to leave France. Las Cases and Madame Bertrand must have recalled painfully the praises of England that they had sung at Rochefort. And a few others, unwilling to sacrifice their freedom if it could be avoided, began to seek a way out for themselves.

In Paris and London diplomats had nearly settled the problem of what to do with Napoleon. In Paris, Castlereagh had gained Allied acceptance of England's offer to assume responsibility for Napoleon's safekeeping, but was finding the Powers insistent about being allowed to send commissioners to keep Napoleon under surveillance at his place of detention. Several articles of a proposed formal convention relating to the detention were scheduled to be discussed. In the meantime, France was urging that Savary and Lallemand be returned to face trial for treason.

In London, Bathurst had found the Court of Directors of the East India Company amenable to his request that the Crown assume control of the administration and security of St. Helena. The ministers were formulating the specific conditions that would govern Napoleon's incarceration on the island and were working on the letter that would inform Napoleon of the fate intended for him.

They meant to present him with a fait accompli. They felt that they owed him nothing. The Allied Powers had denied him the protection of the law, so he should consider it fortunate that his life was being spared. His letter to the Prince Regent? To acknowledge receipt of it would be to extend to Napoleon a recognition that would conflict with the decree of outlawry. England would dispose of him without debate and without delay. Melville expressed this intention in a letter to Keith:

The sooner that Bonaparte is disposed of, and despatched to his destination, the better for all concerned. Sir George Cockburn means to embark at Spithead, and whenever he arrives at Plymouth and takes charge of his companion you will be relieved from further trouble on that subject.

When we communicate to Bonaparte our final intentions concerning him, I think it probable that you may have to visit him; at least I do not expect that we shall be able to come to a conclusion on all matters without your having a personal communication with him.

On the morning of July 27 Napoleon acted—or, more accurately, he reacted to the developments of the past three days. When Maitland went ashore to see Keith, Napoleon gave him his original letter to the Prince Regent and requested that Keith forward it to London. It was impossible to hope any longer that Gourgaud would be permitted to deliver it to the Prince Regent. The copy of the letter, which Napoleon knew the ministers must have seen by this time, had elicited no reply or acknowledgment; he could only hope that the original would be more favorably received. The fate of the letter was of paramount importance to Napoleon. For if it were accepted by the ministers and presented to the Regent, he would have succeeded in directly communicating with the government. Once official recognition was granted him, he could no longer be kept in a passive role. The government would have to deal directly with him; it would be forced to accord him a hearing. However, if the letter were not received, he could not expect that any subsequent writings would be; and he would remain shut out of the case, with little doubt remaining about his fate. The release of the letter was only one move in Napoleon's campaign to win a hearing. According to Lord Keith, Napoleon, in conversation with Maitland on the morning of the 27th, claimed that

> many ways of escape had been pointed out and recommended to him [in Rochefort], but which he declined.—That the Army on the Loire had sent to invite him to take command of 70,000 as General of France, and that the Garrisons of Rochelle, Ile De Re, etc., had offered to escort him to join that Army, but this he also declined, preferring to throw himself upon the humanity of England.—He read in the papers that he was to be sent to St. Helena, which idea was dreadful. He would prefer Death.—He would be content to be put in the Tower, or in any place of confinement in England, but above all to be permitted to live in privacy in any part of the Kingdom within a limited space.

These were more than private remarks. They were an attempt by Napoleon to insinuate his views into the government's deliberations. He was trusting that Maitland would report his words to Keith and that Keith would pass them on to London. Thus the government would be informed of some of the arguments that he could advance in support of his claim to asylum and some of his attitudes toward being confined. Its knowing these might make a difference in the manner in which it disposed of him. At any rate it would know that he could not forever be kept supine and silent.

Maitland carried Napoleon's letter to the Regent to Keith. He also reported in detail what Napoleon had said to him, and mentioned the growing restlessness that the newspaper stories concerning St. Helena were breeding in Napoleon and the officers of his suite. Lastly, he repeated Napoleon's desire to see the admiral and his willingness to waive all ceremony and be considered as a private person. Keith, who by this time had received both the Admiralty's orders of July 25 and Melville's letter of the same date, answered, "I shall now have no difficulty whatever, having received full instructions as to the manner in which he is to be treated. He is to be considered as a General Officer, and have the respect due to that rank paid him, and no more. You may therefore say I shall wait on him tomorrow forenoon." So far as is known, Keith did not mention Melville's displeasure at the report that Napoleon had been "allowed to assume a great deal more state, and even authority, and had been treated with more submissiveness, than belongs to his station." Nor does any record exist to show that he even hinted to Maitland that a sterner regimen should be imposed on the prisoner. Keith trusted his captain's prudence and sense of propriety. Maitland had brought Napoleon in without firing a shot or losing a man; he had kept him and his suite aboard his ship, making sure that not one untoward incident occurred. He was performing a difficult job with laudable skill and diplomacy, and Keith chose not to interfere with his interpretation of his orders. In fact, though Melville might consider it unwise, Keith himself would visit Napoleon the next day.

Before Maitland left, Keith presented him with a copy of the Admiralty's orders of July 25 and directed him in writing "forthwith to carry the same into execution; sending on board the *Liffey* or the *Myrmidon*, . . . such of his suite as are to be withdrawn from the ship you command." After Maitland departed, Keith wrote to Melville:

> Plymouth Dock
> July 27

My Lord,

I am honoured by your Lordship's letter of the twenty-fifth and shall carefully attend to the suggestions therein mentioned, and that part relating to a future destination shall remain a profound secret with me. I have the honour to enclose the letter to the Prince Regent which had been withheld by the French general but who is now on board the *Bellerophon.*

Later in the day, he wrote the First Lord again, this time more informally. He thanked Melville for his private letter "concerning the rank and way in which Napoleon is to be considered, for I felt awkward, as he had sent repeatedly desiring to see me." Then, after recounting what Maitland had reported about Napoleon's statements concerning his opportunities of escape while in France and his hopes from England, he continued, "but it strikes me if he has got the idea of St. Helena into his head he may by means of money attempt an escape, and I shall enjoin Captain Maitland to be as vigilant as possible by day and night, to double the Centinels at night and load the Arms. The Guard Boats shall also be cautioned, and changed frequently."

When Maitland announced that several of the officers not attached to Napoleon's personal service and some of the servants were to be removed from the *Bellerophon*, Napoleon's uneasiness could only have increased.* Although none of the principal members of the suite were among those being transferred, the next day might see them also ordered to be moved. It could well be that this was the first step toward their deportation to St. Helena, if such was their destination, for it had become obvious that the *Bellerophon* would not convey them to that island. Since her arrival, the frigate had taken on board only enough supplies to meet her ordinary needs, and none of the other usual preparations for an extended voyage had been in evidence. Perhaps some other ship was waiting for them—ready to depart the moment they had all been transferred on board her. Las Cases observed, "It would be difficult to describe our anxieties and torments: the greater number of us seemed hardly to be living: the least circumstance from land, the most commonplace opinion of any one on board, the least authentic article, supplied us with subjects for the gravest arguments and caused continual oscillations between hope and fear."

They were heartened, however, when they learned from Maitland that Keith would call on Napoleon the next day. At last, someone in authority on shore was recognizing his existence. A breach, however small, was being made in the high wall of of-

* Twenty-one officers and servants were transferred to the *Liffey* on July 28.

ficial silence surrounding him. The admiral might inform him
about the government's deliberations. But even if Keith could
not or would not do so, Napoleon could repeat the declarations
he had made to Maitland that morning, increasing the chances
that they would reach the Ministry. At the least the meeting held
promise of being an amicable one; and by this time a friendly
voice from shore would be a blessing.

In informing Napoleon of Keith's forthcoming visit, Maitland
did not tell him that he was to be considered and addressed as a
General Officer.* One imagines that even if Maitland had been
ordered to inform Napoleon of the status assigned him by the government, he would have done so reluctantly and with distaste—
motivated not only by feelings of humanity but also by a correct
assumption that such an assignment lay outside the sphere of his
responsibilities. He would address Napoleon in the manner ordered, but he would not make an issue of it.

The number of shore boats packed around the *Bellerophon* on
the 27th was the largest yet. Every available craft in the area, it
seemed, had been employed, but still there were not enough to
meet the demand. So keen was the competition among the curious
that some parties paid as high as sixty pounds to hire a boat for
the day. "One would have said that the harbor of Plymouth had
become the rendezvous of all the curious people in England. . . .
The harbor was like a vast square where the curious populace
crowds and presses to see something that it has never seen before."
The guard boats could not prevent the other boats from loitering
or approaching too near the *Bellerophon*; inexorably, they and
their perspiring crews were pressed toward the frigate, at times
almost touching her sides. Many of the people in those tossing
shore boats had traveled to Plymouth from London and still
more distant towns and shires, and they were not amenable to
being kept at more than arm's length from the man they had

---

* Nor did Keith mention it when he visited Napoleon on July 28.

invested time and money to see. Nor were they willing to suspend their efforts to see Napoleon until the next day. He might be gone by then; or, if not, the crowd would get larger. People were converging on Plymouth "as if on a pilgrimage, in the hope of seeing for an instant the features of the legendary man. There were not horses enough on the road between London and Plymouth, so great was the throng of travellers who wanted to be able to say one day to their children: 'I have seen Napoleon!' " Many could hardly believe that "this Man is now actually in Plymouth Sound. How incredible all this is! How astonishing! I cannot think of it coolly, it bewilders me."

The visitors were amply rewarded for their persistence. "Napoleon remained on deck this day longer than usual. He came out after breakfast and continued upwards of an hour"; and he "showed himself to them before and after dinner." When he appeared, "there were acclamations from all sides; everybody moved about and stood on tiptoe to see him the better. . . . The greater part of the visitors had their hats off and those nearest saluted the Emperor with respect; ladies waved their handkerchiefs. I saw a boat containing several officers come pretty near, and these officers took off their hats and made profound bows."

Many of the boats contained fashionably dressed women. Napoleon took special notice of them and was highly impressed by their beauty. He asked Maitland which of them were the ladies and which the common folk, declaring that they were all so well dressed that he could not distinguish them. The officers of Napoleon's suite often remarked ruefully that they were placed "in the situation of Tantalus—so many beauties in view, without the possibility of approaching them."

That afternoon Napoleon and Maitland were favored by a visit from one of the ladies. Mrs. Maitland came alongside the *Bellerophon* in a boat with Sir Richard and Lady Strachan. Napoleon was strolling on deck at the time; and when Maitland told him that his wife was alongside, he went to the gangway to meet her. He pulled off his hat and, smiling, asked if she would not come up and visit him. She shook her head; and Maitland informed Napoleon that his orders were so strict that he could not allow even his wife to come on board. "That is very hard," Napoleon commented; then to her he said, "Milord Keith is a little too severe, is he not, Madam?" Turning to Maitland, he remarked, "By my faith, her portrait is not flattering. She is handsomer than it is." When Maitland told him that Sir Richard Strachan was second in command of the Channel Fleet, Napoleon bowed to him and observed to Maitland, "He appears a very young man to hold so high a rank."

All told, the day had been a rewarding one for Maitland. Besides seeing his wife, he had received a most welcome letter from the First Secretary of the Admiralty, acknowledging Maitland's announcement of his arrival in Tor Bay and his report of his proceedings, prior to Napoleon's embarkation, "of which their Lordships have been pleased to . . . signify their approval."

The responsibilities of his present assignment allowed him meager time for self-congratulation, however. A letter from Keith that evening emphasized how much remained to be done: "From the representation you have made to me of the dissatisfaction expressed by Buonaparte, on observing by the newspapers that he was to be sent to St. Helena, it will be necessary that you redouble your vigilance to prevent his escape; and you are therefore to station double sentinels, and resort to every other means that may be necessary for frustrating any such intention."

In addition to attracting scores of onlookers, Napoleon was providing England's newspapers with copy that their editors could hardly refuse to print; the demands of readers for every detail relating to his surrender, his detention and activities on board the *Bellerophon*, and his probable fate were too importunate to be profitably ignored. Even *The Times*, after originally professing that "What relates to Buonaparte is not much, neither is it a matter of essentially great interest," later yielded to its readers' insistence for information and filled columns with reports of the events surrounding Napoleon's surrender and of the activities in Tor Bay and Plymouth Sound. *The Courier*, the *Morning Chronicle*, the *St. James's Chronicle*, and others were already devoting prime space to everything that they could collect on the affair.

Read today, these accounts display an amalgam of fact and error, firsthand evidence and hearsay. But at that time, any news of Napoleon, no matter how apocryphal, was eagerly sought. Unable to go to Tor Bay or Plymouth themselves, readers wanted to know what visitors to those places had heard and seen, and they were no more critical than many of today's readers. In the *St. James's Chronicle* they read, "On board the *Bellerophon* Bonaparte still played the Emperor. Captain Maitland showed him his own cabin, and said he should have the whole of it, except one corner, which the Captain said he would close for his own bed. Bonaparte said he must have the whole of it to himself, which the Captain politely yielded; and shortly afterwards Napoleon invited him to dinner." *The Times* reported that "Bonaparte's suite consisted of upwards of forty persons, among whom were Bertrand, Savary, Lallemand, etc. He had also been allowed to take on board carriages and horses, but was denied admission for about 50 cavalry for whom he required accommodations." The same paper also stated: "In conversing with the Admiral, Napoleon said, 'I have given myself up to the English; but I would not have done so to any other of the Allied Powers. In surrendering to any of them I should be subject to the caprice and will of an individual: in submitting to the English I place myself at the mercy of a nation.' " It added that he

talked with great freedom on the present state of things, said it was impossible for the Bourbons to govern France, and that Napoleon II. would very soon be recalled to the throne, that Fouche was an ass, and totally unfit for the office assigned to him. He acknowledged that England alone had ruined all his grand plans, and that but for her he had now been Emperor of the East as well as of the West. He walked on the poop and quarter deck, conversed with the seamen, and affected great gaiety and unconcern.

Items stated that Gibraltar and the fort at Valletta on Malta had been designated as places of detention for him; the majority of the newspapers, however, still preferred St. Helena. They somehow acquired copies of Napoleon's letter to the Prince Regent and printed it verbatim, stating that it was "signed 'Napoleon' only—not in the character of a private individual; for he claims still to be Sovereign of Elba, though no longer Emperor of the French." They published information of Cabinet's decisions, leaked to them by the offices of the ministries, which revealed that Napoleon would be considered and treated on the footing and rank of a mere general, and would also "be separated from his suite, having not more than two or three persons with him."

Editorials discussed Napoleon's possible destiny, some insisting that he be tried and executed; but the *St. James's Chronicle* advocated a more humane policy:

Whatever may be his ultimate destination, we are persuaded that Britain will be found incapable of unnecessarily trampling on a man who has no longer the power to resent it; and will, by her magnanimity, show herself worthy of the victories which her arms have acquired. Future generations, when they read the narrative of our triumphs, shall not say they were stained by one blot from malignity or vindictiveness; but when they see us forgive even him who never forgave, and generously treat him who was so generous to none, and least so to Britain, [they] shall recognize in us that manly virtue, which scorns to make the vices of an offender an apology for our own, and that Christian benevolence which delights to forgive an enemy.

By no means so charitably inclined toward Napoleon, *The Times* featured long letters from a reader who signed himself "Probus." These philippics against Napoleon showed no forgiveness or leniency. "I cannot but think," Probus wrote on July 23, "that the age will be for ever disgraced, and the cause of justice will endure a most fatal shock, if Napoleon Buonaparte be not brought to *solemn trial*, and to *public execution*." Probus proposed sending Napoleon back to France to face trial for treason against Louis; or, that failing, trying him in England for the murder of Captain Wright. "If, however," he continued, "the different powers of Europe, from motives of a weak and cowardly policy, should be afraid to do justice upon this unparalleled villain, there is one place to which I should earnestly hope they would not refuse to send him. Let him be transported to Hayti; let him be put at the disposal of the countrymen of Toussaint;* and I will venture to answer for it, that the blood of that just man will not long cry to Heaven unrevenged."

On July 24, Probus expressed his further sentiments, this time with reference to reports that Napoleon was to be sent to St. Helena.

This man is to be suffered to escape *a second time*!—and the guilt, the folly, the base contemptible cowardice of refusing to inflict justice on him, is now to be set down to the account of England alone! ... Now that we have paid for his guilt by a more lamentable waste of gallant lives than were ever before lost by us, in any single battle,— now *we* are to become his protectors! Gracious Heaven! What a strange confusion of ideas! What an incomprehensible inconsistency of conduct!

It is said, this monster is to be sent to St. Helena, and there to be guarded by an English regiment. . . . We do not employ a whole regiment to guard a single individual. Perhaps, however, this is a guard of *honour*! And as some of our brave regiments bear on their standards the ennobling inscriptions of "Waterloo," "Vittoria," "Salamanca," "Busaco," or are entitled "The King's Own," "The Prince's," "The Queen's," etc.; so we shall hereafter hear of "The Corsican's Favourites," or see their colours embroidered with "Ajaccio." ... He trusts himself to those whom he has most injured, as Daniel braved the fury of the lions, or as the three Brethren walked through the fiery furnace—and our folly, our cowardice, works the miracle of his safety! As long as he lives, therefore, treason and rebellion must be every where at work. . . .

---

* Leader of a revolution in Haiti against the French colonial rulers. After his surrender, Toussaint was arrested and shipped to France, where he died in prison, possibly by assassination.

Statements such as these, however, were but the preliminary exchanges in what developed into full-scale battle among the newspapers. The anti-administration Whig journals, who up to this time had waited for an opportunity to use *l'affaire Napoléon* as ammunition against the Ministry, were readying themselves for a frontal attack.

At eleven o'clock in the morning, on Friday, July 28, Keith's barge came alongside the *Bellerophon*. The admiral, resplendent in full-dress uniform, was piped aboard with honors and met at the gangway by Maitland, who escorted him across the quarterdeck, through the state room—in which the members of Napoleon's suite had gathered—and into Napoleon's cabin. There, Bertrand introduced Keith to Napoleon, after which he and Maitland withdrew, leaving the two men alone.

The contrast in physical appearance between Napoleon and Keith was striking. Keith was a spare, big-boned man of well over six feet, his erect carriage still unbowed by age, the ruddiness of his cheeks accentuated by his thick shock of white hair; and Napoleon was a corpulent five-feet-six, sallow-complexioned, dark-haired. Keith noted that he looked "like a man in perfect health, thick calves, thin ankles, clear eyes and a thin mouth—like as possible the picture."

They conversed in French. Keith again thanked Napoleon for the attention he had shown his nephew at Waterloo. He inquired about the comfort of Napoleon and his suite and said that he would be happy to do anything he could to increase it. The two talked of places that had figured in their careers: Toulon, where in 1793 Keith had braved the batteries of Napoleon's artillery to evacuate a large number of Royalist fugitives, Egypt, the East Indies. Keith likely informed Napoleon that he had forwarded the letter to the Prince Regent to London. This brought from Napoleon a repetition of the arguments for his being granted asylum that he had voiced to Maitland the previous day. "I am no more and can disturb nobody," he asserted. "Cannot I live in England?" He asked Keith to write the Prince Regent that he wished to become an English subject. This would have been highly irregular for one in Keith's position, and he refused. "But," he said, "any communication you might incline to make I will transmit to the Ministers."

Napoleon asked if he might be allowed to walk on shore, with officers attending him. Keith replied negatively.

Did the admiral know what was to become of him? "That does not belong to me," Keith said. "I probably never shall know."

Did Keith imagine that it would be long before his fate was determined? "I have no access to know this," Keith answered. "It might require a communication with Paris and the other sovereigns assembled there."

A short while later Keith took his leave of Napoleon. Before quitting the ship, however, he spent some time in the state room with the members of the suite, to whom Maitland introduced him. The admiral found Madame Montholon "good looking, but not a good figure." Of Madame Bertrand, he noted that she spoke English perfectly. Indeed, she supplied him with ample evidence on which to base this judgment; for, taking him aside, she protested that it would be a gross injustice to send them to St. Helena. She also attempted to persuade Keith to interfere in preventing Bertrand at least from going, should Napoleon be sent there. On breaking away from her, the admiral may have reflected wryly on the troublesomeness of wives. For Lady Keith was at that moment on board the *Eurotas*, hoping to catch sight of Napoleon from its deck. Although Keith had earlier kept her from going to Tor Bay "upon the chance of [her using] the influence of the name to get on board the *Bellerophon*," he evidently had settled for this compromise arrangement and had most likely taken her to the *Eurotas* when on his way to the *Bellerophon*.

Besides its generally friendly character, the meeting with Keith had yielded little that was encouraging or helpful to Napoleon.

He had not discovered what the government intended to do with him. He had learned that Keith, though seeming personally well-inclined toward him, would in no way either alter or relax the official restrictions that had been imposed upon him, act as his mediator with the government, or serve as a private source of information for him. But though Keith had been circumspect in his replies to Napoleon's questions, he had let slip one statement that revealed a great deal to Napoleon. When Keith had said that the determination of Napoleon's fate might require consultations with the sovereigns assembled in Paris, he could hardly have stated something of which he had had no notice. Assuming that his words constituted more than a personal surmise, they indicated to Napoleon that his letter to the Prince Regent had proved a lost gamble. It had not been able to separate England from her allies and so enable him to treat with her alone. Though he was on an English ship, he was apparently still considered the prisoner of the Coalition, and if that were so, the reference in his letter to England as "the most powerful, the most constant, and the most generous" of his enemies would hardly incline Russia, Prussia, and Austria to leniency toward him.

For Keith the visit had proved more rewarding. It had enabled him to ascertain the effectiveness of the security measures he had ordered taken and to observe the accommodations and treatment that had been extended to Napoleon and his suite on the *Bellerophon*. It had also enabled him to repay his personal obligation to Napoleon, to determine how equably he was bearing the restraints and uncertainties of his situation, and to satisfy his curiosity about the kind of man Napoleon was. Keith had been particularly fascinated by Napoleon's conversation. Before leaving the ship, he spoke to Maitland about his meeting with Napoleon, mentioning that Napoleon had expressed a wish for an interview with the Prince Regent. "Damn the fellow," Keith said. "If he had obtained an interview with his Royal Highness, in half an hour they would have been the best friends in England."

Writing to Melville that day, Keith confided,

Everything goes on as quietly as possible here; it is certainly desirable that Buonaparte be removed as soon as possible; so long as he remains so near France, there will be a fermentation and various intrigues no doubt; I had forgot to mention the way in which it is intended he and his suite shall be maintained, at this moment his own provisions being exhausted, he draws upon Captain Maitland, and I send him what this place affords, and am glad to do what I can to render them comfortable.

He informed Melville that he had been to see Napoleon, and he related the details of their conversation. "I then visited the *Liffey* and *Eurotas* to see that those of the French sent to the former were properly accommodated. Upon the whole," he concluded, "notwithstanding the extreme curiosity, the Boats all kept at a proper distance, and the General seems perfectly satisfied."

For the Frenchmen on the *Bellerophon*, the remainder of the afternoon following Keith's departure passed quietly, broken only by one somber incident. Lieutenant John Bowerbank of the *Bellerophon* recorded it in his journal:

This day several transports passed very near the *Bellerophon*, bringing over the French prisoners taken in the battle of Waterloo, many of whom were wounded. Several of these poor fellows with their bandages, etc., were on deck. I am unable to speak as to the effect this sight (if he were witness of it) may have had upon Bonaparte, as he was at the time in his cabin. His officers beheld them pass from the poop, the ideas with which it must have been associated could not but render it an affecting scene, and to do them justice they appeared to feel it.

Other than this, the day followed the pattern that by this time was becoming routine: "Bonaparte appeared on deck for about half an hour before and after dinner. Being completely surrounded by boats he stood alternately on each side of the ship, bowing and smiling to the spectators."

In London, the Cabinet Council, which had met at the Foreign Office from one until after four o'clock that afternoon, had finally completed arrangements for Napoleon's detention. In the future St. Helena would be under His Majesty's control. Although the ships of the East India Company would still be allowed to touch there, the company's garrison on the island would be replaced by a King's regiment under a governor and officers appointed by the Prince Regent. Admiral Sir George Cockburn, who would convey Napoleon to the island, had already met several times with Liverpool, Bathurst, and Melville to discuss the nature of his command and the measures drawn up to ensure Napoleon's secure custody. A letter to Keith from Melville, informing him of the government's intentions respecting Napoleon and giving him permission to communicate these to Napoleon, was ready for delivery to Plymouth:

Admiralty, 28th July, 1815

Private.

MY DEAR LORD,

Major-General Sir Henry Bunbury* will convey this letter and another I have addressed to you on the subject of Bonaparte's destination. As it will probably be more agreeable to you that some person should accompany you at the conference which it will be necessary for you to have with Bonaparte, and as it will also be convenient that, besides your written details, we should have a verbal report of such matters as you could not well introduce into your statement of what passed at the conference, Sir Henry Bunbury will attend you on board the *Bellerophon* if you see no objection to it. Bonaparte will probably ask many questions, and make many demands, on points which are not noticed in my other letter; in answer to all which you can only refer him to Government and undertake to convey his wishes. If he desires to have Bertrand with him as one of his attendants, and Madame Bertrand and her family are also asked for, I scarcely think that we should be entitled to refuse it; but of course the matter must be referred to us.

The arrangements mentioned in your letters of the 26th instant, respecting the *Bellerophon*, are perfectly proper. I hope that our instructions are as full as you desire.

The other letter mentioned by Melville was the government's statement of its intentions regarding Napoleon.

---

* Undersecretary of State for War.

At the same time a letter from Liverpool was on its way to Castlereagh. The Prime Minister wrote:

Fife House, July 28, 1815

MY DEAR CASTLEREAGH—

We have completed all the arrangements for conveying Buonaparte to the island of St. Helena. Melville writes to Lord Keith tonight, to desire that he will announce to him his destination. Sir George Cockburn is to have charge of him, and to convey him in a line-of-battle ship.

Bathurst has written to Sir Hudson Lowe, to offer him the military government of the island. It will be garrisoned by King's troops, and all ships of every description will be excluded, excepting ships of war, and those of the East India Company. The Court of Directors have shown every disposition to accommodate in every part of the business. The question of the security of the station has been most fully discussed. We have taken the best opinions upon it, and listened to all those who had any objections to make to it. It is, however, now generally admitted that, provided neutrals are excluded, it is the safest station that could be found for such a purpose. St. Helena is perhaps the only place in the world from which neutrals can be excluded without any material inconvenience.

We certainly concur with you in opinion, that a Convention should be signed between us and the Allies, by which Buonaparte is to be considered as a *common* prisoner, though in our custody, and that we should not give him up or release him, except by joint consent. You will perhaps employ somebody to draw up the draft of such a Convention.

But the work of the staffs of the ministries was not ended. More correspondence passed between the War Department and the Lords Commissioners of the Admiralty:

War Department, 28 July, 1815

MY LORDS,

I have it in command from His Royal Highness The Prince Regent to signify to you ... that your Lordships should take the necessary Measures to convey General Napoleon Buonaparte, and such of his suite as will be permitted to attend him, to the Island of St. Helena, which is to be the place of his future residence.

His Royal Highness has commanded that one of His Majesty's regiments of foot and a detachment of Artillery should be sent at the same time to St. Helena for the greater security of the Island; and your Lordships will be pleased also to make arrangements for the conveyance of these troops.

Orders went by express to the military barracks in Portsmouth, directing that a captain, a lieutenant, 40 men of the Royal Artillery, and the 1st Battalion of the 53d Regiment, commanded by Sir George Bingham, prepare to embark. At the Admiralty, the staff was busily engaged in consulting its records of the numbers, positions, and readiness of the vessels required for Napoleon's transportation to St. Helena. The *Northumberland,* still at the Nore, was ready to proceed to Spithead and from thence to Plymouth to take Napoleon on board; but the Admiralty would not risk sending her alone to St. Helena. It meant her to be convoyed there by a company of ships formidable enough to discourage or repulse any attempts by Bonapartists to effect a rescue at sea. It posted orders to Captain Hamilton of the frigate *Havannah* "to cause the stores of His Majesty's Ship *Havannah* to be completed at Plymouth to a proper porportion for foreign Service, with all the dispatch that may be," and it pored over its lists of other ships in harbor, seeking an additional half-dozen to join her and the *Northumberland.* It assigned the troopships *Bucephalus* and *Ceylon,* then lying in Portsmouth harbor, to carry the regiment of infantry and the detachment of artillery to St. Helena. It looked for storeships for the trip: at least one would be needed to accompany the squadron.

The original of Napoleon's letter to the Prince Regent, forwarded by Keith the previous day, had still not reached the Ministry. Napoleon had waited too long before sending it—not that it would have mattered if he had not delayed its submission. The British government never notified him of its receipt of the letter.

VI

Arrangements for the "Unemperoring"

RAIN fell continuously on Plymouth and the Sound on Saturday, July 29. The thick weather confined the Frenchmen on the *Bellerophon* to their quarters for most of the day. When any of them did venture out on deck, they found the waters empty of all boats save those of the guard, who continued their monotonous circling of the ship. During the morning a lighter with water for the ship came alongside, and the sailors were employed in clearing her and starting the water into the casks in the hold. At eleven the *Eurotas* unmoored and shifted her berth a little farther from the *Bellerophon*. But these activities only emphasized the emptiness of the day. The rain slanted down, obscuring the low, dark hump of Drake's Island at the northern end of the Sound, the bulk of Charles II's citadel on the eastern edge of the lofty Hoe, and the old martello tower on the summit of Mount Batten. The *Bellerophon* creaked at her moorings, water dripping steadily from her rigging, yards, furled sails, and guns, and glistening on the masts and hardwood decks and railings. It was a day to foster gloomy thoughts.

By this time the stamina and emotional stability of the suite were being tested to the utmost. They had been in England more than five days now, and their hopes for a warm reception had been blighted. They had read the newspapers' assertions that they would be held as prisoners on St. Helena; they had received no word from the British government concerning their fate; they had been sent from Tor Bay to Plymouth Sound, where two frigates and armed guard boats kept close watch over them; they had been separated from a number of their company, who had been removed to the *Liffey*; finally, any reassurance or information that they had expected from Keith's visit to Napoleon had not been offered.

They were helpless. They could not officially protest against their lot; that prerogative belonged to Napoleon. But he, too, was helpless. Against what could he protest: newspaper reports, ill treatment, insult? They could only wait—dreading the blow they were quite sure would fall, but by now almost wishing it would descend soon. The terrible uncertainty of their present condition was becoming more unnerving than any terrible knowledge could be.

For one member of the suite the fears and tensions were growing unbearable. Madame Bertrand was using her last resources of self-control in her battle against panic. At Rochefort she had been one of the most outspoken in recommending that Napoleon seek asylum in England. She had foreseen a good life there for her family and herself—a life of comfort and perhaps excitement, and the enjoyment of the prestige that would attach to the intimates of Napoleon. But the events of the past few days had replaced her dreams with nightmares. The prospect of herself and her family being exiled to St. Helena terrified her, but there seemed no escaping it. Bertrand was ignoring her pleas that he try to dissociate himself from Napoleon, vowing to accompany the Emperor to St. Helena if he were sent there. Madame Bertrand could do or say nothing to make him alter his decision. She had besought Maitland to help prevent Bertrand from going, but he could not aid her. She had even pleaded with Keith to intervene; but, although he listened politely, he remained noncommittal. Her desperation grew.

Major General Sir Henry Bunbury, Undersecretary of State for the War Department, sped on his way to Plymouth, having left London early that morning accompanied by Earl Bathurst's son and Mr. Guy, a messenger of the King. He carried the government's decision about its prisoner, enclosed in a letter from Melville to Keith. The *Northumberland*, at length under weigh from the Nore, headed under full sail for Spithead to meet Admiral Sir George Cockburn. Meanwhile, letters and orders continued to issue back and forth in the ministerial offices in London. The Lords Commissioners of the Admiralty wrote to Bathurst:

My Lord—

We have received your Lordship's letter of yesterdays date . . . and in return we have to acquaint your Lordship that Rear Admiral Sir George Cockburn having been appointed Commander in Chief of His Majesty's Naval Force at the Cape of Good Hope and in the adjacent Seas, he will be ordered to proceed without delay to that Station, and will be directed to convey General Buonaparte to St. Helena, in obedience to His Royal Highness's Commands. . . .

A conveyance will also be provided in Sir George Cockburn's Flag Ship, and in two other of His Majesty's ships, and they may be embarked either at Portsmouth or Plymouth.

To His Majesty's ships the brigs *Zephyr*, *Zenobia*, *Icarus*, *Leveret*, *Redpole*, and *Peruvian* went orders from Barrow commanding them to "be completed at Plymouth with a proper proportion of stores for foreign service, with all the dispatch that may be," and "to put themselves under the command of Sir George Cockburn."

Instructions from Bathurst arrived at the Admiralty:

War Department
29th July 1815

My Lords,

. . . I have now to acquaint you that the 1st Battalion of the 53rd Regiment under the command of Sir George Bingham has been ordered to proceed to St. Helena, and I request your Lordships would give the necessary Instructions for its being received on board the Troop Ships which may have been appointed for its conveyance.

The same day, Bunbury, at Bathurst's direction, wrote to Barrow requesting the Lords Commissioners to "give Orders that Camp Equipage for 500 Men, which will occupy about Twelve Tons, should be received at Portsmouth on board the Troop Ships destined to carry out a Battalion of the 53d Regiment to St. Helena."

Barrow then sent a series of Admiralty orders to Admiral Sir Edward Thornbrough at Portsmouth:

I am commanded by my Lords Commissioners of the Admiralty to signify their directions to you to cause the 53d Regiment to be embarked on board His Majesty's Ships *Ceylon* and *Bucephalus*; and in the event of these ships not being able to receive the whole, you will order the remainder, with a detachment of artillery, to be put on board the *Northumberland*.

Give the necessary orders that camp equipage for 500 men, which will occupy about twelve tons, should be received on board the Troopships at Portsmouth, which may be ordered to carry out a battalion of the 53d regiment to St. Helena.

A call for money went from the Admiralty to the Treasury, requesting that the sum of £1500 be advanced to Admiral Cockburn for the expenses he would incur en route to St. Helena.

A letter from Melville to Keith kept the admiral informed of these various developments:

Admiralty, 29th July, 1815

Private.

MY DEAR LORD,

I have little with which to trouble you today, except to acknowledge receipt of your letters of the 27th instant with the letter from Bonaparte to the Prince Regent. I have sent the latter to Lord Bathurst.

The *Northumberland* was paid this morning at the Nore, and we understand by telegraph that they meant her to proceed so far this afternoon. She will probably be two days at Spithead, where the 53rd Regiment and a party of Artillery will embark in the *Bucephalus* and *Ceylon,* and if they are not sufficient the *Northumberland* will take the remainder. The *Havannah* Frigate, and six brigs, which have been placed under Sir George Cockburn's orders, are to assemble at Plymouth.

I was not surprised that Bonaparte does not relish the idea of St. Helena, as I have understood before that he disliked it particularly. That circumstance does not alter my opinion as to its being the most eligible situation for him. I am glad, however, that he submits quietly to be unemperored; and I trust that all our Officers and men will agree so far with him and consider him only in his true light.

A most practical consideration dictated that these orders be carried out quickly—namely, money. For England during the Hundred Days had spent thirty million sterling in helping to defeat Napoleon and now was finding him a costly prisoner. At least sixteen ships were presently under assignment because of him, some of which the Admiralty had planned to pay off or reduce before this time. Now some of them had to be refitted, their provisions replenished and their crews maintained at full strength. Therefore, the sooner Napoleon was debarked on St. Helena, the sooner the government could effect some much desired economies —even though the Treasury rather than the East India Company would now bear the cost of administering and garrisoning St. Helena. One other consideration underlay the government's desire for Napoleon's speedy departure: despite the stringent measures instituted for his secure custody while he remained in English waters, it was still feared that he might escape.

Despite a rainy morning and a cloudy afternoon, Sunday, July 30, brought shore boats out on the Sound in greater numbers than on any previous day. "I am certain I speak within bounds," wrote Maitland, "when I state, that upward of a thousand were collected round the ship, in each of which, on an average, there were not fewer than eight people. The crush was so great, as to render it quite impossible for the guard-boats to keep them off." Packed so closely together that no water was visible between them, they bobbed and rubbed sides with each other. Their occupants were dressed in a colorful variety of suits, frocks, bonnets, and shawls. Here and there the vivid uniform of a navy or army officer stood out sharply. Many of the spectators had adorned their button-holes with carnations, a Bonapartist emblem. Bands of musicians in several of the craft played popular French airs, hoping to attract Napoleon's special notice whenever he should appear.

The sightseers chatted gaily among themselves or with people in neighboring boats, ate the lunches they had brought along, applauded the music, commented on the guard boats, and urged their boatmen to work nearer the *Bellerophon*. They cheered lustily whenever members of the frigate's crew displayed a board on which they had chalked brief descriptions of Napoleon's ac-tivities—"At breakfast," "In the cabin with Captain Maitland," "Writing with his Officers," "Going to dinner," "Coming on deck." They waved handkerchiefs and hats in salutation to the members of the suite when any of them showed on deck. And on several occasions they screamed and cursed, when one of the guard boats, trying to keep the crowd at a decent distance from the *Bellerophon*, charged violently against the nearest shore boats, almost overturning them. These rough proceedings greatly incensed the French officers who observed them. "Is this your English liberty?" they complained to Maitland. "Were such a thing to happen in France, the men would rise with one accord to throw that officer and his crew overboard."

The people in the boats were not the only spectators of the scene. At low tide a few enterprising boatmen enjoyed a brisk business by ferrying scores of persons out to the breakwater. Though it was still under construction, its upper surface was above water at low tide; and there these adventurous ones stood pre-cariously in a line a mile long, straining their eyes toward the *Bellerophon*. On land, crowds of those who could not afford or locate boats for the trip out on the Sound gathered on the Hoe, on the parapets of the citadel, on Mount Edgcumbe and Mount Batten, on Staddon Heights, and on the shores of Cawsand and Bovisand Bays. Telescopes and pocket-glasses were at a premium here.

Plymouth was in a holiday mood, enjoying—and profiting handsomely from—the event which had made her the cynosure of England and indeed of the world. Not since the days of Drake and the Armada had she been thrust so prominently and excitingly into the news. The most famous captive in history was hers, and her citizens talked of little else besides Napoleon: his appearance, his habits, his treatment on board the *Bellerophon*. Some persons expressed indignation because the officers and crew of the ship removed their hats when Napoleon came on deck. He should be treated like the common criminal he was, they contended. Others asserted that the officers and men had acted spontaneously: Napoleon went about the ship with such an imperial air that they uncovered every time he passed. Rumors ran rampant. It was stated that Napoleon regularly drank the health of the Prince Regent and that the Regent himself was on his way to Plymouth to have a look at "Boney." Wagers were laid on what Napoleon's fate would be. Nothing concerning him was too insignificant or incredible to believe.

Admiral Lord Keith did not share the merry mood of the residents and visitors in Plymouth. "I wish he was sent away," he complained in a letter to his daughter, "for I am plagued to death; the women go near the ship and the guard boats have been desired to fire. Lady Duckworth and a party went with Mrs. Maitland so near as to speak. . . . General Browne in full uniform went also too near on board, but was driven away by the guard boats."

Napoleon, who had kept the crowds waiting for his appearance most of the day, at last came on deck about five-thirty. His arrival there was signaled to the spectators by the sight of the officers removing their hats. In spite of the efforts of the guardsmen, the mass of boats surged in closer to the frigate's sides. After walking the deck a short time, Napoleon went to the gangway, where he could be seen. The spectators stood up in the boats to see him and waved. He responded to their acclamations with salutes. "He again expressed his admiration at the great beauty of the women," Lieutenant Bowerbank noted,

viewing them through his glass, and occasionally taking off his hat. Upon his quitting the gangway (after remaining there about twenty minutes), many of the spectators cheered. Being close to him I immediately fixed my eyes upon him and marked the workings of his countenance. I plainly perceived that he was mortified and displeased and not a little agitated, attributing the shout, and I believe justly, to the exultation which they felt at having him in our possession. After he had retired we were told he was taken ill.

Bowerbank also noted, when Napoleon had first come on deck, that "for the first time since he had been on board he was not shaved. This surprised us as we had been accustomed to remark his great and peculiar personal neatness. We could only ascribe the change to the anxiety respecting his fate." Bowerbank was correct; for the day had been especially trying for Napoleon. When Maitland had returned from seeing Keith that morning, he had informed Napoleon that Sir Henry Bunbury was expected to arrive during the day with the government's decision on Napoleon's future. Although Napoleon questioned him closely about it, Maitland would reveal no more. He had been told by Keith that Napoleon definitely was to be sent to St. Helena, but he had been cautioned to keep that intelligence secret.

And so the hours of the day had passed in waiting for Bunbury. Napoleon could have little doubt now about what the government's notification would be. St. Helena was waiting to receive him. And it was improbable that he would ever leave it alive: a government scarcely incarcerates a man on an island two thousand leagues from Europe if it considers paroling him in the future. No one in his retinue harbored any longer the hope that Bunbury would bring good tidings from London. The officers who had been transferred to the *Liffey* therefore addressed a letter to Keith requesting permission to see Napoleon before their final separation from him.

The newspapers of July 28, which had now arrived on board, carried the ordinance issued by Louis XVIII at Paris on July 24. Article I stated, "The Generals and Officers who betrayed the King before the 23d of March, or who attacked France and the Government with force and arms, and those who by violence gained possession of power, shall be arrested and brought before competent Courts-martial, in their respective divisions." The names of Bertrand, Savary, and Lallemand were among those listed. Bertrand treated the news with derision, but Savary and Lallemand were acutely alarmed by it. They asked Maitland if he thought the British government would deliver them to Louis. "Decidedly not," Maitland said. "You have been received on board an English man-of-war, and it never can be the intention of the Ministers to deliver you over to punishment." Despite these assurances, however, the two men remained noticeably apprehensive.

Madame Bertrand, too, had grown more distraught. She sought out Maitland again; and her pleading elicited the following letter on her behalf from the captain to Keith:

> *Bellerophon*—Plymouth Sound
> July 30, 1815

DEAR LORD KEITH,

The Countess Bertrand has been so extremely urgent for me to write to your Lordship on the same subject that I spoke to you this morning that I know not how to refuse her; she requests I will entreat Your Lordship to take measures to prevent her husband accompanying Napoleon Bounaparte to St. Helena should he be sent there, which she is convinced can only be done by an order of our government as he has declared to her he will follow Bounaparte wherever he goes. In writing this letter to Your Lordship I am actuated only by the distress in which I see an unfortunate woman who declares positively she will poison herself in preference to quitting Europe, and she takes this step without the knowledge of her husband.

So the Frenchmen waited for Bunbury. And in London—working even though it was a Sunday—Bathurst issued more directives to the Admiralty regarding St. Helena and Napoleon. The first notified the Lords Commissioners that ships needing water or supplies might touch at the island to receive these, but that their crews would not be allowed to communicate with the shore; after a certain time, intercourse between British or neutral ships and the island would be wholly prohibited, except for His Majesty's ships and the ships of the East India Company. The second directive included the War Department's orders governing Napoleon's removal to St. Helena.

War Department
30th July 1815

My Lords,

I have to desire that your Lordships will have the goodness to communicate a copy of the enclosed Memoranda to Rear Admiral Sir George Cockburn for his Information and guidance during the time that General Buonaparte may remain in his Custody.

In committing so important a Trust to British Officers, the Prince Regent is sensible that it is not necessary to impress upon them His anxious desire that no greater measure of severity with respect to confinement, or restriction, be imposed than what is deemed necessary for the faithful discharge of that duty which the Admiral as well as the Governor of St. Helena must ever keep in mind—the perfect Security of General Buonaparte's Person.

Whatever, consistent with this great object, can be allowed in the shape of Indulgence, His Royal Highness is confident will be willingly shewn to the General:—and He relies on Sir George Cockburn's known Zeal and energy of Character that He will not allow Himself to be betrayed into any improvident relaxation of his duty.

The Memorandum read:

When General Buonaparte shall remove from the *Bellerophon* to the *Northumberland*, it will be a fit Moment for Admiral Sir George Cockburn to direct an examination of the Effects which the General shall have brought with Him.

Admiral Sir George Cockburn will allow all Articles of Furniture,

Books and Wine, which the General may have brought with Him, to be trans-shipped on board the *Northumberland*.

Under the Head of Furniture is to be included His plate, provided it be not such an amount as to bespeak it to be rather an article of convertable property than of domestic use.

His Money, Diamonds, and Negotiable Bills of every description are to be given up. The Admiral will explain to the General that it is by no means the Intention of the British Government to confiscate his Property, but simply to take the Administration of these Effects into their own Hands for the purpose of preventing their being converted by Him into an Instrument of escape.

The Examination must be made in the presence of some Person appointed by General Buonaparte, and an Inventory of the Effects, so to be retained, must be signed by this Person, as well as by the Rear Admiral, or any one appointed by Him to make out the Inventory.

The Interest, or the Principal, (according to the amount of the Property) will be applicable to his maintenance; and the disposition of it, in that respect, left chiefly to his own choice.

He will for that purpose from time to time communicate his Wishes to the Admiral, until the new Governor of St. Helena arrives, and to the Governor afterwards;—and unless the Proposition be objectionable, the Admiral, or Governor as the case may be, will give the necessary orders, and the Bills will be paid by Bills drawn upon His Majesty's Treasury.

In the Event of His death, the disposition of his Property will be determined by His Will—the contents of which He must be assured will be strictly attended to.

As an attempt may be made to represent part of the Property as belonging to Persons in his Suite, it must be understood, that the Property of those who go out with Him is subject to the same Regulation.

The disposition of the Military allotted to guard Him must be left to the Governor—the Governor being instructed to attend to the wishes of the Admiral in the instances hereafter to be mentioned.

The General must be always attended by an officer appointed by the Admiral, or Governor as the case may be—if the General be permitted to move beyond the Boundaries where the Sentries are placed, the officer should be attended by one orderly at least.

In the Event of Ships arriving, so long as they continue in sight the

General must be confined within the Boundary where the Sentries shall be placed—He must during that Interval be prohibited from all Intercourse and Communication with the Inhabitants. They who accompany Him to St. Helena must be subject at this period to the same Regulations—. They are to reside with Him, and it is left to the discretion of the Admiral in the first instance, and to the new Governor afterwards, to establish such Regulations with respect to them at other times as may appear expedient—

The Admiral will not take on board any Individual belonging to General Buonaparte's Suite for the purpose of conveying Him to St. Helena with the General, except with his full consent after it has been explained to Him that He thereby becomes liable to all the Regulations, which it may be deemed necessary to subject Him for the Security of the General's Person.

The General must be given to understand that in the Event of his attempting to Escape, He will be afterwards subject to close Custody —and they who go out with Him must also understand that if they shall be detected in contriving means for his Escape, they will be separated from Him, and placed in close Custody.

All Letters addressed to Him, or his Attendants, must be first delivered to the Admiral, or to the General [Sir Hudson Lowe] as the case may be,—who will read them before they are delivered to the Persons to whom they are addressed—all letters written by the General or his attendants must be subject to the same Regulation.

No letter, which has not been transmitted to St. Helena by the Secretary of State, should be delivered to the General, or to those who accompany Him, if it be written by any Person not residing in the Island—and all their letters addressed to Persons not resident in the Island, must be sent under cover to the Secretary of State.

The General must be given clearly to understand that the Governor and Admiral are strictly instructed to forward to His Majesty's Government any Wish, or Representation, which He may think proper to make to the British Government, and in that particular they are not at Liberty to exercise any discretion—but the Paper on which such application or Representation may be written must be left open for their joint inspection, in order that if in transmitting it, they may be enabled to accompany it with such observations as they may think expedient.

Until the arrival of the new Governor, the Admiral must be considered as entirely responsible for the security of General Buonaparte's Person, and His Majesty's Government entertains no doubt of the disposition of the actual Governor to concert with the Admiral for this purpose.

The Admiral is authorized to keep the General on board, or re-embark Him, if the security of His Person cannot, in the Admiral's opinion, be otherwise obtained.

On the representation of the Admiral upon his arrival at St. Helena, the Governor will take measures immediately to convey either to England, or to the Cape, or to the East Indies, according to the Circumstances of the Case, such Non-Commissioned officers and privates in the Military Corps at St. Helena, as the Admiral may deem expedient to relieve from their military duty in the Island by reason of being Foreigners, or on account of their general character and disposition.

If there are any Foreigners in the island, whose residence there appears to the Admiral calculated to be instrumental to General Buonaparte's escape, measures must be taken for their removal.—

The whole Coast of the Island, and the Vessels and Boats frequenting it, must be placed under the control of the Admiral. He will regulate the places which Boats may frequent; and on His representation the Governor will station a sufficient guard at those places at which the Admiral may think precaution necessary.

The Admiral will take the most effectual Steps to watch the arrival and departure of every Ship, so as to prevent any Intercourse with the Shore except such as He may approve.

An order for preventing, after due Notice, foreign Ships and Ships belonging to the private Trade, from resorting to St. Helena, will be forthwith given.

If the General should be attacked by any serious Indisposition, the Governor, and the Admiral will each direct a Medical Person, in whom they may have confidence, to be in attendance on the General in addition to his own Medical assistance, and direct them severally to report daily on the State of His Health.

In the Event of his Death, the Admiral will give orders for his Body being conveyed to England.

VII

The Sentence

S IR Henry Bunbury did not reach Plymouth until evening on July 30, too late to go on board the *Bellerophon*. When Maitland called on Keith the next morning, the admiral announced that he and Bunbury would visit Napoleon around ten o'clock. Keith showed Maitland the government's notification of its decision respecting Napoleon and gave him permission to reveal its contents if Napoleon inquired about them.

To grant such permission was irregular, since it was Keith's responsibility to communicate the information to Napoleon, and it may indicate Keith's distaste for his role. Or Keith may have desired to afford Napoleon an opportunity to prepare himself to hear the official announcement with dignity and composure. Whatever the case, in essence the forewarning constituted a gift, another repayment by Keith of the debt he owed Napoleon. Keith never told Bunbury what he had done.*

Maitland returned to his ship and informed Napoleon that the admiral and Bunbury would arrive shortly. Napoleon asked if Maitland knew what they would tell him, and the captain replied that he understood it had been determined that Napoleon would be sent to St. Helena. Napoleon received this information without marked emotion. The newspaper reports together with

---

* In his memorandum of the visit with Napoleon, Bunbury wrote that Napoleon "appeared as if he had been previously aware of what was to be communicated to him."

his confinement to the *Bellerophon* and the government's refusal to correspond with him had prepared him for it. Nevertheless he complained strongly to Maitland of the injustice of the decision. The conversation was curtailed by the announcement that the admiral's barge was approaching, and Maitland went on deck to receive Keith and Bunbury.

Although it was only ten-thirty, Keith's barge had to thread its way to the *Bellerophon* through the throng of shore boats that had already assembled around the ship. The efforts of the guardsmen to keep them off were meeting stiff resistance: while they were forcing one segment of the encroaching circle to retreat, another would be edging closer. The people in the boats knew that Bunbury was in Plymouth; and, cognizant of his mission, they were determined not to miss his visit to the *Bellerophon*. Those who had not yet seen Napoleon knew that their time for doing so was running short. Once his fate had been announced to him, he might be sent off without delay.

Maitland met Keith and Bunbury at the gangway and took them directly into the after-cabin, where Bertrand announced them to Napoleon. Bertrand and Maitland withdrew, and after Keith had introduced Bunbury and answered a few trivial questions put by Napoleon he produced Melville's letter containing the orders of the government, and tendered it to Napoleon. Napoleon asked if it were written in French, and when Keith replied that it was in English, he remarked that it would thus be useless to him and would have to be translated. Keith then began to read the letter in French, but Napoleon "appeared not to hear distinctly or not to comprehend; and after a line or two had been read he took the paper from Lord Keith's hands" and proposed that Bunbury translate it.

Bunbury read,

MY LORD—

As it may be convenient to General Buonaparte that he should be apprized, without further delay, of the intentions of the British Government respecting him, your lordship is at liberty to communicate to him the information contained in this letter.

It would be inconsistent with our duty to this country, and to His Majesty's Allies, if we were to leave to General Buonaparte the means or opportunity of again distrubing the peace of Europe, and renewing all the calamities of war: it is therefore unavoidable that he should be restrained in his personal liberty to whatever extent may be necessary to secure our first and paramount object.

The island of St. Helena has been selected for his future residence. The climate is healthy, and its local situation will admit of his being treated with more indulgence than would be compatible with adequate security elsewhere.

Of the persons who have been brought to England with General Bounaparte, he will be allowed to select (with the exception of Generals Savary and L'Allemand) three officers, who, together with his surgeon, will be permitted to accompany him to St. Helena. Twelve domestics, including the servants of the officers, will also be allowed. It must be distinctly understood that all those individuals will be liable to restraint during their attendance upon him and their residence at St. Helena, and they will not be permitted to withdraw from thence without the sanction of the British Government.

Rear-Admiral Sir George Cockburn, who is appointed to the chief command at the Cape of Good Hope and the adjacent seas, will convey General Buonaparte and his attendants to St. Helena, and will receive detailed instructions respecting the execution of that service. Sir George Cockburn will probably be ready to embark in the course of a few days; it is therefore desirable that General Buonaparte should make without delay the selection of the persons who are to accompany him.

MELVILLE.

During the reading, Napoleon listened calmly and attentively and did not interrupt. When Bunbury had finished, Keith asked Napoleon if he wished to have a written translation of the document made. Napoleon declined, stating that he had comprehended the substance perfectly, for the translation had been sufficiently good.

Bunbury handed him the letter; he took it and laid it on the table. He paused, glanced at the letter, at the two men; and then he spoke. He declared, first, his solemn protest against the proceedings of the British government. It did not have the right to dispose of him in this manner, he said, and he now appealed to the British people and to the laws of the country against its decision. Next he asked if there was not a tribunal where he might prefer his appeal against the illegality and injustice of the decision taken by the government. Bunbury could only reply that he was little more than the bearer of the dispatches to Lord Keith and that he was not authorized to enter into discussions.

"I am come here voluntarily," Napoleon went on,

to throw myself on the hospitality of your nation, and to claim the rights of hospitality. I am not a prisoner of war. If I were a prisoner of war, you would be obliged to treat me according to the law of nations. But I am come to this country a passenger on board one of your ships of war, after a previous negotiation with the commander. If he had told me I was to be a prisoner, I should not have come. I asked him if he was willing to receive me and my suite on board and to carry me to England. Admiral Maitland answered that he would; and this after having received, and after telling me that he had received, the special orders of his Government concerning me. It was a snare, then, that had been spread for me. In coming on board a British ship of war I confided myself to the hospitality of the British people as much as if I had entered one of their towns—a vessel, a village, it is all the same thing. As to the island of St. Helena, it would be my death sentence.

I protest against being imprisoned in a fortress in this country. I know indeed that I cannot be admitted to the rights of an Englishman at first—some years are requisite to entitle one to be domiciliated. Well, let the Prince Regent place me during that time under any surveillance he may think proper. Let me be put into a country house in the center of the island, thirty leagues from every sea. Place a commissioner about me to examine my correspondence and to report my actions—and if the Prince Regent should require any paroles [pledges of honor], perhaps I would give it. There I could have a certain degree of personal liberty and I could enjoy the liberty that literature affords. In St. Helena I should not live three months. With my habits and constitution, it would be immediate death. I am used to ride twenty leagues a day.

What am I to do on this little rock at the end of the world? The climate is too hot for me. No, I will not go to St. Helena—Botany Bay is better than St. Helena. If your Government wishes to put me to death, they may kill me here. It is not worth while to send me to St. Helena. I prefer death to St. Helena.

And what good is my death to you? I can do you no harm: I am no longer a sovereign; I am a simple individual. Besides, times and affairs are altered. What danger could result from my living as a private person in the heart of England, under surveillance and restricted in any way that the Government might imagine necessary?

He paused again and looked at Bunbury and Keith as if for a reply; but they merely repeated that they were not authorized to discuss the matter. Bunbury stated that he could only undertake to hear Napoleon's representations and communicate them to the King's ministers.

Napoleon again mentioned the circumstances surrounding his surrender, insisting that he had been perfectly free in his choice and that he had preferred entrusting himself to the hospitality and generosity of the British to taking any other course. "Why should I not have gone to my father-in-law?" he asked.

Or to the Emperor Alexander, who is my personal friend? We have become enemies because he wanted to annex Poland to his dominions, and my popularity was in his way; but otherwise he would not have treated me in this manner. If your Government acts thus, it will disgrace itself in the eyes of Europe, and even your own people will disapprove and blame its conduct. Besides, you do not know what a feeling my death will create both in France and Italy, and how greatly the character of England will suffer if my blood rests here. There is high opinion of the justice and honor of England. If you kill me your reputation will be lost in France and Italy, and it will cost the lives of many Englishmen. There never has been a similar instance in the history of the world. What was there to force me to the step I took? The tricolor flag was still flying at Bordeaux, at Nantes, at Rochefort. The army has not submitted at this hour! I should have joined them— or, if I had chosen to remain in France, what could have prevented my remaining concealed for years among a people who were all attached to me? But I preferred to settle as a private individual in England.

He referred once more to his going on board the *Bellerophon,* repeating the assurances he claimed Maitland had given him and citing the honors and attentions shown him by Maitland and Admiral Hotham. "And after all," he commented bitterly,

this has been a snare laid for me! If you now kill me, it will be an eternal disgrace to the Prince Regent and to the nation. That will be an unparalleled cowardice. I hold out to the Prince Regent the brightest page in his history. I am his enemy, and I place myself at his discretion. I have been the greatest enemy of your country; I have made war upon you for twenty years—and I do you the highest honor and give you the greatest proof of my confidence by placing myself voluntarily in the hands of my most constant and inveterate enemies! Remember what I have been, and how I stood among the sovereigns of Europe. This courted my protection; that gave me his daughter; all sought my friendship. I was Emperor—acknowledged so by the powers of Europe except Great Britain—and she had acknowledged me and treated with me as Chief Consul of France.

He turned back to the table and laid his finger on the letter. Angrily he said,

Your Government have not the right to style me *General* Bonaparte. I am at least First Consul, and I ought to be treated as such if treated with at all. When I was at Elba, I was as much a sovereign as when I was on the throne of France. I was as much a sovereign in Elba as the King was in France. We had each our flag. I had my flag; we had each our ships, our troops. To be sure, mine were on a small scale. I had six hundred soldiers—and he had two hundred thousand. At length I made war upon him, defeated him and dethroned him. But there is nothing in all this to alter my position or to deprive me of my rank as one of the sovereigns of Europe.

Bunbury remarked that he felt convinced that the government's chief motive in deciding upon St. Helena was that its geographical situation would make it possible for Napoleon to enjoy a greater degree of liberty and personal independence than could be allowed in any other part of Great Britain. Napoleon immediately replied, "No, no, I will not go to St. Helena. You would not go there, sir, were it your own case—nor, my lord, would you. You found me free," he continued. "Send me back again; replace me in the same state in which you found me and which I quitted only under the impression that your admiral was to land me in England. If your Government will not do this, and will not permit me to reside here, let me go to the United States. But I appeal to your laws—and I throw myself upon their protection to prevent my being sent to St. Helena or being shut up in a fortress."

He asked when the *Northumberland* was likely to arrive and be ready to sail, and entreated Keith to take no steps toward removing him from the *Bellerophon* before the government had been informed of what passed on this occasion and had made its final decision. As to going on board the *Northumberland,* he would not do it. "I shall not go—I shall not leave here," he declared. Keith replied that should the *Northumberland* arrive soon a delay might be granted until the final decision of the government was learned. When Napoleon turned to Bunbury for confirmation of this point, the undersecretary answered that he could give no opinion upon it, but that it rested with Keith to decide. Napoleon urged Bunbury to acquaint the government at once with what had passed at the meeting; Bunbury assured him that he would send a written report immediately and would remain in Plymouth until the next day, in case Napoleon should have anything further to state.

Keith asked if Napoleon wished to put his answer to the government's decision in writing. Napoleon shook his head. "No. This gentleman understands French well, he will represent me. He is in an eminent position and he must be an honest man. He will render to the Government the response that I have given." He paused awhile, then began again. "He went over the same grounds," Bunbury recorded,

dwelling particularly upon his having been free to come or not, and his having decided to come here from understanding that Captain Maitland, acting according to the orders of his government, would undertake to bring him in safety; upon the illegality of sentencing him to Death or Imprisonment; and his desire to appeal formally to the

Laws and the People of England;—upon the disgrace which would attach to the nation and particularly to the government.—He repeated his desire to live in England as a private citizen, under any Restrictions and with a commissioner to watch over him ("who would also be of great use to me for the first year or two in showing me what I ought to do")—and He added, "I will give my word of Honour that I will not hold any Correspondence with France, and that I will not engage in any political affairs whatever." Finally he repeated his fixed Determination not to go to St. Helena.

The meeting ended; Keith and Bunbury made their bows and retired to the forecabin, where the suite had assembled to be introduced by Maitland. The group was no less affected by Melville's letter than Napoleon had seemed to be. Savary and Lallemand were particularly distressed and demanded to know what would be done with them—irately protesting that their being given up to France would be a breach of all faith and honor. Madame Bertrand followed Keith to the quarterdeck, where she drew him aside. Trembling with agitation, she said, "My husband is so weak as to be attached to that *man*, and he will go with him. I have three children. My health is bad; I shall never reach the island. We have no money. If I stay behind, I must starve. Besides, to leave my husband would kill me."

Keith, in reply to Maitland's letter on her behalf, had instructed the captain to inform Madame Bertrand that he considered it the duty of every good wife to follow the fortunes of her husband. Now he found little to say that would comfort or reassure her. As quickly as possible he left her and prepared to go ashore.

Napoleon, however, had not yet finished. He sent word to Keith, begging to see him again. When the admiral reentered the cabin, Napoleon asked him to advise him.

Keith replied, "I am an officer and have discharged my duty. I have left the heads [i.e. a list] of my instructions with you, in order that you may observe upon them if you consider it necessary. Sir," he added, "if you have anything more to urge, I must beg to call in Sir Henry Bunbury."

"Oh, no," said Napoleon; "it is unnecessary. Can you, after what has passed, detain me until you hear from London?"

Keith answered, "That will depend upon the arrival of the other admiral, of whose instructions I am ignorant."

"Is there any tribunal to which I can apply?" Napoleon asked.

"I am no lawyer," Keith said, "but I believe none. I am satisfied there is every disposition on the part of the British Government to render your situation as comfortable as is consistent with prudence."

Flushing, Napoleon picked up Melville's letter. "How so?" he said angrily. "St. Helena?"

Keith replied, "Sir, it is surely preferable to being confined in a smaller space in England or being sent to France or perhaps to Russia."

"Russia!" Napoleon exclaimed. "God preserve me!"

Bowing again, Keith left.

When Keith and Bunbury had left the ship, Napoleon asked to see Maitland. He showed the captain the letter that Bunbury had read and, when Maitland had finished reading it, continued his complaints against being sent to St. Helena:

The idea of it is a perfect horror to me. To be placed for life on an island within the tropics, at an immense distance from any land, cut off from all communication with the world and everything that I hold dear in it! It is worse than Tamerlane's iron cage. I would prefer being delivered up to the Bourbons.

Among other insults—but that is a mere bagatelle, a very secondary consideration—they style me General! They have no right to call me General. They may as well call me Archbishop, for I was head of the church as well as the army. If they do not acknowledge me as Emperor, they ought as First Consul. They have sent ambassadors to me as such; and your King, in his letters, styled me brother.

Had they confined me to the Tower of London or one of the fortresses in England (though not what I had hoped from the generosity of the English people), I should not have so much cause of complaint. But to banish me to an island within the tropics! They might as well have signed my death-warrant at once, as it is impossible a man of my habit of body can live long in such a climate.

Nor was this the end. Napoleon informed Maitland that he wished to write another letter; and that same afternoon Maitland carried it to Keith, who forwarded it at once to London. It stated:

Bellerophon, July 31, 1815

My Lord,

I have read with attention the extract of the letter which you sent me. I have given you my views in detail. I am not a prisoner of war, but I am the guest of England. I came to this country on the *Bellerophon* man-of-war, after informing its Captain of the letter which I was sending to the Prince Regent, and obtaining from him an assurance that he had been given instructions to receive me on board and to take me with my suite to England, if I were to approach him with this object. A similar statement has since been made to me by Admiral Hotham.

From the moment that I came of my own free will on board the *Bellerophon,* I considered myself to be under the protection of the laws of your country. I would rather die than go to St. Helena, or be confined in some fortress. I desire to live in the interior of England, a free man, protected by and subject to its laws, and bound by any promises or arrangements which may be thought desirable.

I do not wish to keep up any correspondence with France nor to interfere in any political matters. My intention, since I abdicated, has always been to make my home in one or other country—the United States or England.

I trust, my Lord, that you and the Under Secretary of State will faithfully report all the arguments I have adduced in order to make clear to you the rights of my position. It is in the honor of the Prince Regent and in the protection of your country's laws, that I have trusted and that I still continue to trust.

Napoleon.

This letter, added to his statements of that day, reveals that the really significant event of July 31 was not Napoleon's receipt of the formal notification of the government's decision. Although it was important, the announcement was not unexpected. His reading of the newspapers had prepared him for it, and his lengthy, and at times repetitive, reply shows that he had prepared his arguments against it. The truly significant event was Napoleon's replies. Now, for the first time since his arrival, the burden of silence had been lifted from him. His words would be recorded by Keith and Bunbury and reported to the Ministry; his arguments would be studied, would go into the official records, would attain permanence. It was unlikely that his protestations would in any material way influence the government, but that was not the essential point. For Napoleon was doing more than answering the British government—he was addressing the future and, through it, seeking ultimate victory over his captors.

The British government and its Allies could imprison him on St. Helena and keep him there until he died. But if history were to declare that he had been unjustly incarcerated there, his enemies would have enhanced rather than diminished his heroic stature. Then there would be a return from St. Helena, at least in spirit, as surely as there had been an actual return from Elba. His name would serve as a talisman and an inspiration for those who would arise to renew the revolution that he had for so long personified. The confrontation that had begun with the writing of his letter to the Prince Regent was continuing—raised now to a more critical level by the government's decision to send him to St. Helena. Until he died, Napoleon would maintain his position with every resource at his command.

In his conversation with Keith and Bunbury, Napoleon was not wholly truthful. His protestations against the government's decision repeatedly emphasized two points—the voluntary nature of his surrender and his negotiations with Maitland about being conveyed to England in the *Bellerophon*. Half of his reply to Keith and Bunbury was devoted to these points, and nearly the same proportion of his letter to Keith dealt with them. But, as has been seen, his decision to surrender to England was not an entirely free choice—it was a gamble made necessary by and intended to obscure the increasing precariousness of his situation off Rochefort. Even less honest was the claim that Maitland had declared that he had received special orders from the British government to convey him and his suite to England if he approached

Maitland with that proposal. If Maitland had reiterated any point in his discussions with Las Cases, Savary, and Lallemand, it was that in taking Napoleon on board his ship and conveying him to England he was acting solely on his own authority and could not guarantee what kind of reception Napoleon would meet with. So, Napoleon lied. But then he had never proved himself so devoted a servant of truth as to let it stand between him and his ends. Also he knew, and was relying upon, the propensity of many people to give greater credence to a dramatic lie than to the prosaic truth.

Shortly before dinner Napoleon joined Maitland on deck and showed himself to the surrounding spectators—much to Maitland's surprise, for he had been convinced that Napoleon was too depressed by the day's events to appear. And at dinner Napoleon conversed as usual, again astonishing the captain "with what elasticity his spirits regained their usual cheerfulness, after such trials and disappointments." Maitland wondered if Napoleon were really as angered as he had seemed.

Maitland had little time to speculate about Napoleon's vacillating moods, however. Other problems claimed his attention, particularly the one relating to Savary and Lallemand. During the day the two had appealed continually to him concerning the injustice of their being given up to France by Britain. Neither doubted that this would happen; their having been prohibited by the Ministry from going to St. Helena, considered with their having been proscribed by Louis, seemed proof of their fate. Naturally, they feared being returned to France. "Were I allowed a fair and impartial trial," Savary declared, "I should have nothing to fear, never having accepted a position under Louis. But at present, when faction runs so high, I should inevitably be sacrificed to the fury of party. Lallemand's case is quite different," he went on. "He held a command under Louis, and on Napoleon's return from Elba joined him with his troops. Therefore his situation would at any time be a dangerous one. But I lived in the country all the time Louis was in France and did not come forward until Bonaparte's arrival in Paris, when he directed me to take the command of the *gendarmerie*."

"My reason for coming on board the *Bellerophon* with Las Cases on the morning of the 14th," Lallemand said, "was to ascertain whether there would be a risk of any of the Emperor's followers being delivered up to the French Government, in the event of their accompanying him to England—when you assured me there could be no danger of it."

Maitland tried to reassure them. "My answer to you," he stated,

was that I was of opinion there could be no risk of the British Government taking such a step; and I see no reason now to alter that opinion. As I have received you on board the *Bellerophon*, I consider you under the protection of the British flag, and myself in a great measure responsible for your personal safety. And under that impression I will write on the subject to Lord Melville, as the Minister under whose immediate control I act, that your minds may be set at rest—though, I repeat, you run no hazard of being sent to France.

Maitland was not as confident of their safety as he would have had them believe, however. Louis's proscription of Savary and Lallemand and their subsequent exclusion from the group Napoleon could take with him to St. Helena had filled him with doubts and worry about their future destiny. If they should be turned over by Britain to France and there be tried and executed, or imprisoned, for treason, Maitland felt that the damage to his personal honor could never be repaired. What would it matter to him then that he had taken Napoleon? He wrote to Melville that night:

H.M.S. *Bellerophon*
Plymouth Sound, 31st July, 1815

My Lord,

I am induced to address your Lordship in consequence of having observed, in the intimation delivered to Napoleon Buonaparte of the number of persons allowed to accompany him to the Island of St. Helena, that the names of Savary and Lallemand are expressly ex-

cepted, which, together with their being proscribed in the French newspapers, has created in them a belief that it is the intention of His Majesty's Government to deliver them up to the King of France. Far be
it from me to assume such an idea; but I hope your Lordship will make
allowance for the feelings of an officer who has nothing so dear to him
as his honour, and who could not bear that a stain should be affixed
to a name he has ever endeavoured to bear unblemished. These two
men, Savary and Lallemand (what their characters or conduct in
their own country may be I know not), threw themselves under the
protection of the British flag; that protection was granted them with
the sanction of my name. It is true, no conditions were stipulated; but
for I acted in the full confidence that their lives would be held sacred,
or they should never have put foot in the ship I command, without
being made acquainted that it was for the purpose of delivering them
over to the laws of their country.

I again beg leave to repeat to your Lordship, that I am far from
supposing it to be the intention of His Majesty's Government to deliver these men over to the laws of their country; but, as they are
strongly impressed with that belief, and I look upon myself as the
cause of their being in their present situation, I most earnestly beg
your Lordship's influence may be exerted that two men may not be
brought to the scaffold who claimed and obtained at my hands the
protection of the British flag.

Maitland had to contend with another critical and unexpected
problem that day. Madame Bertrand, faced with the terrifying
prospect of exile on St. Helena and defeated in all her efforts to
escape it, surrendered to despair. Walking on deck with Bertrand
shortly before nine o'clock that evening, she pleaded with him
again not to follow Napoleon; but he, as faithful as ever to his
master, rejected her appeals. Frantic, her last vestiges of self-
control gone, she whirled away from his side and darted into Napoleon's cabin, where he was listening to Las Cases translate the
newspapers. Throwing herself at Napoleon's feet, she cried, "Sire,
do not go to St. Helena. Do not take away my husband!" Then—
as Napoleon stood immobile, staring at her in surprise—she rose
and dashed out as swiftly as she had entered. She went into the

wardroom, where Maitland and the ladies and officers of the suite were enjoying an evening drink.

"Will you sit down and take something?" Maitland invited. But she shook her head, muttered an incoherent answer, and fled into her cabin. Montholon, who had noted her tense, distraught expression, rose at once and followed her—and not a moment too soon. She had crossed the cabin and was trying to throw herself out of the quarter gallery window and into the sea, four decks below. Already, she had forced most of her body over the protective bar across the window. Hanging suspended from it, she gave a loud scream as she attempted to thrust herself headlong into the dark water. Montholon rushed forward, caught hold of her legs, and shouted for help.

The scream and Montholon's cry for aid threw those in the wardroom into an uproar. They rushed to the door of Madame Bertrand's cabin, all trying to press through it at once. Someone shouted, "The Countess is overboard!" Montholon was tugging at Madame Bertrand, struggling to pull her back into the cabin, while she was attempting to kick herself free from his grasp. In a moment the others had helped him drag her back over the bar and carry her to her bed, where she lay sobbing and talking hysterically, her hair disheveled and the glazed look of panic on her face.

Maitland, who had hurried on deck at the shout to spot her body in the water and begin rescue operations, soon satisfied himself that the shout had been a false alarm. He returned to the wardroom, looked into Madame Bertrand's cabin, and saw her on the bed. The women and Bertrand were trying to calm her, but she tossed about unheedingly, all the time pouring out a stream of invective against England and its government—speaking mostly in English, but lapsing at times into French. The members of the suite who had returned to the wardroom milled about and buzzed in excited comment. Lallemand was walking up and down, his eyes flashing and his mouth drawn into a thin line. "It is horrible," he exclaimed bitterly, "to bring a set of people on board the ship for the purpose of butchering them."

The remark snapped Maitland's patience and Scots reserve. "Monsieur Lallemand," he retorted, "what a woman says in the state of violent irritation that Madame Bertrand at present is, I consider of little consequence, and am willing to make every allowance for the situation you are placed in. But I cannot stand by and hear such terms used of the government of my country; and if you do not desist or make use of more respectful language I shall be under the necessity of taking measures that will be very unpleasant both to you and myself."

Lallemand fell silent at this; and eventually the bustle in the wardroom subsided. Maitland, satisfied at length that some serenity had been attained, went to his cabin to write to Melville on behalf of Savary and Lallemand. He had scarcely begun when Lallemand, Montholon, and Gourgaud came into the room. They barraged him with further complaints about the cruelty and injustice of their situation, and then added, "You may depend upon it, the Emperor will never go to St. Helena. He will sooner put himself to death. He is a man of determined character and what he says, he will do."

"Has he ever said he will put himself to death?" asked Maitland.

"No; but he has said he will not go, which amounts to the same thing. And were he to consent himself, here are three of us who are determined to prevent him."

"You had better consider the consequences well before you venture on a measure of that kind," Maitland warned. As they left, however, he noted that their looks remained obdurate.

This sudden eruption of violence and threatened violence, though startling, was not surprising. And Maitland—no one— could know for certain what might follow. Madame Bertrand might well attempt suicide again. Lallemand, Montholon, and Gourgaud might attempt to kill Napoleon; they still possessed their arms, which Maitland was not empowered to seize. Or Napoleon might end his life himself; shipboard rumor stated that he carried a supply of laudanum on his person. Or—even though such an effort would be doomed—the Frenchmen might try forcibly to escape. As matters stood, Maitland might be unable to preclude these possibilities. He could only be watchful and hope for the best. As the ship quieted down for the night, several men were reassessing their positions in light of the sentence that had been passed upon Napoleon. Paramount in their minds was the question: "What will happen now?"

For Napoleon, the answer was clear: his protest and reiterated appeals for hospitality and justice would go unheeded; no arguments were likely to alter the government's fiat. Though it was true that the future might bring a change of ministers, the death of a prince or of a confidant, or a dispute that would lead to the commutation or relaxation of his sentence, such eventualities were fragile bases for hope. He could expect to remain a prisoner on St. Helena until he died, without the company of Marie Louise and his son, his mother, his brothers and sisters, and others who, for good or ill, had been tied closely to him during his years of glory.

The members of his suite were scarcely more optimistic than he about the future. Savary and Lallemand—fearful, angry, full of doubts—analyzed the possible perils that they faced. Bertrand lay beside his unsleeping wife and considered the price his sense of honor was exacting; for even his wife's attempt at suicide had not shaken his determination to accompany Napoleon. The surgeon, Dr. Maingaut, who had suffered greatly from seasickness during the passage from Rochefort, decided that he would refuse to go to St. Helena. Others wondered whether they would be asked by Napoleon to accompany him. If they were, what answer should they give? If not, what would happen to them, left behind in England?

Only one group on the *Bellerophon* joyfully contemplated the future—the ship's company. Since arriving in Tor Bay they had had no respite from duty. They had had to stand watches, take water and provisions on board, clean the decks, quarters, and holds, and work with sails and rigging—without enjoying their usual shore leave. In a sense they had been as confined as their prisoners. Now, however, they could see an end to it all.

The government's decision respecting Napoleon drew cries of outrage from some London newspapers. *The Times* condemned the Ministry's action in an editorial on July 31:

We cannot any longer, we suppose, refuse our belief to the reports generally in circulation, that instead of bringing him to justice, we are to impose upon ourselves the disgraceful trouble of conveying his body to a distant island, and there watching it. It is an honourable occupation for us! It is a worthy result of that glorious victory at Waterloo! and we know not which we are to congratulate most, the warriors who are to guard him; or those, who have bravely bled, as it now appears, *to ensure his safety*! The French army could not protect him! His old guard, and his new guard, and his middle guard, and all his guards, failed; and at last he must owe his preservation to the British *Life Guards*, and their irresistible charge, which drove him to seek shelter in the very country that gave birth to these heroes: with a generous inconsistency we sent *them* out to *destroy* him, and have taken *him* in to *preserve* him. Is this reason? Is this common sense? Is this the end and object of war? Answer, ye counsellors of humanity! No, we say, if he is to be saved, put us—put the people of England to no expense for his worthless life. We have been at expense enough already, in bringing him into this situation; put us to no more to extricate him from it. What will be the cost of fitting out those vessels that are to convey him and his associates to St. Helena? And who is to bear it? The people of England? No! we explain again, the people of England have no right to bear it, if it were but twenty pounds they have borne enough and more than enough already, on his account. If we have not the heart to bring him, or send him to the justice which his crimes merit; if he has still too many friends among us for that, why then, we say, turn him loose again upon the continent, and let him work his worst; there nobody fears him, and may the next man that catches him, be actuated by a more proper sense of his atrocious and criminal life, than the people of this country have been. May he come within the reach of some man, who is related to, or once knew the brave Captain Wright!

A different note of remonstrance had been sounded on the previous day, however, by the *Independent Whig*, as rabid an anti-Ministry journal as London offered. It wrote:

Appearing, however, as it does, to our judgments, that the LAWS, and not the *Ministers*, can alone legally decide upon the fate of a person situated as Napoleon was, after his surrender, and decisively as the Laws of England deny to the Crown all *discretionary* power as to the punishment of any individual, without a distinct accusation having been preferred, and a formal trial instituted, we cannot conceive a more outrageous act of arbitrary usurpation, than the banishment of Napoleon to the Island of St. Helena, merely at the will of the Crown. The character and dignity of the country is not only outraged in such an assumption of power, but the Bill of Rights is actually made a dead letter.

The battle of the newspapers was about to be joined in earnest.

At midnight in Plymouth Sound the *Bellerophon* slept, swinging to her cable while the *Erotas* and the *Liffey* rode astern and abeam of her. In Spithead, nearly 150 miles away, the *Northumberland* lay moored. She had arrived that afternoon and had taken on board seven marines and 31 seamen; and the next morning she would be provisioned for the voyage to St. Helena. Admiral Sir George Cockburn had not yet arrived to assume command of her, but he was expected to do so any day. He had just that day received his orders from the Lords Commissioners of the Admiralty.

Whereas by our commission dated the twenty-first of last month, we appointed you commander in chief of His Majesty's Ships and Vessels to be employed at the Cape of Good Hope and in the Seas adjacent, as far Northward as the equinoctial line, as far Westward as the fifteenth degree of West Longitude, Southward to the sixtieth degree of South Latitude, and Eastward to the sixty-fifth degree of East Longitude; we do hereby require and direct you to repair forthwith to Spithead, and there hoisting your flag on board His Majesty's Ship *Northumberland*, take the said Ship under your command, together with the *Ceylon* and *Bucephalus* Troop Ships, on board of which Ships a Battalion of the 53d Regiment and a detachment of artillery have been ordered to be embarked; and, having so done, proceed with the three ships with all possible dispatch to Plymouth Sound.

On your arrival at that anchorage, you are to receive on board the *Northumberland* General Buonaparte with his baggage and such part of his Suite as shall be allowed to accompany him; and putting to sea with the ships before named, and also with the ships and vessels named in the margin,* the commanders of which have received directions to put themselves under your orders, proceed with the whole to the Island of St. Helena, and there take upon you the charge of the service intrusted to your care, according to the enclosed instructions, which have been communicated to us by Earl Bathurst, one of His Majesty's Secretaries of State, by command of His Royal Highness the Prince Regent. . . .

You will employ the Sloops under your command in such manner as may be best calculated to carry into effect the important service entrusted to your charge, sending one of them home to report your arrival at St. Helena, with such communications respecting your proceedings and passengers, and such information with regard to the state of the Island as may be proper for our knowledge and you may be able to collect: and while you continue employed upon the service in question you will from time to time report your proceedings and occurrences, as you shall see occasion, for our information.

In committing to your charge the important trust of the person of Buonaparte, we are fully persuaded that the zeal, ability and discretion manifested by you in His Majesty's service on various occasions are the best pledges that can be given for the performance of the Prince Regent's Intentions, as signified to Us in the letters of Earl Bathurst communicating the instructions for your guidance.

Given under our hands the 31st of July 1815.

MELVILLE
J. S. YORKE
N. PAULET.

---

* These were the *Havannah*, the *Zenobia*, the *Peruvian*, the *Zephyr*, the *Leveret*, the *Redpole*, and the storeship *Weymouth*.

VIII

Questions of Law

AUGUST First found Admiral Lord Keith angry and worried. His anger had been aroused the previous day when he had seen the shore boats defying the guard boats' efforts to keep them clear of the *Bellerophon*. Jammed together, a thousand strong, filled to capacity with chattering, gaping curiosity-seekers, the boats had been as irresistible as a tidal wave, and at one time had forced the guard boats back against the frigate's sides. The mob cared nothing for orders, discipline, or restraint, its one purpose being to work as close as possible to the captive Napoleon.

Though under sentence, Napoleon was still creating unrest and setting Englishman at odds with Englishman. When he showed himself on deck, the spectators saluted him as though he were a popular hero; and it was the crews of the guard boats at whom they scowled, shook their fists, and cursed. What particularly inflamed Keith was that some of the most flagrant violators of his orders were navy men, whose uniforms he had noticed in the crowd. Even his own relatives were not exempt from the madness sweeping over the English. "I am miserable with all the idle people in England coming to see this man," he wrote to his daughter. "Here is among others my niece Anne, with 'dear friends' she never saw before, arrived from Exmouth. Sir J. Hippisley and Sir H. McLean and family—people all the way from

Birmingham—not a bed in all the town. Windsor [i.e. the Windsor Hotel] makes up 50, so you may guess my trouble and anxiety. I wish him at the ———— or anywhere but here."

If Keith were to hold his captives safe, he would have to institute more stringent measures against the trespassing shore boats. He had tried somewhat to indulge their holiday humor, but they had pushed him too far. Keith ordered additional guard boats to assist those already on duty, and he issued a General Order stating that

the Commander-in-Chief has observed with regret that boats of every description are allowed to approach much too near the *Bellerophon.* . . . If any officer in His Majesty's service or any persons of their families persists in breaking through the rules laid down, or approach nearer the *Bellerophon* than 30 yards, the guard boats are to ascertain by any means in their power the names of such persons and report the same to him; and if any shore boats attempt to resist the guard boats, the officers are to report the names of the rowers and of the boats, that measures may be taken for withdrawing their licenses to ply in future.

Adding to Keith's wrath was Maitland's report of the French officers' threat to kill Napoleon, reminiscent as it was of the defiance of authority that he had contended with years before at the Nore. "You may tell those gentlemen who have threatened to be Bonaparte's executioners," he informed Maitland bluntly, "that the law of England awards death to murderers and that the certain consequences of such an act will be finishing their career on a gallows."

Worry gnawed at Keith, too. The combination of the confusion alongside the *Bellerophon* with the threatened violence on board her could have disastrous results. Now that Napoleon knew his fate, he might make a final bid for freedom by attempting to force his way ashore in order to win popular support for his claim to refuge. Should he succeed, it did not matter that he would be recaptured; his temporary success would render England, and Keith, targets for the world's derision and would possibly lead to grave political complications with the Allied Powers. Even if he should fail, and perhaps be wounded or slain in the venture,

England and Keith would suffer enormous embarrassment. Keith did not intend that either should happen, but the presence of the shore boats complicated the problems of security. Yet, wearied, angered, and apprehensive as he was, Keith carried on as always and scrupulously excluded any hint of his personal feelings from his official correspondence. Writing to Melville, he said,

The concourse of people to this place is beyond all imagination. The Taverns are full and the Sea covered with Boats. Yesterday they pressed so much on the ship as to touch the side in defiance of the Guard Boats which induced me to issue an order which I sent to the Board this day; and it is become necessary that I am most careful, for the General and many of his Suite have an idea that if they could put foot on Shore, no Power could remove them, and they are determined to make the attempt if at all possible, they are becoming most refractory and talk of resisting the Emperors being taken out of the ship. I desired Captain Maitland to inform these Gentlemen that if such language was continued I should feel obliged to have recourse to a more rigorous mode of confinement.

Maitland, on August 1, was still deeply concerned about the fate of Savary and Lallemand and his involvement in it. When visiting Keith that morning, he showed the admiral his letter to Melville. Keith read it, then remarked that although he did not agree that Maitland's honor or character might be compromised by the affair he saw no harm in the letter. Even this, however, did not entirely reassure the captain. He sought out Sir Henry Bunbury, who was preparing to return to London, and repeated his plea for leniency toward the two Frenchmen, begging the undersecretary to tell Melville that "I should consider myself dishonoured for ever, if they suffered death through my means." Bunbury promised to inform the Ministers of what Maitland had said.

When Maitland returned to the *Bellerophon*—passing as usual through the scores of shore boats that had already assembled around it—he went at once to see Madame Bertrand. She was still in bed, her face drawn from a sleepless night, her hands moving restlessly on the blankets. After inquiring how she felt, Maitland asked, "Madame, how could you be so indiscreet as to attempt to destroy yourself?"

"Oh, I am driven to desperation!" she exclaimed. "I do not know what to do. I cannot persuade my husband to remain behind, he being determined to accompany the Emperor to St. Helena." At the thought of Napoleon, her brows drew down and her lips tightened. "If his ends are served," she accused, "he does not care what becomes of other people. 'Tis true, he has always given Bertrand lucrative and honorable situations; but the expense attending them is such that it was impossible to save money. And he has never given him a grant of land or anything that permanently bettered our fortune."

Self-pity and a feeling of insecurity, then, had been the sources of her despair and panic. She said nothing about renewing her attempt to take her life; nor did she again try to do so. Indeed, the incident had been so sudden and startling that some persons found it difficult to credit her attempt as sincere. Maitland, for one, inquired of Montholon if he thought that Madame Bertrand truly had intended suicide. Montholon had no doubt of it. Even after he had grasped her, he said, she had fought to free herself and plunge overboard. Napoleon, smiling incredulously, asked the *Bellerophon*'s surgeon, Barry O'Meara, "Do you really think, Doctor, that she meant to drown herself?"

We cannot know what Bertrand thought of or felt about his wife's action. But he must have felt his code of honor challenged by her attempt to take her life, and must have balanced his duty to Napoleon against his duty to her and to their children. He also must have asked himself how many of the suite would follow Napoleon to St. Helena if he, the highest ranked among them, declined to go. The best he could do was seek a compromise to placate his wife.

Death did come at Plymouth Sound, on Tuesday, August 1. That evening a shore boat carrying Deputy Purveyor Raymond, a Mr. Hartley and his wife and child, and a gentleman from the dockyard turned shoreward from the *Bellerophon.* Unnoticed and unnoticing until it was too late, one of the bulky guard boats bore down upon them at full speed. There followed a moment of stunned awareness of danger, then a woman's scream, shouts of alarm and command, frantic flailing of the oars in an attempt to stave off collision—and then the blunt, heavy bow of the guard boat rammed into the shore boat, crushing through its strakes, cutting it nearly in two, then riding it over onto its side and flinging its dazed occupants into the Sound. The thrashing of bodies in the water and the cries of pain and fright mingled with the shouts of onlookers and the sounds of hard-driven boats converging on the scene of the accident. Mr. Raymond, a capable swimmer, saved Mrs. Hartley, and others saved the child; but "the Gentleman sunk to rise no more, leaving a wife and four little children to deplore his loss."

No shore boats lingered late around the *Bellerophon* that evening.

Men in other ports and cities besides Plymouth had been working long hours on Napoleon's account that day. In Portsmouth the troops of the 53d Regiment had vacated their barracks and embarked on board the troopships *Bucephalus* and *Ceylon.* At Spithead that morning the *Northumberland* had received on board three Royal Artillery officers, 40 men, and four field pieces complete with carriages and other equipage; and in the afternoon she had taken on provisions and water from the six dockyard vessels that had met her on her arrival the previous afternoon. The supplies came aboard so speedily and in such quantity that the crew were hard pressed to keep up with their unloading; stowing would have to wait until the next day. Mounds and stacks of sacks, cases, casks, barrels, and butts grew on the decks and in the holds: 14½ tons of bread, 5½ tons of flour, 3½ tons of pork and beef, 3,700 gallons of wine, brandy, and rum, 40 butts of water, 400 gallons of vinegar, a ton and a half of sugar, more than a ton of suet and raisins, 1,200 pounds of tobacco, and cases, barrels, and sacks of other miscellaneous provender.

The seamen sweated and grunted as they wrestled these heavy, unwieldy stores on the crowded decks, muttering angrily at their unceasing flow and at the sharp-tongued bosuns and officers who urged them to keep things moving handsomely. They scowled as they labored on. They should by rights have been paid off at the Nore the week before. They had served their time in the war; they were entitled to a rest or to discharge. Instead they were bound for St. Helena, down at the empty end of the globe, sentenced to cruise its rocky perimeter for God only knew how long, keeping an eye on Boney! They hated the men who were sending them there—men who, in their experience, looked on the ordinary Jack-tar as no more than a sod to be kicked about, a galley slave to be sworn at because he did not gulp his biscuit and rum fast enough and run back to crack his spine working. But, look out. They were getting a bellyful of such treatment.

In London that afternoon, Rear Admiral Sir George Cockburn left his house in Cavendish Square, took his leave at the Admiralty, and departed for Spithead to join the *Northumberland*. At the same time the reading public continued scanning the newspapers for the latest information about Napoleon. Most of the daily summaries of his activities made much of the fact that when he appeared on deck the British as well as the French officers bared their heads and stepped aside respectfully. Napoleon's meeting with Keith and Bunbury was described, and in a mixture of fact and error, the conditions of his detention were reported. "According to one account," wrote the *St. James's Chronicle*,

Buonaparte's attendants are to be limited to six persons, of whom two are to be selected from his officers and four from his domestics, at his own option; while the remainder of his suite will be landed in France except Rovigo, Bertrand and Lallemand, who, in conformity to the late Royal Ordinance, will be given up to the Government. Another account says Buonaparte is to have the choice of any three persons to attend him, with the exception of Rovigo and Lallemand; and this is perhaps more probable, since the constancy of Bertrand to his master seems to have been his only crime: it cannot in truth be denied, that be the former what he may, the fidelity of Bertrand has almost universally gained him the good opinion of the public. His physician and Surgeon and a certain number of domestics will of course be also permitted to accompany their master. The amount of bills and cash which Buonaparte is said to possess is £200,000 sterling; but it is added, with no great probability indeed, that such things and such sums of money only as are indispensable to his comfort will be put on board the *Northumberland*. It is said a residence with a plot of 25 acres will be allotted near the Governor's house on the high lands for this extraordinary man to whom the Empire of the West, as he himself said, was too circumscribed. It is moreover said that Sir Hudson Lowe declines the appointment of being his Keeper, and we do not know what other Officer has been selected for the purpose. The Island it is now said is to remain in the hands of the East India Company, whose troops, under Colonel Mark Wilks, will continue to occupy the bay, harbour, and low lands; and a King's regiment, with a Commandant, will be stationed on the high land, as his body guard. This is the final arrangement made with the Company, so that their ships touch there as usual in there homeward passage. Already, as we are informed, it has been notified to Bonaparte that he is to be treated on the footing of a captured General, and he is said to have received this notification with great dissatisfaction. It is not indeed improbable, that ere this, Bonaparte has sailed from our shores; for the *Northumberland*, destined to convey him, sailed down the river on Sunday, and was in the Downs by night. . . .

Most interesting of all the articles was one in the *St. James's Chronicle* that concerned the legality of Napoleon's sentence:

We understand, that to warrant the detention of Bonaparte in Britain, an Act of Parliament must be passed for the occasion; the same authority is required to authorize the custody in any British settlement. Such an Act will be prepared against the meeting of Parliament, to authorize and regulate the confinement in St. Helena. We suppose this Act will be passed without much difficulty, although certainly not without observation; for however justifiable and proper, and even indispensable, the measure may be, it is, in a constitutional sense, the greatest innovation in British law and practice, since our Constitution has been matured to its present perfection, to make a British settlement a state prison. . . . The principle of detention, to secure good behaviour, is the only one in our law that affords analogy for this measure, and that principle will be in this instance carried to an extent before unknown. The thing altogether will constitute an era in the history of the British Constitution as well as of the British arms; and we look forward with particular curiosity and interest to the debates which will attend the passing of the Act. Till the meeting of Parliament, the Cabinet will proceed upon its constitutional responsibility, as if already fully authorized. An Act of Indemnity will, we conceive, be necessary, to discharge the Minister from penal consequences, as soon as Parliament shall meet.

An Act of Parliament authorizing and setting the conditions of Napoleon's detention on St. Helena was passed during the next session of Parliament, on April 11, 1816.

Although it was unprecedented, and at the time unauthorized by Parliament, the Ministry's action in ordering Napoleon to St. Helena was undoubtedly taken in good conscience. But in preparing the act the administration blundered, to say the least; for in so doing, it opened the door for the "very nice legal questions . . . which would be particularly embarrassing" that Liverpool had mentioned in his letter of July 21 to Castlereagh. The passage of the act gave Napoleon and his adherents further grounds for contending that England's treatment of him was contrary to every code of justice. They could thereafter not only emphasize that the Ministry had flouted the English Constitution in sentencing Napoleon without granting him a hearing or allowing him an appeal, but could also claim that it had afterward influenced Parliament to legalize its action.

In Paris, the final draft of the Convention that stipulated the measures the Allied Powers were taking to dispose of Napoleon was ready. It would be signed the next day by the representatives of England, Russia, Austria, and Prussia.

And in Marseilles, Major General Sir Hudson Lowe, having that day received Earl Bathurst's letter recalling him from France to assume the custody of Napoleon on St. Helena, departed immediately for Paris.

On Wednesday, August 2, London's Tory and Whig newspapers engaged in full-scale battle over Napoleon's fate. Before this there had been only light skirmishes with the Tory papers enjoying a clear advantage. They could exult in Napoleon's surrender and detention, freely express their hatred for him—the enemy, the bloody tyrant, the scourge of the world—and advocate that the harshest retribution be meted out to him. Against this heavy barrage of invectives, the Whig newspapers could only hold their fire or engage in minor sniping actions, aware that a counterattack would result in their being charged with lacking patriotism or having pro-Bonapartist leanings. Besides, their primary foe was not the Tory newspapers, but the Tory administration; and until the government officially announced its intentions respecting Napoleon, the Whig journals had to restrain their impatience to attack it. They did, it is true, decry the harsh punishment that unofficial reports said was being prepared for Napoleon, and they did point out the glory that would attach to England if she displayed Christian mercy toward her illustrious captive. With the possible exception of the *Independent Whig*, their editorial statements on the affair were circumspect. But when Napoleon's fate became public knowledge, they hit viciously at the Ministry. They attacked the decision to detain Napoleon on legal grounds, holding it up as another illustration of that callous disregard for the liberties of the individual of which they accused the Tory government.

The *Morning Chronicle* opened the engagement. "There is a strong sentiment," it wrote,

that Bonaparte, being within the jurisdiction of the Admiralty, is entitled to *Habeas Corpus*. . . . Having touched England, by being within the jurisdiction of the Admiralty, he is entitled to the benefit of our laws. A slave cannot touch it without being free; and no man, however criminal, can be transported without a judgment. We object to no measure that is indispensable to public security, but let not the laws of England be violated.

There followed a letter on the subject from Capel Lofft, an independent and constitutional lawyer who was a proponent of abolition and other reforms. Lofft's letter denied that Napoleon could be regarded as a prisoner of war, that he could be tried either by England or by the Allies, and that he might be executed without trial. He claimed that ⁸

all persons within the Realm of England, which includes the adjoining seas, are temporary subjects if aliens, or permanent if natural born.

Though not on the British soil he [Napoleon] is within the protection of the British Law. If at Plymouth, he is in a British county. An *Habeas Corpus*, if issued, must be obeyed. . . .

I am of opinion that deportation, or transportation, or relegation, cannot legally exist in this country, except where the law expressly provides it on trial and sentence.

.   .   .

. . . the Writ of *Habeas Corpus* is the legal Mode of investigation, as to all persons, whether their liberty be legally or illegally restrained, and all restraint of liberty is illegal, of which the legality is not clearly and strictly proved.

I know of no law of ours which supports such a conduct, as is asserted to have already taken place, and to be further determined.

That evening's *Courier* contained a reply:

There was a strange report this morning that it is the intention of those who think the tyrant of the human race an object of compassion, to apply for a Habeas Corpus, in order to prevent his being sent beyond the seas. . . . We stop for a moment to express our utmost astonishment that any Briton can view Buonaparte with the least feeling of pity or respect. Is it because he is no longer in a condition to repeat the assassinations that sent the last hope of the House of Conde, and Pichegru, and Toussaint, and our own Captain Wright, and Palm to the grave, that he is to become an object of compassion? If he has "fallen from his high estate," is he not fallen by his own crimes, by his own inordinate and remorseless ambition, that was not to be satiated at a less price than the conquest of all Europe and the ruin and subjugation of this country.

But it will be said by Mr. Loft, perhaps, that these considerations have nothing to do with the point of law. Is Buonaparte or is he not entitled to his *Habeas Corpus?* What a strange change in the state of affairs and persons—that we should now be quietly discussing whether the former Emperor of France, King of Italy, Mediator of Switzerland, Protector of the Rhenish Confederacy, the absolute disposer of the lives and fortunes of upwards of 50 millions of human beings, the enemy to freedom, particularly to British freedom, the violator of all laws, should, being a prisoner in our custody, be entitled to the protection and provisions of one of those great laws, which have kept us free from his power, and have enabled us at last to destroy that power! This *Habeas Corpus* Act . . . provides that "no inhabitant of England shall be sent prisoner to Scotland, Ireland, Jersey, Guernsey, or any places beyond the seas within or without the King's dominions." If inhabitant of England mean every person foreigner as well as native, who may come to this country, or be within the limits of British local allegiance, no doubt Buonaparte is such an inhabitant, and is entitled to his writ of *Habeas.*—But are foreigners or aliens so considered? If they are, the moment they arrive in any of our ports, they might, as inhabitants of England, demand their *Habeas,* and be brought before a Judge and set at liberty. Yet we know by the Alien Act of May last, that no alien can land without written permission from Government.

But Buonaparte must be viewed as a prisoner of war, and if he be, would it not be absurd to say, that being our prisoner, he has a right to the provision of a law which would make him no longer a prisoner? . . . But Mr. Loft contends, that in *his* opinion Buonaparte is not a prisoner of war. Upon what his opinion is founded, he does not state. The question seems to us to be a very clear one: We were at war with Buonaparte; vessels sailing under his flag were captured; and no doubt had he attempted to put to sea in his two frigates, we should have attacked and made prizes of them. He had at first the intention of putting to sea in contemplation, but he abandoned it, knowing that we should treat him as an enemy. Well: how does he avoid any such act of hostility? by surrendering at discretion. Surrendering in what character? Clearly as a prisoner of war; and this he distinctly and unequivocally understood from Captain Maitland. As a prisoner of war, therefore, how have we a right to treat him? The Law of Nations . . . says, "as soon as your enemy has laid down his arms and surrendered his person, you have no longer any right over his life." We do not intend any thing against his life. But we may secure his person. The same Law of Nations adds, "Prisoners may be secured, and for this purpose they may be put into confinement, and even fettered, if there be reason to apprehend that they will rise on their captors, or make their escape." . . .

Buonaparte is our prisoner of war; a character in which he might claim to be treated with less harshness than being exiled for life to St. Helena—were he not such a prisoner and such a man—had he not broken his parole at Elba and involved Europe again in warfare and slaughter, for his own selfish and ambitious purposes. When a ferocious and dangerous animal is taken, with what justice can he complain of restrictions that prevent him from continuing his career of cruelty and crime?

"Were he not such a prisoner and such a man." Napoleon's stature was at the crux of the debate concerning the legality of the government's action. For if the sentence passed on him was without precedent in law or history, it was so because what the man had been and done and symbolized were unprecedented. In his person and genius resided the force and focus of a revolutionary social and political ideal, which had collided violently with the old order. For England and her allies, Napoleon had become the movement that imperiled the social and political structures of Europe. His defeat would mean its failure, and they meant to ensure that that failure would be complete.

We should not infer that the legality of its action did not concern the British government. It did. But the peace and security of Europe was its primary concern, and could be achieved only by having Napoleon permanently out of the way. Lawyers and scholars might argue about the legal aspects of the government's action; but the government was chiefly interested in the stability of Europe. Nevertheless, the publicity given by the newspapers to the legal questions was disquieting to the Ministry. The rumors that a writ of habeas corpus might be issued made the ministers especially nervous. If a writ were served, it could appreciably delay Napoleon's being sent to St. Helena. While they could not prevent its being issued, they could move to prevent its actually freeing Napoleon from confinement on the *Bellerophon*. And they did. Downing Street sent instructions to J. W. Croker, and the First Secretary relayed them to Keith:

2nd August 1815

My Lord,

   I am to signify to your Lordship the commands of my Lords Commissioners of the Admiralty that you do give positive orders to the officer commanding His Majesty's Ship in which Buonaparte may be that he should on no account permit the General to be removed from his ship, except of course from the *Bellerophon* to the *Northumberland*, or by a subsequent special order from their Lordships; and I have to convey to your Lordship, and to request of your Lordship to convey to Sir George Cockburn on his arrival their Lordships anxious desire that the removal of the general on board the *Northumberland*, and the sailing of this ship in execution of Sir George's orders should be hastened by every possible means.

   In a letter to Keith that day, Melville mentioned, among other matters, this order and the reasons for its being issued:

Admiralty
Aug. 2

My Lord,

   You will perceive by my other letters what you probably anticipated, that we cannot allow of any alteration in our instructions respecting the disposal of Bonaparte. He must therefore submit, and I hope that he will not compel Sir George Cockburn or Captain Maitland to resort to measures of personal compulsion. . . .

   You will receive what is perhaps, and most probably, unnecessary—I mean official instruction *on no account* to permit Bonaparte to come on shore. In some of the newspapers a notion is held out that he may be brought out of the ship by a writ of habeas corpus. The serious public inconvenience and danger which would arise from such an occurrence, even though he might not escape and be remanded by the

judge as a prisoner of war, renders it indispensably our duty to prevent it, and also to protect you, or rather Captain Maitland and Sir
George Cockburn, by the peremptory order which we have sent you.
If we were to receive an intimation of any such proceeding going
forward here, we should order the *Bellerophon* to sea, and to cruise
off the Start or elsewhere, on some assigned rendezvous to meet the
Northumberland. We may possibly have to apply to Parliament for
their sanction to what we are doing respecting Bonaparte and the safe
custody of his person, but we must do our duty in the meantime.

Melville's fears that legal maneuverings might be employed
to release Napoleon from his confinement on the *Bellerophon*
were not unfounded, though they would be confirmed in an un-
usual way. On that very day one Anthony Mackenrot was hasten-
ing toward Plymouth from London. He carried a subpoena issued
him by the Court of the King's Bench in June, and he intended
to serve it on Napoleon. He was party to no organized effort to
secure Napoleon's entry into England; he had obtained the subpoena to further his own, not Napoleon's, cause.*

A quiet day passed on the *Bellerophon*. The shore boats clus-
tered around her gave the guard boats little trouble: the memory
of the drowned gentleman from the dockyard, plus the strict
enforcement of Keith's General Order, served to keep them outside the prescribed limits.† But the people who were present
would wait vainly for Napoleon to appear, and those who were
continuing to pour into the city in large numbers from all parts
of England would be disappointed. Napoleon would not come
on deck again in Plymouth Sound. Bitter, despondent, unwell at

* Mackenrot was the defendant in a libel case brought in 1815 by Sir Alexander
Cochrane, whom Mackenrot had charged with cowardice for not having engaged a
French West Indies fleet in 1807. Mackenrot intended that Napoleon should act as a
witness in his defense because Napoleon knew the state of readiness of the fleet at the
time referred to in his accusation. The writ is in Appendix II.

† In a letter to Keith that morning, Captain Lillicrap of the *Eurotas* enclosed the names
of persons and boats refusing "to keep a cable's length from the *Bellerophon* after having
been ordered to do so by the officers of the guard boats." Of the eleven men named,
seven were Navy personnel, and another was the quartermaster general of Plymouth
barracks. One of the Navy men was from the *Ville de Paris*, Keith's ship in Hamoaze;
and a midshipman had been in Sir John Duckworth's barge.

times because of a bad liver and stomach—from now on he would keep to his cabin the greater part of each day, coming out only for his meals.

He had had half an hour's conversation with Maitland in his cabin that morning before the captain went ashore to visit Keith. Again he had complained of the government's cruelty in sending him to St. Helena. He continued to assert that he would not leave the *Bellerophon* to go into any other ship, but conceded that he would submit to being confined in a fortress in Great Britain. He asked Maitland many questions about St. Helena, inquiring "as to its extent, climate and productions, whether it would be possible to take exercise on horseback, if there was game upon it of any kind, etc." Maitland, who had no firsthand knowledge of the island, could only answer what he had read or heard of it. Hoping that Napoleon's interest in the island might indicate a lessening of his resolve not to go there, Maitland asked if he would now consent to nominate the persons who were to accompany him there. Napoleon declined.

His refusal was only prudent since as yet he had received no reply to any of his protests against his sentence. Although the possibility that it might be alleviated was negligible, it did exist. If, however, he now named those he wanted to accompany him, he would seem to acquiesce in his sentence and thus forfeit any possibility of its being mitigated. Until the government reported its final decision, therefore, he would maintain silence.

Napoleon remained in his cabin most of the day, quitting it only for breakfast and dinner. He brooded on the approaching years of inaction, which would be broken only by riding or walking, reading, and talking with the handful of the faithful who would accompany him to St. Helena. Bertrand, who was with him frequently during the day, tried vainly to revive his spirits. At dinner, Napoleon spoke little. He did not look good; the tensions of the past few days had kept him from sleeping soundly, and his drawn face expressed his physical pain. That evening he sent for Las Cases. He spoke with him about St. Helena. What sort of place was it? Was it possible to exist there? "But after all," he mused, "am I quite sure of going there? Is a man dependent on others, when he wishes that his dependence should cease?"

For a minute the two men continued to pace the cabin—Napoleon calm, though affected and somewhat absent, Las Cases studying his expression. "I have sometimes an idea of quitting you," Napoleon continued, "and this would not be very difficult. It is only necessary to work up a little mental excitement, and I shall soon have escaped. All will be over, and you can then tranquilly rejoin your families. This is easier, since my internal principles do not oppose any bar to it; I am one of those who conceive that the pains of the other world were only imagined as a counterpoise to those inadequate allurements which are offered to us there."

Aghast at the idea of suicide, Las Cases contended warmly against it. Poets and philosophers, he reminded Napoleon, had said that it was a spectacle worthy of Divinity to see men struggling with fortune: reverses and constancy had their glory. Such a great and noble character as Napoleon's could not, he insisted, descend to the level of vulgar minds. He who had governed with so much glory and who had excited the admiration and influenced the destinies of the world could not end like a desperate gamester or a disappointed lover. What would then become of all those who looked up to and placed their hopes in him? Would he thus abandon the field to his enemies? The eagerness they had shown to drive him to suicide was surely sufficient reason to make him resist. Besides, Las Cases continued, who could tell the secrets of time or assert what the future would produce?

"Some of these suggestions have their weight," Napoleon admitted. "But what can we do in that desolate place?"

Excitement brightened Las Cases' eyes. "Sire," he said, "we will live on the past; there is enough of it to satisfy us. Do we not enjoy the life of Caesar and that of Alexander? We shall possess still more—you will re-peruse yourself, Sire!"

"Be it so!" Napoleon answered. "We will write our memoirs.

Yes, we must be employed; for occupation is the scythe of time. After all, a man ought to fulfill his destinies. That is my grand doctrine: let mine also be accomplished."

He would have need of occupation on St. Helena, for there was no doubt that he was bound there. On that same day, August 2, a convention signed by plenipotentiaries of the Allied Powers, in Paris, officially entrusted the British government with Napoleon's safekeeping—reserving the choice of place and the provision for security to his Britannic Majesty.* The choice was already clear.

* The convention stated that Napoleon was regarded by the Powers who had signed the treaty of March 26, 1815, as their prisoner. The courts of Austria, Russia, Prussia, and France (if Louis XVIII so desired) would appoint commissioners to "assure themselves of his presence" at the chosen place.

IX

Seaward from Menace

MANY of the *Northumberland*'s crew were in an ugly mood. They had worked all day on August 2, arranging the stores taken on board the day before and receiving and stowing the baggage of Rear Admiral Sir George Cockburn, who had joined the ship and hoisted the red flag of his rank at 10:30 that morning. Weary, and angry at the assignment they felt was unfairly allotted them, the men gathered in the evening in knots on the forecastle and around the masts and gun mounts to mutter their grievances. They should have been discharged by this time. Other ships and men with far less service time than theirs had been paid off. They were being exiled as surely as Boney himself was—sent to rot with him at St. Helena for who knew how long. To make matters worse, they'd be miserably cramped with the artillery troops and Boney's crowd aboard and underfoot.

Well, they'd not stand for it. They were entitled to squarer treatment, and if they didn't get it, they'd take affairs into their own hands. But if they were going to do so, they'd have to step lively: with the supplies all stowed and the admiral aboard, the ship would most likely get under weigh the next day. So the disgruntled ones debated what action to take, formed resolves, and counted those who were firmly with them. They acted the next morning. Twenty-three seamen and one marine deserted while ashore on duty. And that was only the beginning. To the disaffected seamen still on board the ship, the sight of undermanned boats returning from shore and the news of the desertion of their mates served as a spark to dry tinder. Their turn to move came when the ship was ready to be unmoored. What occurred then is described in a letter to Cockburn, who was ashore in Portsmouth, from Captain Charles Ross, the frigate's captain:

> HM Ship *Northumberland*
> 3 August 1815

SIR,

I think it my duty to inform you that the ships Company have been behaving very ill bordering on a state of Mutiny, it began upon my ordering the ship to be unmoor'd—early this Morning the Petty Officers came aft in a very quiet way to say they had served a very long time and if the ship was to remain on a foreign station to know if there woud be any impropriety in asking for their discharge—I told them it was very possible the ship woud not remain the usual time abroad but that their voyage woud be a short one, upon which the whole of them went perfectly satisfied below—when the hands were turned up to unmoor they were very slack and the fore top men positively refused to clap on the nippers and desired the Boatswain's Mates to come aft again and say they woud not go. I had the troops and Marines under arms in a moment and went down on the lower deck and at a word they all went to their stations, I have confined the Fore top men which has been pointed out and am now finishing unmooring but I thought proper to mention these circumstances to you without loss of time.

Cockburn, who had been on the point of embarking when Ross's letter reached him, hurried aboard. He found all quiet there, the men having returned to their duties, but he judged that although the crew's rebelliousness had been subdued, their grievances might remain. The memory of the 24 men who had escaped would feed the discontent of those who remained, and another outbreak might occur at any time. More men might desert when the *Northumberland* put in to Plymouth to take on additional supplies. Or—an exceedingly more ominous prospect—mutiny might flare up again when they were out at sea. Who could foretell what the combination of Bonaparte and an unhappy crew might bring to pass? What if Napoleon should bewitch or bribe them to mutiny, and should escape! That such trouble should occurr on this ship, of all ships, and at this time, of all times, was a development that Cockburn must not have found welcome. He determined that he and Captain Ross, aided by the petty officers, would study the roster of the entire crew, and replace any man who they suspected was a potential recalcitrant.

During the morning the *Northumberland*'s rigging had been set up fore and aft, her topgallant yards crossed, and the ship itself unmoored. At 4:30 that afternoon she weighed and made sail and proceeded to sea accompanied by the troopships *Bucephalus* and *Ceylon*. At six she hove to at St. Helen's to take on a load of planks from a dockyard lighter that came alongside. Then at 7:30 she filled and made sail again, tacking at 8:30 and standing to the southwest under topsails and topgallant sails.

During the day the Admiralty learned that the *Leveret,* one of the ships at Plymouth assigned to accompany the *Northumberland* to St. Helena, was in defective condition and would have to be replaced.

The Lords Commissioners of the Admiralty were becoming apprehensive over the time it was taking to get everything ready for transferring Napoleon to the *Northumberland* and ridding England of him. The tremendous crowds around the *Bellerophon*, rumored escape attempts by Napoleon and his suite, reports that a writ of habeas corpus would be served—all fostered extreme anxiety. Napoleon's detention on the *Bellerophon* had been devoid of incident thus far; but the calm and quiet might not last indefinitely. Each day that he remained in Plymouth Sound increased the Commissioners' fears that somehow he might discover a way to thwart them. Thus Croker sent the following orders to Keith:

3rd August

Secret and Confidential.
MY LORD,

As it appears that considerable inconvenience is occasioned by the continuance of General Buonaparte in Plymouth Sound, I have to signify to your Lordship the commands of my Lords Commissioners of the Admiralty that you do immediately on the receipt of this letter, order Rear Admiral Sir Benjamin Hallowell, in the *Tonnant*, to take the *Bellerophon* under his command together with any frigate you may please to appropriate to this service, and putting to sea with all possible expedition proceed to cruize with the three ships (the *Bellerophon* having the general and his suite on board) off the Start, or such other rendezvous as your Lordship may judge proper, until they shall be joined by Sir George Cockburn in the *Northumberland*, when General Buonaparte and the persons who are to accompany him to St. Helena are to be transferred to the latter Ship which is to proceed immediately afterwards in execution of their Lordships' former orders.

In case of unfavourable weather Sir Benjamin Hallowell is to be authorized to take shelter in Torbay or such other anchorage as your Lordship may appoint; and the transfer of General Buonaparte to the *Northumberland*, if it cannot be made at sea, which would be more desirable, may be made at the said anchorage.

Sir George Cockburn may perhaps fall in with the squadron before he reaches Plymouth, but as it is conceived that he may have some short arrangements to make which may make it convenient to him to come to Plymouth, Sir Benjamin Hallowell should acquaint him that he should proceed to the Sound or Cawsand Bay, for that purpose, and should afterwards return to rejoin Sir Benjamin on the rendezvous appointed, for the purpose of taking Buonaparte on board.

On the arrival of Sir George at Plymouth, your Lordship will communicate these instructions to that officer, and you will urge him to make his arrangements at that port, and sail again in execution of his orders, with the greatest expedition.

My Lords reckon confidently on the zeal and vigilance of Sir Benjamin Hallowell to keep the *Bellerophon* in sight and to prevent any communication with her whatsoever, and when the general and those who accompany him shall be safely on board the *Northumberland*, and that ship has proceeded on her voyage, he is to return with the ships to Plymouth Sound, the remaining part of Buonaparte's Suite continuing on board the *Bellerophon* for further orders.

Those persons of Buonaparte's suite who are not on board the *Bellerophon* [i.e. the servants on the *Myrmidon* and the *Liffey*] should be transferred to the *Tonnant*, unless they should already be in the Frigate which may be appointed to accompany these ships.

It has been stated to their Lordships, that some persons of the general's suite on board the *Bellerophon* have used violent and threatening language; Your Lordship will therefore if you should judge it necessary, take measures for removing any such persons from the *Bellerophon*, into the *Tonnant*.

In the event of General Buonaparte, or any of his suite escaping to the shore, which, however, it may be hoped is impossible, your Lordship will take the most active measures for securing them and sending them back on board ship.

Croker added the postscript, "It seems hardly necessary to observe to your Lordship that the most profound secrecy should be observed on the subject of the proceedings directed in this letter, which indeed need be communicated only to Sir Benjamin Hallowell and Sir George Cockburn."

The withdrawal of the *Bellerophon* from Plymouth Sound would free her from the inconvenient crowds of shore boats, materially reduce the chances of Napoleon's escaping, and minimize the possibility that he might gain a temporary reprieve with a writ of habeas corpus. The ship's sudden and secret departure was intended to provide additional assurance that Napoleon could be transferred to the *Northumberland* quickly and without incident. The Admiralty wanted no fanfare to announce the finale of this episode.

Peripheral matters relating to the case would have to wait until Napoleon was safely on his way. Melville wrote to Keith on August 3 that he would not answer "Captain Maitland's extraordinary communication" on behalf of Savary and Lallemand until Napoleon had sailed.

The Ministers as well as the Lords Commissioners were anxious about the security of their prisoner. "Bonaparte is giving us great trouble at Plymouth," Liverpool informed Castlereagh. "We have been obliged to order the ship to cruise, by telegraph, till the *Northumberland* can come round. We have had abundant proof that it would have been quite impracticable to have detained him here, without the most serious inconvenience."

But even the certainty of his isolation on St. Helena was not a guarantee of complete security. The Ministry wanted to prevent disagreements among the Allies that might work to Napoleon's advantage. "With respect to the Commissaries," Liverpool continued, "might not an agreement be made with the Allies, that they should have alternately a Commissary at St. Helena, who should remain a year. This would be a considerable saving of expense to the Allied Powers; it would fulfil their principle; and one man would be much less likely to intrigue and give trouble than three or four."

The Ministers were no more edgy than Keith and Maitland had become after ten days at Plymouth. Keith, especially, felt the strain: "I am worried to death with idle folk coming, even from Glasgow, to see him," he confided to his journal; "there is no nation so foolish as we are! ... I look for the *Northumberland* every day to take Monsieur le General off my hands." He thought he saw evidence of a number of plots to free Napoleon: the Frenchmen, though more quiet than usual the day before, had been inquiring "if it was possible to swim on shore or if the gunboats would fire on them." Then "a Frenchman calling himself Chevalier de St. Grieg went off to the *Bellerophon* the other day and when stopped by the guard boat said he wanted to see the Emperor and presented papers, which I have," he wrote, "but the officers did not secure the man. I have sent to seek for him and if he cannot give a good account of himself I will send him to prison and his papers to the Admiralty." Keith refused the request of an English youth who was Savary's servant to visit friends in Surrey, "at least until Bonaparte shall have sailed."

Maitland went ashore on the morning of August 3 to call on Keith, without having first seen Napoleon. At Plymouth Dock he met the admiral, who was then escorting a group of ladies and Sir William Lemon to the barge of the *Ville de Paris*. Sir William told Maitland of a rumor that a boat had been under the *Bellerophon*'s stern at ten o'clock the previous night for the purpose of taking off Napoleon. Although Maitland doubted the report, he returned at once to the ship, summoned First Lieutenant Mott, and asked him if Napoleon had been seen that morning. Mott said that Napoleon had not been at breakfast, and that no one but his own people had seen him. Was the report, then, possibly true? Maitland sent to the *Eurotas,* which lay astern, to ask if anyone there had seen Napoleon at the stern windows of the *Bellerophon.* The *Eurotas* sent back her answer: Negative. Maitland summoned a midshipman and ordered him to go out on the spanker boom and look in the cabin windows to discover if Napoleon might be sitting on the sofa. While the young man was about this task, Maitland inquired of Bertrand about Napoleon. Bertrand replied that he had spent a bad night and was too ill to leave his quarters. The midshipman returned. He reported that he had been unable to see Napoleon in any part of the cabin.

Maitland was genuinely alarmed now. Had Napoleon in truth escaped the night before, slipping past sentinels, guard boats, and frigates? Was he even now ashore and in hiding while he pondered new intrigues—or perhaps at sea and on his way to the United States? Had Bertrand lied, trying to win every minute's advantage for his master? Calling his servant, Maitland sent him into Napoleon's cabin to bring out some paper. It was a flimsy pretext for entrance, but Maitland had to discover if his captive was still on board. His hand gripping his sword hilt, he waited long minutes for the man's reappearance. When at last the servant rejoined him, the smile he wore told Maitland that his fears had been groundless. The man reported that he had found Napoleon lying stretched out on his bed and looking extremely unwell.

Maitland released his breath in a long sigh of relief. But that night, when he heard Napoleon and another person, whom he assumed to be Bertrand, pacing up and down the cabin until after eleven o'clock, he notified the officer of the watch and the sentries to be doubly watchful; and he ordered one of the guard boats to lie under the *Bellerophon*'s stern all night. Only then, well past midnight, did he seek his bed.

Rumors continued to be broadcast in Plymouth. One stated

that the Prince Regent was coming down immediately and that
orders for his reception had been received at Saltram, a few miles
east of Plymouth; another, that the Duke of York was expected
any moment. The most persistent and widely current one, however, was that Napoleon's suicide was imminent. He had vowed,
it was said, not to leave Plymouth Sound alive, and when told
that his intended suicide would be prevented he had replied that
he had friends about him who would kindly shoot him. The
belief that he carried a quantity of poison on his person added
to the circulation of certain of his remarks to Keith and Bunbury
and twisted versions of the threat to his life made by Lallemand,
Gourgaud, and Montholon, helped lend an air of authenticity to
the report. Most convincing of all to the credulous, however, was
Napoleon's failure to show himself on deck the past two days
and his refusal to name those who would go with him to St.
Helena.

So the shore boats continued to converge on the *Bellerophon*
and ring her round with thousands of the morbidly curious. Hour
after hour they sat cramped together, perspiring freely in the
sun that beat down upon them and reflected glaringly off the
water into their faces—waiting to be in at the death.

There were some in the country who might have received news
of Napoleon's suicide with mingled regret and rejoicing. *The
Courier* expressed their opinion of the punishment awaiting him
on St. Helena: "Let him live!—live to lament that he ever *did*
live—live to die as many deaths as he has caused, for fear of dying
that one death, which he cannot escape and dare not encounter."
Others, however—those who from the beginning had clamored
for his execution—would have greeted his suicide with exultant
shouts, preferring it to what they judged the leniency with which
he was being treated. "When all the world acknowledges that he
ought not to be suffered to go at large," the *Morning Post* stated,
"it might be deemed high time to send him, loaded with fetters
to a dungeon. But though the guilt of the culprit exceeds all forms
of the most vindictive justice, we choose to rest contented with

the mildest punishment for felony known to the Constitution; and even for this excess of lenity, his abandoned crew of admirers presume to insult us."

That "abandoned crew of admirers," and especially Capel Lofft, were receiving a concentrated fusillade from the Tory newspapers for questioning Napoleon's status as a prisoner of war and the legality of his being detained. *The Times* wrote on August 3:

We rather suppose that some wag may have been assuming Mr. Capel's name, for the purpose of ridicule; if not, why then, Mr. Capel himself is a very facetious man. He says, "The intelligence that the great Napoleon will not be permitted to land, is almost overwhelming to him," from which some people might suspect that the writer was a bit of a traitor as well as a bit of a lawyer. *"He does not know,"* indeed, "that the Emperor can be regarded as a prisoner of war:" but is inclined to think "that he cannot," and upon this presumption he coolly discusses the said Emperor's claim to the protection of British laws as a British subject. But would it not have been as proper to have settled the point first, *whether* Buonaparte could be considered as a prisoner or *not*; and then to have proceeded to the discussion of the rights, emanating from his situation. However, as Mr. Capel Lofft, or the writer in his name, seems to possess an inquisitive mind, we shall propose to him a character in which he shall consider Buonaparte, and let him settle what are the rights and privileges resulting to him from that character. View him as the author of the dark and mysterious murderer of Captain Wright, his prisoner of war, while acting Monarch of France; and now that he has himself fallen into the hands of that Sovereign, whose subject Captain Wright was, and whose commission he bore, what are his rights and privileges, we ask, as resulting from that character.

In the *Morning Chronicle,* anti-Ministry though it was, a letter from one Mary Ann Bulmer challenged Lofft's position by claiming that Napoleon was a prisoner of war because England had been at war with him when he surrendered. "It [the right of the conqueror over the conquered] is not a question of precedent," she contended.

It is one altogether of principle. The moral right of detaining the person of an enemy, of keeping him in a severe and rigorous, or relaxed and mitigated custody, must depend wholly on the prisoner, his capacity to do further mischief, the character of the hostility he carried on against you and the probability of a renewal of that hostility, were he to be set at large. The *place* of his custody is a mere accident, as a logician would call it. If he cannot be secured in one place, he may be carried to another. The sources of this moral authority are the common safety and expedience.

And the *St. James's Chronicle*, commenting on the charges that the Ministry's treatment of Napoleon was illegal, declared,

The following appears to us to be the plain state of the case.—Our civil law (if security cannot be otherwise obtained) places in safe custody him who threatens the peace, happiness and life of another, and the tenor of whose life shows that he is not to be trusted to his own free agency. This civil law, however, *applies not* to a nation or its chief; nor to any case for which it does not specifically provide; and to talk of any *violation* of it in the case of Bonaparte is quite absurd. It is by a law of much more extensive and general kind that Bonaparte is held in detention—the law of nature and nations—a law which, though it differ in extent, differs not in spirit from the civil law. The latter is indeed strictly founded on and illustrates the former. It is obvious then that this international law, exercised as in this case it actually is, by the allied nations of Europe, through their chiefs as their organs, applies to a particular nation or its chief precisely as does the civil law of a particular nation to a particular individual.

Capel Lofft stood his ground. He wrote again in the *Morning Chronicle* on August 3:

See the situation of the greatest of living men; trusting to the Prince Regent and his Ministers, the justice, freedom and humanity of the English laws, and the generosity of the British character. And observe the daily and horrid calumnies in the public prints against him; thus coming to England and thus received, calumny, though not more generous, is a safer instrument of destruction than *poison*. And if (at which they have been aiming at every opportunity) they can drive his great and firm mind into *suicide*, they will triumph in their success. Their work will have been then done; though they may perhaps force some crocodile tears.

Hence, perhaps, their savage joy, and possibly exaggeration on the project soon to be determined, and instantly to be executed, of transporting him a prisoner for life to the deserted island of St. Helena. A project, which on deliberate consideration, I affirm to be a breach of Magna Charta, the Act of *Habeas Corpus*, 31 Car.II.c.2 & 12, and a violation of the Bill of Rights, which, declaratory of the common law, denounces unequal and arbitrary punishments. And a violation of our *whole* criminal law, which permits not transportation, unless in cases for which Statute Law has expressly provided. It may be dangerous to speak: but when it would be so criminal to be silent, what *Englishman*, what *Man*, can help it who is worthy of the name?

Lofft was not alone in his sympathy for Napoleon and in his attack on the Ministry's action. A letter signed "Walsingham," asked:

But is it fitting that so distinguished an actor in the theatre of the world, be his imperfections what they may, should, after throwing himself on the honour and generosity of a British Prince and Government, be treated like a paltry felon, and condemned to that Siberian confinement, which is, perhaps, but one shade better than the dungeons of Magdeburgh or Spandau?

The noble muse of Dryden, in his immortal Ode has well painted the manly emotions of Alexander, for the fallen fate and fortunes of Darius.

Dryden's was a truly English Muse. The inference is obvious.

Admiral Lord Keith prepared to go to sea. "The crowds of people and their very ill behaviour obliged me to put to sea with this Reptile to wait the arrival of Sir George Cockburne," he wrote testily in his journal. However, other reasons had helped him decide to sail. On the night of August 3 an indistinct telegraphic message from London had reached him: "*Tonnant* . . . frigate . . . sail . . . Start." The next morning's post brought the orders from Croker to quit the Sound and cruise off Start Point

until the *Northumberland* arrived. At three that morning, therefore, Keith notified Maitland that the *Bellerophon* probably
would be required to weigh and put to sea at a moment's notice.

Although Keith's orders from the Admiralty had specified that
he order Rear Admiral Hallowell in the *Tonnant* to take the
Bellerophon and another frigate under his command and cruise
off Start Point, Keith decided to perform that task himself, rather
than remain behind in Plymouth. Consequently, he assumed command of the *Tonnant,* sending Hallowell ashore for the time
being. Two considerations fostered this move. The first was
Keith's desire to be present for the final act of the affair he had
so far directed. The second was that unforeseen events might
occur, requiring important and immediate action; and as the
officer in charge of Napoleon's detention in England Keith wanted
to be present to make and implement decisions.

The second consideration was the more important one. Keith
had heard that a writ of habeas corpus had been issued to obtain
Napoleon's release from the *Bellerophon* and land him on English soil, and that a lawyer was on his way from London to serve
it. As Commander in Chief of the Channel Fleet, Keith was the
logical person to whom the lawyer would apply for permission
to serve the writ. For him to refuse the permission or in other
ways seek to hinder the writ's being served would be for him to
defy the authority of the King's Bench, and thereby become
liable to prosecution. To say that the *Bellerophon* had left Plymouth Sound and that it was under Hallowell's flag would not
delay matters, since both the ship and Rear Admiral Hallowell
were under his orders. To leave Plymouth, then, seemed Keith's
most prudent course.

Maitland waited on Keith soon after seven o'clock to report
that at daybreak he had had the *Bellerophon* unmoored and hove
short, the topgallant sails bent, and other preparations made to
weigh at short notice. He added that the French officers had
watched these preparations with signs of alarm and annoyance
and had frequently inquired about the reason for all the activity.

Keith instructed Maitland to say that the government intended that Napoleon's removal to the *Northumberland* should take place at sea and that the *Bellerophon* was going out to meet her. He also revealed to Maitland his information about the habeas corpus and requested the captain to be ready to put to sea whenever the signal was given. He himself, Keith said, would board the *Tonnant* that morning.

Keith had been gone from his home only a short time when he was brought disconcerting news from James Meek, his secretary. Hardly had the admiral left, Meek related, when a lawyer* named Anthony Mackenrot had called at the house, asking for Keith and announcing that he bore a summons to serve on Napoleon. Meek, who had been on the point of joining Keith to go on board the *Tonnant*, had put off Mackenrot by suggesting that he seek Keith at one of the admiral's offices; then he had set off at full speed to warn Keith of the approaching danger. Keith lost no time in being rowed out to the *Tonnant*, which was at anchor in the Sound.

Mackenrot bore, not a writ of habeas corpus, but a subpoena for Napoleon to appear as a witness in a trial in which Mackenrot was the defendant. He did not prove at all easy to evade. Failing to locate Keith at his offices, and learning that he had gone to the *Tonnant*, Mackenrot hired a boat and set out to waylay the admiral in the Sound. Warned of the man's approach, Keith left the *Tonnant* for the *Eurotas*. Mackenrot pursued him there, and while he was attempting to get on board at one side of the frigate, Keith was clambering out the opposite one and urging the crew of his barge to row to sea. ("Neither of the Captains were in their ships [so much for wives!]," Keith later wrote.) Keith next turned toward land at Cawsand; Mackenrot followed him closely, failing to overtake him only because Keith's 12-oared barge out-rowed Mackenrot's smaller craft. At length—

---

* So Meek and Keith believed; actually Mackenrot was an indigent West Indies merchant.

harried, wearied, and fuming with anger—Keith fled out to the point at Rame Head and there boarded the *Prometheus*. He remained on that ship until dark, when he saw Mackenrot land at Cawsand. Keith still was apprehensive lest his pursuer should make another attempt in a sailboat during the night, so he cautioned the captain of the *Prometheus* to keep off boats of all kinds.

The day had been a physical and emotional ordeal for the admiral. He shuddered to think what the consequences of Mackenrot's apprehending him might have been: "I should have been had up before the Justice; and Bony under my wing till November next!"

Meanwhile, Maitland had returned to the *Bellerophon*, shortly after eight that morning, and had found Napoleon anxious to speak with him. Napoleon urgently requested to know why the ship was preparing for sea. Maitland told him what Keith had said earlier: that the government wished Napoleon's transferral to the *Northumberland* to take place at sea and that the *Bellerophon* was going out to meet her. This news was one more hatchet stroke to whatever hopes for a mitigated sentence that Napoleon may still have had. Since July 31 he had had no word from the government, and now time was running out. Had any word reached Keith—and, if so, why had the admiral not informed him? If there were no word, why was he being taken so unexpectedly to sea to meet and be put on board the *Northumberland*? He at least deserved not to be spirited away in silence.

Napoleon requested that Maitland write Keith at once to say that Napoleon wished very much to see him. The admiral might be able to explain what was taking place. He might also be useful in helping Napoleon gain time and win some concessions from the government.

Maitland did write to Keith, who was then on the *Tonnant* (Mackenrot's marathon chase had not yet begun), and soon after received Keith's reply. Keith declined to meet Napoleon, stating that on disagreeable subjects criticism was unpleasant, that he had no power, and that to hear or discuss the matter could only affect his and Napoleon's feelings. "I . . . shall be glad to hear the determination of the General," he continued, "whom you may inform that the answer is arrived from London, and that I have no authority to alter, in any degree, any part of the former communication [regarding Napoleon's sentence]; which induces me to wish the selection of the persons he is inclined should attend him."

Bertrand carried Keith's reply to Napoleon, who was in his cabin. When Bertrand came out, Maitland pressed him again on the subject of Napoleon's naming those who would accompany him to St. Helena. Bertrand's reply was short: "The Emperor will not go to St. Helena."

Soon after nine the *Bellerophon* received a signal to prepare to weigh, and at nine-thirty the signal came. The anchor was heaved up, sail made, and the ship immediately started, accompanied by the *Eurotas*. The wind was blowing right into the Sound and the flood tide was against the ships; consequently, Maitland sent the guard boats ahead to tow the *Bellerophon* out to open water. As they made way slowly out past the breakwater and toward the mouth of the Sound, Maitland noted a man in a small boat approaching his ship. At once, he ordered one of the guard boats to cast off its towline and not allow the shore boat "on any pretext, to come near us."

That was fortunate, for the man in the boat was none other than the indefatigable Mackenrot. Having failed to intercept Keith, he was now attempting to cut off the *Bellerophon*, board her, and serve his writ through Maitland. But the guard boat prevented him from getting near the frigate; and after a time he gave up this chase, too. He returned to his room at the King's Arm Tavern in Plymouth Dock, from whence he that evening addressed this letter to Keith:

My Lord,

I arrived this morning from London with a writ issued by the Court of the King's Bench to subpoena Napoleon Bonaparte as a witness in a trial impending in that Court.

I was extremely anxious of waiting on your Lordship, most humbly to solicit your permission to serve such a process on your said prisoner, but unfortunately could not obtain any admittance into your presence, neither at your own house, nor at the two offices, nor on board HMS *Tonnant*, where your Lordship was said to be.

I humbly entreat your Lordship to consider that an evasion to give due facility to the execution of any process would amount to a high contempt against that Honourable Court from whence it issued and that under the continuance of such circumstances I shall be under the painful necessity of making my return accordingly. Leaving the issue to your Lordship's discretion, I shall remain here until tomorrow night. And to remove all doubts from your mind I beg leave to enclose a copy of the writ for your persual, having exhibited the original to Sir Thomas Duckworth as likewise to your secretary and have the honour to subscribe myself with greatest respect.

The writ would prove of no benefit to Mackenrot—or to Napoleon. With both Keith and Maitland out of reach at sea, it could not be served; and, even had Mackenrot succeeded in serving it, it is doubtful that Napoleon would have been taken ashore. Maitland, answerable for Napoleon's safety as a prisoner and having no authority from the Admiralty to release him, would not have obeyed the writ.

The *Bellerophon* spent most of the afternoon beating out of Plymouth Sound. At 3:40 she upped her mainsail and hove to off Rame Head, joining the *Prometheus*, which was flying Keith's flag. The *Tonnant* also was tacking her way out of the Sound; and at length Keith was able to transfer to her from the *Prometheus*, hoisting his flag on board at seven that evening. At eight, the *Tonnant*, the *Bellerophon*, the *Eurotas*, the *Myrmidon*, the cutter *Nimble*, and the express schooner that Keith had ordered to join them set a southeast course that would take them past Bolt Head and on toward Start Point to rendezvous with the *Northumberland*. That ship, along with the *Bucephalus* and the *Ceylon*, was working her way westward. St. Catherine's Point, Needles Rocks, and the Needles Light came and went as she narrowed the gap between her and Napoleon.

For the members of Napoleon's suite on the *Bellerophon,* their unexpected and rather mysterious departure from Plymouth Sound caused much agitation and speculation. "Our curiosity was greatly excited," Las Cases wrote.

The newspapers, official communications, and private conversations, told us we were to be conveyed to St. Helena by the *Northumberland*: we knew that this ship was still fitting out at Portsmouth or Chatham, so that we might still calculate on eight or ten days' delay. The *Bellerophon* was too old for the voyage, she had not provisions enough; moreover the wind was contrary; when therefore we saw the ship returning up Channel, our uncertainty and conjectures were renewed; but whatever these might be, every thing was welcome when compared to the idea of transportation to St. Helena.

Of all the uncertainties, two in particular kept the Frenchmen, and the British, in suspense. By far the most important question was whether Napoleon would accept his fate and go into exile and imprisonment. Then, if he should, whom would he choose to accompany him? Savary and Lallemand, of course, had been ruled out by the British government on July 31. Bertrand—with his wife and children—was sure to go. Napoleon's favorite valet, Marchand, a young man devoted to his master, would in all probability make the trip. But what other two officers would Napoleon nominate? Which of the domestic servants? Las Cases reports that on the evening of August 1 Napoleon asked him if he would go to St. Helena and that he had without hesitation or qualification said yes. Savary knew of this agreement the next morning. Perhaps the other members of the suite were aware of it; perhaps not. But even if they were, the question of who Napoleon's third choice would be remained. Each of them, with the exception of the young surgeon Maingaut, declared that he was ready to accompany Napoleon, if chosen. Even Madame Bertrand was trying to face the inevitable with composure and good grace. Some men in the suite must have fervently hoped to be chosen. The Elysée, the battlefield, St. Helena—all were one to them, provided they could serve Napoleon. But there were doubtless some whose conception of service and loyalty did not include sacrificing themselves to an indeterminate tenure on St. Helena; who, despite their present circumstances, hoped to fashion profitable futures for themselves. For the present, they would help maintain the appearance of unanimous fidelity to Napoleon; there would be time enough to reveal their true feelings if they chanced to be chosen.

As for Napoleon, his hopes for clemency had died by now. No further appeal, no conceivable advocate, was left him. Deeply depressed, he confined himself to his cabin from that time on, "never coming on deck, or appearing at breakfast or dinner. He was not served from the table, but what he ate was prepared and carried in to him by Marchand." He spent a great deal of time with Bertrand and Las Cases; and that evening he worked long over a paper with them. It was his famous letter of protest, which was directed not really to any person or government, but to History—or, more appropriately, to the legend of Napoleon. It read,

I hereby solemnly protest, in the face of Heaven and of men, against the violence done me, and against the violation of my most sacred rights, in forcibly disposing of my person and my liberty. I came voluntarily on board of the *Bellerophon*; I am not a prisoner, I am the guest of England. I came on board even at the instigation of the Captain, who told me he had orders from the Government to receive me and my suite, and conduct me to England, if agreeable to me. I presented myself with good faith to put myself under the protection of the English laws. As soon as I was on board the *Bellerophon*, I was under shelter of the British people.

If the Government, in giving orders to the Captain of the *Bellerophon* to receive me as well as my suite, only intended to lay a snare for me, it has forfeited its honour and disgraced its flag.

If this act be consummated, the English will in vain boast to Europe of their integrity, their laws, and their liberty. British good faith will be lost in the hospitality of the *Bellerophon*.

I appeal to History; it will say that an enemy, who for twenty years waged war against the English people, came voluntarily, in his misfortunes, to seek an asylum under their laws. What more brilliant proof could he give of his esteem and his confidence? But what return did

England make for so much magnanimity? They feigned to stretch forth a friendly hand to that enemy; and when he had delivered himself up in good faith, they sacrificed him.

NAPOLEON.

On board the *Bellerophon,*
4th August, 1815.

Once again Napoleon portrays himself as a tragic hero ensnared and sent to his doom by a cunning enemy who has neither honor nor pity. The image of Themistocles, to whose situation Napoleon compared his own at the time of his surrender, recurs. Against the overwhelming treachery and injustice of his betrayal, Napoleon protests to Heaven, to men, and to History, passing judgment upon his judges. The portrait loses something, however, by being overdrawn and transcending reality: Napoleon is both helpless and guileless; England is without virtue or even humanity. The genius evident in these lines seeks for effect rather than for truth, and there is little truth in them.

The Napoleon who insists that he is not the prisoner but the guest of England had, at midnight on July 13, told Bertrand, "There is always some danger in trusting to one's enemies, but it is better to risk reliance on their sense of honor than be in their hands as a prisoner by law." The Napoleon who insists that he is not a prisoner, since he voluntarily boarded the *Bellerophon,* had been forbidden to set foot again on French soil, had faced arrest if he remained off Rochefort any longer, and would have confronted British ships of war if he had attempted escape by sea.

When he writes that he boarded the *Bellerophon* at the instigation of Maitland, who had said he was authorized to receive him, Napoleon blatantly lies, in light of the evidence available for the period of July 10–15, for Maitland's letter of July 10 to Bertrand refutes him. The argument made by a few partisans that Maitland orally asserted his authority to receive Napoleon is unsound; no officer in his senses would have jeopardized his career with such a lie. Further, it is interesting that Napoleon's letter to the Prince Regent made no reference to his having boarded the *Bellerophon*

at Maitland's instigation or to his having been told that Maitland
was under orders to receive him and his suite and conduct them
to England and asylum. Although the letter had been written on
July 13, the original was not sent to London until July 27, the
day after the *Bellerophon* moved to Plymouth from Tor Bay.
The letter was sent then, at Napoleon's request, after it had been
made apparent—by the presence of the *Liffey* and the *Eurotas*,
by the patrolling guard boats, and by the newspapers that had
been received on board ship—that he and his suite were prisoners.
If what Napoleon now claimed were true, it is almost inconceivable that he would not have revised his letter, adding this
vital information when it would have been most likely to help
him. It is strange, too, that he did not mention any of this to
Keith when the admiral first visited him. The charge of government duplicity has all the weakness of a lie that is told too late.

"They feigned to stretch forth a friendly hand" may be effective rhetoric, but it is hardly an accurate or convincing description
of the events that occurred while Napoleon was at Rochefort and
on board the *Saale* off the Ile d'Aix. The British government
had ignored his request for a passport, had sent a fleet of warships
to prevent his escape, and had even informed him in writing
(through Maitland's letter to Bertrand) that an attempt to depart would be forcibly opposed.

Napoleon could appeal eloquently to history—could even, in
his egoism, presume to supply it with its verdict on the affair.
But history reserves its verdicts to itself, and in this case it does
not expose England's perfidy, but Napoleon's mendacity. The
Protest was written, as Las Cases confessed, to "be a weapon in
the hands of our friends, and leave causes of remembrance as
well as grounds of defence with the public."* It has served these
purposes admirably.

---

* Las Cases claimed in his *Mémorial de Sainte Hélène* that it was he who prepared the
Protest, with Napoleon only "suppressing a few phrases and correcting others." This is
hardly credible, however; the style and the arguments employed are indisputably Napoleon's.

X

Rendezvous and Remonstrance

THE *Bellerophon* and her escort vessels marked time on August 5, running along the shore toward Start Point, making or shortening sail occasionally, or hauling to the wind on starboard or larboard tacks. The weather, fine at dawn, turned foggy at eight o'clock, cloudy at noon; the moderate breezes freshened, kicking up the sea. Her decks wet with spray, the *Bellerophon* pitched and tossed. The Frenchmen, discomposed, mostly kept to their cabins.

Near noon, with Start Point nine leagues away to the east-northeast, Keith signaled Maitland to a meeting on board the *Tonnant*. Before Maitland left, he told Bertrand that he was going to the admiral and would convey anything that Napoleon had to communicate to Keith. Bertrand asked him to wait until a letter then under preparation could be finished. It was, he said, intended for Maitland, but a copy was to be presented to Keith also. Maitland waited for nearly an hour, until at last Bertrand brought him the letter. It was Napoleon's "Protest."

Keith immediately forwarded it to Melville, sending it to shore in one of the small vessels. Later in the day, in a letter to Melville, he wrote,

I send a formal protest from General Bonaparte against all proceedings on the part of the Government, but he mistakes one point: Captain

Maitland, in common with all the other captains, had orders to take
them and detain his person, but no one foresaw that Captain Maitland
was to take him, nor could it be foreseen that to avoid a greater evil he,
Bonaparte, was to fly on board any one particular ship. Had the General been on board of an American ship and found a British ship coming fast upon them and got into a boat and come to the British ship,
could that have been considered a voluntary surrender or a capture?

Admiral Keith, still fatigued from his strenuous efforts to elude
Mackenrot, eagerly looked for the arrival of the *Northumberland*. His approaching retirement seemed especially desirable because of the demands of this assignment. "I suppose I shall not
be long at Plymouth after I return," he wrote hopefully to his
daughter; "perhaps till a peace is signed, such as it is to be."

Time drifted, the minutes hanging as heavily as the cloudy
canopy that stretched to the horizon. The heaving of the ship,
the montonous creaking and cracking of her timbers, and the
snapping of her sails punctuated the slow procession of the hours.
In the afternoon the ships tacked to the westward, foresails set,
waiting for the sails of the *Northumberland* to show. At four,
thick weather set in, with rain pocking the slopes of the spumey
waves, obscuring the cliffs and rocks between Start and Prawle
Points, and hanging a gray curtain over the high lands of the
Devon coast. The *Bellerophon* hove to: "Joined Company HMS
Actaeon. 4:30 filled and hove Ship—set the foresail—6 Moderate
and hazey with rain at times. Admiral N by E 1 mile. *Eurotas,
Actaeon* and *Nimble* Cutter in Company. Bolthead NE by N 6
miles."

The Frenchmen, quiet for the most part, stayed in their cabins
or in the wardroom, occupied with their private thoughts, or with
seasickness. Napoleon was still shut up in his cabin, waited upon
occasionally by Bertrand. On the lower decks, seamen and marines lounged and talked, wondering when the *Northumberland*
would be sighted. At dinner Madame Bertrand informed the
company that Napoleon's legs had swelled considerably due to
lack of exercise during the past few days. This observation caused

some of the suite to aver that he would not survive a year under the conditions prevailing on St. Helena. Madame Bertrand said to Lieutenant Bowerbank, "I promise you, you will never get the Emperor to St. Helena. He is a man, and what he says he will perform." Bowerbank, unconvinced, asked Marchand how Napoleon did that evening, and Marchand replied, "Very low-spirited at the thought of being sent away; but he has made a very good dinner."

Later that evening Napoleon and Las Cases walked in the stern gallery. Napoleon suddenly drew a kind of girdle from under his waistcoat and handed it to Las Cases, saying, "Take care of that for me." Las Cases secreted it under his own waistcoat, learning only later that it contained a diamond necklace worth two hundred thousand francs, given to Napoleon by Hortense when he left Malmaison. Shortly afterward darkness fell, as the wind and rain continued. Some distance away the *Northumberland* bore steadily westward.

In London that day the newspapers printed long descriptions of Napoleon's meeting with Keith and Bunbury, detailed narrations of the past days' events at Plymouth Sound, and editorials and letters to the editors on the subject of vengeance or leniency toward Napoleon. A barrister who signed himself "Generosus," explaining, "I am so professionally placed, that I dare not, without injury to my own family give my name," wrote to the *Morning Chronicle* giving his opinion that "the intended imprisonment and banishment for life" would, upon inquiry, be found "a breach of the laws of the realm."

As to the *policy* of the measure let me say a word. The great object is to prevent Napoleon Bonaparte returning to France; and I will ask any man with an usual allowance of brains whether he will be safer in the interior of England or Scotland (say the Castle of Stirling . . .) or in the island of St. Helena? In England or Scotland, as soon as the first burst of curiosity was past, he would gently sink into comparative insignificance. He could have no abettors, no helpmates if he wished for them; secure in our possession of him, we should be without alarm or uneasiness. Send him to the rock of St. Helena, we shall be shaken by perpetual stories of his escape, and after havng been in a feverish state of inquietude, shall, when we least expect it, hear of his reappearance where we least wish him to be.

An editorial in *The Times* scoffed at reports of Napoleon's threat to commit suicide:

Nor is it very usual with men who threaten suicide to commit it, yet we recollect two ridiculous lines in Cowley's "Davideis"; where speaking of the giant Goliath's weapon of war, the poet says, "A sword so great that it was only fit / To cut off his great head that came with it."

Perhaps after all, this great man may be too great a villain to die by any other hands than his own; yet we should want better evidence than his assurance, before we believed it.

"Probus" reappeared in *The Times* that day. He was filled with "apprehensions of the consequences to be expected from sending Buonaparte to St. Helena." He feared that the island was "an unsafe spot for the confinement of a state prisoner." The passing days had not mitigated his hatred of Napoleon, and he was hardly reconciled to any retribution less than death for "so infamous a monster." However, since exile on St. Helena had been decreed, "I say, then," he wrote, "that this atrocious murderer should be loaded with irons, and shut up for ever in a dungeon from the light of the sun, and from the sight of every one but a preacher of the gospel, to be employed in the difficult work of stirring up repentance in his blood-guilty soul." Should Napoleon go to St. Helena as an honorable exile,

the inhabitants of that island, far removed from the scene of his villainies, will receive him as a person whom not justice but policy has banished from Europe, to whom crimes have indeed been imputed, but on grounds too vague and slight to be noticed by the Governments, whose envy or jealousy has driven him into banishment. From the respect with which he is treated, they will learn to respect him. The soldiers will easily believe that he is the soldiers' friend. The disorderly and disaffected—such there are in every settlement, and in every garrison—will readily listen to his plausible professions. They will at least be accessible to bribes, and Cambaceres,* with the other unpunished traitors in France, will readily contribute to bribe them. An American vessel will always be ready to take him off. . . . In short he will once more escape; and all the bloodshed which his flight may occasion, will rest on the heads of those men, who have dared to treat the most atrocious of murderers with lenity, the most infamous of traitors with respect.

The *Morning Post*, whose assessment of Napoleon was that "nothing ever preceded his footsteps but horror and massacre—nothing ever followed them but desolation!," printed a lengthy piece of doggerel entitled "Habeas Corpus," in which one corrosive couplet after another attacked Napoleon and Capel Lofft's arguments against the detention. It ended,

> . . . so brush up your law,
> Get the writ signed and sealed by old Lucifer's claw;
> And e're to Helena we ship off the Porpuss,
> *Direct to the Devil your* HABEAS CORPUS.
>
> Signed OLD BAILEY

If nothing else, this made for amusing reading in some of the London clubs, where even at this date wagers were being laid that Napoleon would not be sent to St. Helena.

During the early morning hours of August 6 Keith's squadron continued to cruise offshore between Start Point and Bolt Head—tacking, heaving to, filling and making sail again, trimming sail as needed—the sailors frequently scanning the eastern horizon for the *Northumberland*. On board the *Tonnant*, Keith passed the time writing a letter to Melville. He was still disturbed by the Mackenrot episode.

---

* Cambacérès was a jurist; he served as Napoleon's Minister of Justice following the return from Elba.

Off the Start
Aug. 6

My Lord,

Sir John Duckworth sent me your Lordship's note which is dated the 3rd and I received it last night. By the same conveyance I received the enclosure* which had been left at my house. . . . I submit to your Lordship whether it is better to take no notice of the letter at all, as it cannot be proved that it was delivered and is only a copy; or to state that I got it at sea at a given time and place so long after the date that no reply could be made to the letter as I was out of the kingdom at the time. It does not appear that the person is an officer of the Court, but this may be only a pretence. I am certain he was not refused access to any ship on which I actually was, nor was I in any ship at the time of his coming alongside to enquire for me. I have always left the ship before he came too near and at last went out to sea. Soon after sunrise he manned a fast rowing boat and rowed round all the ships. A signal was made not to suffer communication. We were ten miles off the land. . . .

On the *Bellerophon* an unpleasant development surprised Maitland. He was already perturbed by Napoleon's refusal to name his companions and by his insistence that he would never go to St. Helena; if Napoleon remained adamant, Maitland would forcibly have to remove him to the *Northumberland*. The thought of taking such a measure offended Maitland's sense of propriety. What happened next, therefore, must have seemed an especially malevolent stroke of circumstance.

He was walking the deck in the morning with Las Cases, when the Frenchman for the first time mentioned that, at their meetings off the Basque Roads, he had understood Maitland to have assured him that Napoleon would be well received in England and allowed to reside there. The announcement shocked Maitland. He had had no idea that he would be accused of treachery in relation to Napoleon's boarding his ship; though he had worried about his authority to receive Napoleon on board, Hotham's,

---

* A copy of Mackenrot's writ.

Keith's, and the Admiralty's statements had eased his mind. The fate of Savary and Lallemand, and his involvement in it, was still troubling him. But this! His astonishment gave way to barely controlled anger. "I cannot conceive how you could so far misunderstand me," he told Las Cases, "as I constantly, in my communications with you, stated that I could make no promises whatever; that I thought my orders would bear me out in receiving him on board and conveying him to England. But even in doing that, I acted very much upon my own responsibility. You questioned me frequently as to my private opinion," he confessed, "and as I was quite ignorant upon the subject, I could only say I had no reason to believe he would be ill received."

Maitland thought bitterly that the imputation against his integrity was deliberate. Las Cases might attempt to placate his feelings by terming the matter a misunderstanding; but Maitland considered it a lie. "If there was any misunderstanding, (which I cannot allow to have been the case)," he later wrote, "Monsieur Las Cases has himself to blame."

When he came on board of the *Bellerophon* for the purpose of treating, he concealed his knowledge of the English language; which, as I had considerable difficulty in expressing myself in French, could only be intended for the purpose of throwing me off my guard, that he might take advantage of any expressions that fell from me, or the officers I had always present at our meetings. Even after he was on board with Buonaparte, though he acknowledged he could read English, and always translated the newspapers for his master, he affected not to be able to speak it.

Maitland also had a lengthy conversation with Napoleon that morning, his first since August 4, and found that Napoleon's grievances against England still flourished. Napoleon complained bitterly of the government's conduct, then spoke again of the state of his affairs when he had decided to board the *Bellerophon*. "There still was a large party in the South that wished me to put myself at its head," he said.

The army behind the Loire was also desirous of my return. At ten o'clock of the night before I embarked, a deputation from the garrison of Rochelle waited upon me with an offer to conduct me to the army; in addition to which, the troops that were in Rochefort, Bordeaux, and the Ile d'Aix, amounting to twelve thousand men, were at my disposal. But I saw there was no prospect of ultimate success, though I might have occasioned a great deal of trouble and bloodshed, which I did not choose should take place on my account individually. While the empire was at stake, it was another matter.

He gave no sign that he intended to comply with the government's orders.

At nine o'clock that morning the *Northumberland*, followed at a distance by the *Bucephalus* and the *Ceylon*, at last was sighted. She exchanged numbers with the *Bellerophon* and the *Tonnant*, fired the traditional salute to Keith, and received in return a thirteen-gun salute to Cockburn. On the *Tonnant*, Keith rejoiced: "All our troubles will soon be at an end now," he wrote his wife, "and we may return to quiet again." The crew of the *Bellerophon*, crowding the gunwales and rigging and peering from the gunports of the lower decks, cheered. They could soon break the two weeks' strict confinement under which they had been held in Tor Bay and Plymouth Sound.

The rendezvous produced profound gloom among the Frenchmen on the *Bellerophon*, the *Eurotas*, and the *Myrmidon*. The time of farewell and separation had arrived. Those who were going to St. Helena with Napoleon were binding themselves to him until his death—which, since he was only forty-six, might not occur for many years. Then they would return to Europe; but they would be middle-aged or older. They would return to a world in which they would have little future and by which they might have been forgotten. The years on St. Helena would strain and perhaps sever family connections and old friendships; even their homes, if they still should exist, might seem alien. Those not chosen had somber thoughts too. Some may have wondered why they were not deemed fit to share Napoleon's destiny. Those who had hoped to avoid St. Helena could scarcely have escaped a sense of guilt when contrasting their self-concern with the self-lessness of the others. All who were being left behind knew that Napoleon had lent their lives a luster that would fade now: they would never again be quite what they were when known as "Napoleon's men."

With the raising of the *Northumberland*, the ships of Keith's squadron, which had been cruising in loose formation, closed and bore eastward to join her; and at ten o'clock the rendezvous was made. Hardly had the ships hove to when the *Northumberland* lowered a boat and Cockburn was rowed to the *Tonnant*.

He found Keith anxious to deliver Napoleon into his charge—so anxious, in fact, that when Cockburn reported that the ships under his orders should put in to Plymouth to take on water, beds, and other supplies and equipment, Keith offered to provide them from the *Tonnant* and the *Eurotas* so that Napoleon could be transferred the next day. Keith also said that he would send his flag lieutenant to Plymouth by land with orders to hurry out the vessels that were to accompany Cockburn and that he would station the *Actaeon* off Start Point to direct them to the *Northumberland*. With strong breezes and squally weather prevailing, Keith judged it wise to stand in for the anchorage at Tor Bay, where Napoleon's removal could be effected more quickly and smoothly than at sea.

Cockburn then told Keith about the mutinous incident that had occurred at Spithead and handed him three lists of men whom he wanted replaced or simply removed from the *Northumberland* before he sailed. One list named 40 marine privates; another named 18 malcontent crewmen, including a gunner's mate, a quartermaster's mate, and a captain of the forecastle. These men were exchanged with volunteers from the *Tonnant* and the *Eurotas*. The third list named 18 men who were to be discharged as "being over Complement."

Keith and Cockburn also went over the War Department's Memorandum of July 30 and discussed arrangements for examining Napoleon's effects. They decided to confiscate the weapons of the Frenchmen, although they did not have to do so, in order to minimize the risk of resistance to Napoleon's removal. They talked of Napoleon—of Keith's meetings with him, of his conduct on the *Bellerophon*, of his obstinacy, of what they might expect the next day. They hoped he would prove amenable and thus make their duty, admittedly not a pleasant one, easier to perform.

The *Northumberland*'s arrival induced Napoleon to name the rest of his companions-in-exile: Montholon and his wife and child, and Colonel Nicholas Planat, an aide-de-camp. He still had to obtain a medical attendant to fill Maingaut's place. Subject of late to painful bouts of illness caused by a bad liver and stomach, Napoleon would more than ever require the services of a physician on the island. Casting about for a suitable candidate, he finally settled on Barry O'Meara, the *Bellerophon*'s surgeon. O'Meara spoke Italian fluently, and Napoleon, in frequent conversations with him on the ship, had found him sympathetic and congenial.

That morning, therefore, he had Bertrand send Savary to approach O'Meara. O'Meara agreed to accompany Napoleon if the government and Maitland approved and if certain conditions were met. He went at once to consult with Maitland about the propriety of accepting the offer. Maitland told O'Meara that the matter depended very much upon his own feelings, but that if he had no aversion to it he had better accept—provided the government consented and agreed to pay his salary. The captain considered that an official communication on the subject should go to Keith.

The disclosure of this proposal was welcome information to Maitland. "This was the first intimation I received of Buonaparte having made any arrangement towards complying with the notification he had received from our Government," he wrote. When the squadron anchored off Berry Head in Tor Bay at three o'clock, Maitland went to the *Tonnant* and reported to Keith that Napoleon evidently had decided to move voluntarily from the *Bellerophon*. He also stated that Napoleon was anxious to see Keith and that Bertrand desired an interview with him in order to make arrangements concerning the exiles. Keith agreed to see Bertrand at once. Before Maitland left to return to his ship, Keith told him to expect a written order the next day to remove Napoleon and the selected members of his suite to the *Northumberland*. He also gave Maitland this memorandum: "All arms of every description are to be taken from the Frenchmen of all ranks on board the ship you command; and they are to be carefully packed up and kept in your charge, while they remain on board the *Bellerophon*; and afterwards in that of the captain of the ship to which they may be removed."

Maitland soon delivered Bertrand to the *Tonnant*. Shortly thereafter, Cockburn also returned to that ship, and he, Keith, and Bertrand were closeted for upwards of two hours. Bertrand opened the conversation by inquiring about the government's intentions with respect to Savary and Lallemand. Keith informed him that as yet no orders had come respecting them and that consequently the exception against them remained in full force. Bertrand then told Keith the names of the persons whom Napoleon proposed should accompany him; and Keith requested that the Grand Marshal prepare a written list.

The inclusion of Las Cases led to some discussion. Napoleon, Bertrand said, had specifically requested that Las Cases be permitted to join him as his secretary, in place of the surgeon who was unwilling to accompany him. After considering the request and concluding that the government would not disapprove, Keith and Cockburn acceded to it. But they refused the application of Captain Piontkowski, a Pole who had served Napoleon as a private on Elba and who now wished to go to St. Helena as a domestic servant. As to Napoleon's desire that O'Meara be permitted to accompany him as his surgeon, Keith informed Bertrand that the matter "could only be taken into consideration upon a special application being received in writing, especially as the number of persons allowed by Government would be complete without a surgeon, from the Count de Las Cases' being permitted to go as Secretary."

Before Bertrand returned to the *Bellerophon*, Cockburn gave

him an extract of his instruction from the War Department and
requested that he explain it to Napoleon. He and Keith also arranged to visit Napoleon that evening.

Bertrand reported to Napoleon on the results of the meeting.
Then, aided by Montholon, he spent the dinner hour drawing up
lists of items desired by the French officers and women to make
their voyage to St. Helena more tolerable: packs of playing cards,
a backgammon and domino table, chessmen, books, and wines.
When these had been finished and dispatched to Plymouth via
Cockburn's secretary, Maitland called Bertrand to his cabin and
said that he had received orders to put Napoleon on the *Northumberland* the next day. He also notified Bertrand of the orders
to confiscate the arms of Napoleon and his attendants, stating that
these would be returned to them upon their arrival at St. Helena.
Bertrand appeared stunned at this announcement. To be deprived
of their weapons—badges of their military status, manhood, and
honor—was not usual in the case of officers who were prisoners,
and it must have seemed particularly insulting in the Frenchmen's
present situation. However, Bertrand agreed, without protest,
to see that the arms were delivered to Maitland the next morning.

At half past eight that evening Keith and Cockburn came to see
Napoleon. With Keith was his secretary, James Meek, who accompanied him as a witness "in consequence of Sir George Cockburn's being on the point of leaving the Kingdom." Although the
customary civilities passed smoothly, tension prevaded the interview, for Napoleon's expectations of better things to come, which
had prevailed during his initial meeting with Keith on July 28,
and the glimmer of hope that remained after Keith and Bunbury
had seen him on July 31 were gone. Now, in Cockburn, he faced
the man who would be his warden until the new governor came
to St. Helena. As usual Napoleon did most of the talking. He
"commenced the conversation," Keith reported to Melville,

by protesting against the measures adopted with regard to him by
the British Government, repeating in detail and almost verbatim, the
language and reasoning contained in his Protest—to which he referred,

observing that he came freely on board the *Bellerophon*, that he was not a Prisoner; that he threw himself upon the hospitality of the country upon which he had made war for upwards of twenty years; that he sought an asylum there under the protection of its laws, that he embarked even at the instigation of Captain Maitland, who told him that he had orders from his Government to convey him to England; that as soon as he was on board the *Bellerophon* he was entitled to the protection of the laws of the country, that all Captain Maitland had done was only a snare to entrap him, and that he was entitled to all the privileges of an Habeas Corpus, but was deprived of the means of obtaining it, thereby prevented from frustrating the measures now pursued against his rights and liberty; that with regard to the orders to consider him only as General Buonaparte the Government acted with injustice and inconsistency; as they had treated with him as First Consul, had received his Ambassador, and had sent an Ambassador to him —but added he with a smile—that was a trifle—that was nothing compared with their present conduct towards him—, which was a violation of every principle of justice, humanity and generosity, and which he was morally certain, although he was but indifferently informed of matters in England, was not less contrary to the wishes of the English people than to those of Europe in general.

I then observed that his protest had been forwarded to Government the moment that it had been received, and that as both myself and Sir George Cockburn were officers in the execution of a duty prescribed to us by our superiors, we could only listen to the remarks he had made, but were not authorized to answer them. The General replied that that he was perfectly aware of, but as we were the only persons permitted to approach him, he owed it to himself, and to the World to protest before us, and he did it in the most correct manner, against the measures pursued by our Government with regard to him, adding that he trusted a faithful report would be made of all he had said.—

I then asked General Buonaparte if he had read the Extract of Sir George Cockburn's Instructions which that officer had delivered up to Count Bertrand for his information.—He replied that he had not— that the Count had not yet finished with the translation;—but that it was a matter of no consequence whatever, as the British Government appeared to have taken its course of proceedings with respect to him, and seemed resolved on pursuing that course even to his Death.—

Sir George Cockburn then enquired at what time he would be ready to remove to the *Northumberland*, and he replied at any hour he pleased after breakfast, which was generally about ten o'clock. Some unimportant conversation then ensued as to St. Helena, the extent of Sir George Cockburn's command, etc., and presently afterwards I withdrew.

Though they surely seemed repetitive to Keith by this time, Napoleon's remonstrances were more than emotional outbursts. They constituted pieces in a pattern that he hoped the future would assemble. He did not intend to lapse into mute tractability but to protest unremittingly against his imprisonment, repeating his charges to as many persons and on as many occasions as he could. Through these persons, or some of them at any rate, his arguments would become known to the world. Over the years they would be impressed upon men's memories, and eventually, he trusted, be accepted as true. Perhaps the official aloofness and silence maintained by his captors in the face of his accusations would actually abet his purpose: their refusal to answer him might be interpreted as tacit admission of their injustice; his voice would seem that of a martyr.

Napoleon's stay off the English coast was ending; in the future he would have to wage his battle at long distance, with opportunities for an audience greatly diminished. He wanted to make use of the time that remained before he sailed. Thus, at half-past nine that evening he invited Maitland to his cabin. When the captain entered, Napoleon said, "Bertrand informs me you have received orders to remove me to the *Northumberland*. Is it so?"

Maitland replied that it was.

"Have you any objection," Napoleon asked, "to write a letter to Bertrand, acquainting him of it; that I may have a document to prove that I was forced to quit the ship and that my inclinations were not consulted?"

Maitland said, "I can have no objection to write such a letter, and shall do it this evening." He moved, as if to leave, but Napoleon asked him to remain.

"Your Government," he said, "has treated me with much severity, and in a very different way from what I had hoped and expected, from the opinion I had formed of the character of your countrymen. It is true," he admitted, "I have always been the enemy of England, but it has ever been an open and declared one; and I paid the highest compliment it was possible for a man to do in throwing myself on the generosity of your Prince. I have not now to learn, however, that it is not fair to judge of the character of a people by the conduct of their Government."

Then, in reference to the Ministry, he went on, "They say I made no conditions [i.e., no agreements with the government prior to his surrender]. Certainly I made no conditions. How could a private individual enter into terms with a nation? I wanted nothing of them but hospitality, or, as the ancients would express it, 'air and water.' I threw myself on the generosity of the English nation; I claimed a place by their fires; and my only wish was to purchase a small estate in England and end my life in peace and tranquility. As for you, Captain," he said, "I have no cause of complaint. Your conduct to me has been that of a man of honor. But I cannot help feeling the severity of my fate, in having the prospect of passing the remainder of my life on a desert island." His voice rose emphatically. "But if your Government give up Savary and Lallemand to the King of France, they will inflict a stain upon the British name that time cannot efface."

Maitland said that Napoleon was mistaken in that respect; he was convinced that His Majesty's ministers had no intention of delivering them up.

"I hope so," Napoleon commented; upon which Maitland withdrew.

One more link—an important one—had been added to the chain of communication connecting Napoleon with the outside world. Because Maitland had been the Englishman in closest association with Napoleon, men would be eager to hear his story of Napoleon's surrender, detention, and reaction to his fate. And Napoleon had realized how invaluable a reporter Maitland could be.

That night, as usual, guard boats circled the *Bellerophon*; and

on board double sentinels manned the posts. The masts and
yardarms of the ships of the squadron traced slow arcs under the
few stars visible in the cloudy sky. In the cabins and on the decks
of the vessels men mused on the events of the past fourteen days
and probed tentative imaginings into the future. For all of them
—the French and the English, the main actors in the drama and
their nearly anonymous underlings—that future would be in-
delibly marked by what had happened during the fortnight just
ended.

XI

To the Northumberland

DAWN broke clear and fair on August 7, and a gentle breeze ruffled the blue waters off Berry Head, where the ships under Keith's and Cockburn's commands rode to their anchors. The sunlight flashed off stern-gallery windows, polished brasswork, and varnished masts and spars, and accentuated the whiteness of the furled sails. Overhead, sharp-eyed gulls floated, their thin cries rivaling the notes of the bosuns' pipes that summoned the crews to another day's duties.

But this was no ordinary day for the crews, and no mood of summer serenity prevailed among them. Rather they were keenly expectant, for they would soon witness Napoleon's departure from England and Europe. Meanwhile they had to unsling hammocks, clean quarters, sweep and wash down the decks, turn to in sailroom, gunroom, and storeroom, and load and unload supplies and equipment. The *Tonnant* was running boats to the *Northumberland*, the *Ceylon*, and the *Bucephalus*, supplying them with the tons of fresh water they would need for their long voyage. Besides getting the water on board, the *Northumberland*'s men were setting up the fore- and main-topmast rigging and preparing cabin accommodations for Napoleon and his companions. For the moment their disaffection had given way to a lively curiosity about the legendary man whose keepers they would shortly become, and the excitement over his imminent arrival on board sent them alertly about their tasks. The crew of the *Bellerophon*, conscious of still being the cynosure among the fleet, looked to the condition of their ship and their best uniforms.

The cutter *Nimble* and the guard boats continued to patrol around the *Bellerophon*, for boats from the shore began to appear early in the morning in the vicinity of Berry Head. The people of Tor Bay, their numbers augmented by arrivals from Plymouth and elsewhere, had been alerted to Napoleon's presence and were braving open water in their small craft, hopeful of catching a final glimpse of him.

The Frenchmen on the *Bellerophon* had risen early. Those who were certain they would accompany Napoleon were making final preparations for their departure, and those who expected to stay behind were helping with the packing. Both groups were seeking to fill the dwindling hours before their separation with conversation and activity. Bertrand, who was overseeing all the preparations, also wrote out the list of those who were going to St. Helena, as Keith had requested.

The announcement of the complete list gave rise to a scene which threatened to shatter the dignified solidarity of the suite. When Gourgaud, who was extremely jealous of his relationship with Napoleon, learned that he had not been included, he rushed in to Bertrand in a fury of disappointment and indignation, wildly waving his arms and shouting. Napoleon could not leave him behind! He was a Baron of the Empire, a Lieutenant General; his life had been devoted to serving the Emperor! He had fought in thirteen campaigns, had received three wounds during that time, had even saved the Emperor's life at the Battle of Brienne, and had borne Napoleon's letter to the Prince Regent. And now to be cast aside, to be excluded in favor of some who had neither known nor served the Emperor as long and as devotedly as he! Death was preferable to such a deprivation, such an insult. Bertrand could do nothing to placate the young general, and so at length, in despair, took him to Napoleon. Napoleon listened to Gourgaud's protestations and pleadings, noted the desperation and devotion that shone in his eyes and made his voice tremble, and relented. He directed Bertrand to substitute Gourgaud for Colonel Planat. Profusely grateful, Gourgaud bowed his way out of the cabin.

This scene ended, Napoleon took a seat on the divan while Marchand finished packing his effects. He sat silently in his dressing gown, his face impassive, seemingly untouched by the importance of the day, or perhaps his quietness was a result of his concentrated mustering of the inner resources he needed to face what lay ahead. The prospect must have seemed especially bleak in contrast to the past two weeks. During that time he had been gazed upon by tens of thousands of people and had drawn the attention of millions; his actions and attitudes had been etched upon men's minds, and his words had been amplified for the ages to hear. Now he looked at his final letter to Keith, which he had dictated earlier in the morning:

Bellerophon
August 7, 1815

My Lord,

When leaving Plymouth, I sent you my protest concerning the line of conduct which has been adopted towards me. Yesterday when you did me the honor of coming to see me with Admiral Cockburn I reiterated this protest.

However it appears that without knowing the results of these complaints you demand that I leave the *Bellerophon* to board the vessel destined to take me to the place of my exile. I am dispatching to you Count de Las Cases with a request that you hand him (1) the deed signed by the authorities who, without prior investigation and without hearing the Captain of the *Bellerophon*, nor any of those who received me, have arbitrarily decreed that I am a prisoner of war, in contradiction with evidence since it is obvious that I came of my own free will and in good faith, as is abundantly proved by my letter to the Prince Regent, which the Captain examined before receiving me.

I beg you, My Lord, also to hand him (2) the signed decree which, after having declared that I was a prisoner, directs that contrary to the laws of the country and those of hospitality, I should be forcibly removed from the *Bellerophon* and exiled two thousand leagues away, on a rock lost in mid ocean, in tropical heat. It is obviously a death sentence on one who will hardly be able to withstand a temperature at the same time so high and so suddenly new.

My Lord, I have claimed and am again claiming the protection of your laws, more particularly that of "Habeas Corpus,"* as I am now under your flag, in your harbors, with the offer and promise of the Captain and can only be removed, deprived of my freedom, led and exiled in accordance with your laws and in due form.

Finally, I also request you, My Lord, to hand me (3) the decree signed by those who, without any form or motive other than their own decision, want to deprive me of my properties, though of little consequence, and to impose upon me and members of my suite hardships likely to shock any refined man and to surprise those who are acquainted with, and practice law.

I require notice of these documents in order to enable me to claim in due form the protection of your laws against these decrees and to appeal formally to sovereigns and peoples in regard to this strange and singular affair. You yourself, My Lord, have expressed to me on several occasions the pain that carrying out these orders caused you; I could not therefore wish for a better advocate in order to get their hastiness, rigor and injustice invalidated.

NAPOLEON.

In this letter Napoleon especially emphasizes the English authorities' bypassing of recognized legal processes, and makes a formal appeal to English law for protection against injustice. As in his previous letters to Keith, he contrasts the English rulers, whom he characterizes as hasty, arbitrary, unjust, and vengeful men who have given him what is "obviously a death sentence," and himself, whose good faith has been betrayed and whose protests have gone unheeded, but who believes that the law, if it were only consulted, would render him justice. Assuming that men have a reverence for law and a propensity for becoming apprehensive and protestant when a sentence is imposed on even

---

* This statement was probably inspired by the newspapers' rumors and debates concerning a writ of habeas corpus. There is no evidence that Napoleon or anyone else ever sought such a writ on his behalf.

the most infamous criminal without regard for law, he trusted that his letter would inspire men to question why legal process had been denied him. However, in none of the letters that he wrote after he decided to surrender to England, did he try to defend himself against the Allies' decree of outlawry, hoping instead that sympathy would prove stronger than memory and that men in the future would concentrate on the prisoner sentenced without trial rather than on the outlaw to whom retribution had been promised.

Las Cases applied to Maitland for permission to deliver the letter to Keith, and at eight o'clock that morning Maitland went to the *Tonnant* to obtain Keith's assent. He took with him letters to the admiral from Bertrand and O'Meara. Bertrand's stated:

MILORD,

The French surgeon who was authorized to accompany the Emperor cannot come to St. Helena. The Emperor asks you to approve that he should be accompanied by M. O'Meara, surgeon, whom he met on board the *Bellerophon* and who speaks Italian.

O'Meara's letter informed Keith that he was willing to accompany Napoleon, but on several conditions: that he be permitted to resign if he should desire to; that he be indemnified for the loss of time as surgeon on full pay in His Majesty's navy; that he not be considered a servant of Napoleon but rather a British officer employed by the British government; and lastly that he be told as soon as possible the salary he would receive.

Keith readily gave Maitland leave to bring Las Cases to him. On this day, he would not slight Napoleon by an authoritarian indifference to his desires. On the matter of Napoleon's physician, he had, after consultation with Cockburn, already decided to accede to Napoleon's wish to have O'Meara. Before Maitland returned to the *Bellerophon*, therefore, Keith gave him a letter informing O'Meara that he approved the plan and would submit it to the Lords Commissioners of the Admiralty, who alone could offer precise terms. Keith also supplied Maitland with orders to receive Napoleon's money, which would be given him by Cockburn, and to deliver into Cockburn's charge the following persons:

General Buonaparte

Count Bertrand, his wife, three children, one female servant, and her child

General Montholon, his wife, one child, and one female servant

General Gourgaud

Count de Las Cases and his son

Marchand, head valet

St. Denis, valet

Novarra, valet

Pieron, butler

Le Page, cook

Archambaud, head footman

Gentilini, footman

Bernard, servant of Count Bertrand

Cipriani, steward

Santini, usher

Rosseau, lamplighter

Archambaud, footman

The meeting between Keith and Las Cases began smoothly. Keith received the councillor with extreme politeness and read Napoleon's letter carefully. When he had finished it, he told Las Cases that he would refrain from commenting upon it, but would give his answer in writing.

"This," Las Cases later recounted, "did not stop me. I stated the situation of Napoleon, who was very unwell, having his legs considerably swelled; and pointed out to his Lordship how desirable it was for the Emperor not to be sent off suddenly. He replied, that I had been a sailor, and must therefore see the anchorage was unsafe, which was certainly true." But with this exchange, Las Cases had only begun. In his first opportunity to speak freely with an English official intimately involved in Napoleon's detention, he was anxious to strengthen his relationship with Napoleon by adding his protests to those of his master.

I explained the Emperor's repugnance to having his effects searched and tossed about, as proposed, assuring him, that Napoleon would infinitely prefer seeing them thrown into the sea. The Admiral answered that as this was a positive order, he could not infringe on it. Finally, I demanded whether it was probable those appointed to search would go so far as to deprive the Emperor of his sword. He said, that it would be respected, but that Napoleon was the only person exempted. . . . A secretary who was writing near us, observed to Lord Keith in English, that the order stated that Napoleon himself was to be disarmed; upon which the Admiral drily replied, also in English, as well as I could comprehend, "Mind your own business, Sir, and leave us to ourselves."

Las Cases had not finished yet. Despite Keith's growing restiveness over the direction the conversation was taking, he continued:

I went over all that had occurred from the commencement. I had been the negotiator, I said, and ought therefore to feel most acutely; and had the greater right to be heard. Lord Keith listened to me with marked impatience; we were standing, and his frequent bows were evidently intended to make me retire. When I told him that Captain Maitland said he had been authorized to bring us to England, without exciting a suspicion in our minds that we were to be prisoners of war; that the Captain could not deny we came on board voluntarily and in confidence; that the letter of the Emperor to the Prince of Wales, which I had previously communicated to Captain Maitland, must necessarily have created tacit conditions, since he made no remarks on it; at length the Admiral's ill humour and even anger broke forth, and he replied sharply, that if such were the case Captain Maitland must have been a fool, for his instructions contained nothing of the kind; and he was quite sure of this, for it was from himself they had emanated.

"But, my Lord," said I, "permit me to observe, in defence of Captain Maitland, that your Lordship speaks with a degree of severity for which you may become responsible; for not only Captain Maitland, but Admiral Hotham and all the other officers whom we saw at the time conducted and expressed themselves in the same way towards us: would it have been thus, if their instructions had been so clear and positive?" Saying this, I relieved the Admiral of my presence: he made no attempt to prolong a subject which, perhaps, his Lordship's conscience rendered somewhat painful to him.

Keith's anger and impatience with Las Cases' remarks did not result from a pained conscience, however, but from Las Cases' attack on the integrity of British naval officers, himself included. He had read Maitland's accounts of the negotiations preceding

Napoleon's surrender, and had listened to and read Napoleon's allegations against the Admiralty's orders and Maitland's complicity in their treacherous intent. Certain that the charges were false, he was angered by them. It seemed clear to him that the purpose of this attack was to persuade men that the trap the British government had laid for Napoleon could have been sprung only by dishonorable naval officers. Keith, who had given his life to the navy, and loved it, could not help bridling at this slander against the men who served it. In fairness he would have to investigate Las Cases' charges, if only to gain final reassurance that they had no basis; but at the moment Napoleon's letter required an answer. Keith wrote it and had Las Cases carry it back to the *Bellerophon.* The letter read:

> His Britannic Majesty's Ship *Tonnant*
> 7 August, 1815

Sir,

I have received by the Count De Las Cases the letter which you have done me the honor to address to me, and I beg to assure you that I lost no time in forwarding to my Government the protest you refer to.

The order for your removal from the *Bellerophon* is imperative, and as an officer I am bound to obey it; but it is a document that must remain in my possession in common with all other orders.

I have Captain Maitlands letters before me, by which it appears that nothing like a promise or what could possibly be construed into a promise was made on his part, but on the contrary a simple offer of good treatment, and being carried to England, and I am happy in thinking that both these objects have been fulfilled with all possible kindness and attention.

The orders respecting your property are addressed to Rear Admiral Sir George Cockburn; and as they appear reasonable, and are only calculated to prevent an improper use of an excessive sum, I am sure they will be executed with all possible delicacy.

Of the Laws I am not able to judge—my habits are of a different nature, but my study has always been to obey them in all the different countries I have visited.—

It is true that I have said in the interviews that I have had the honor to hold with you, that it was a painful duty to communicate any thing of a disagreeable nature to any one, and I hope you will do me the justice to believe it true; but still I am to perform the duties of my situation.

As evidence that the last paragraph of the letter was more than mere politeness, Keith sent this order to Maitland: "When the General quits the ship, it is not intended to take his sword from him, but to let him wear it, but not the others. Pistols, guns, etc., must, *as in all instances*, be removed for the safety of the ship, but the arms are carefully to be kept, and restored at a proper occasion."

While Keith and Las Cases were meeting on the *Tonnant*, Maitland was occupied on the *Bellerophon* with a multiplicity of tasks—checking preparations for the formalities that would accompany Napoleon's departure from the frigate, arranging for the transferal of those French domestic servants who were to go on board the *Northumberland*, seeing that Napoleon's baggage would be ready for examination when Cockburn came on board, and tending to the collection of the Frenchmen's arms. In addition, he wrote and presented to Bertrand the letter that Napoleon had requested the night before:

> His Majesty's Ship *Bellerophon*
> 7th August, 1815
>
> Sir,
> I beg to acquaint you that I have this day received orders from Lord Keith, Commander in Chief of the Channel Fleet, to remove General Buonaparte from the ship I command, to his Majesty's ship *Northumberland*; and I have to request you will intimate the above to the General, that he may prepare for the removal.
> I likewise enclose a copy of an order respecting the arms of General Buonaparte and the whole of his attendants, and request you will give directions for their being delivered to me, that they may be disposed of as the order directs.

Accompanying the letter was a copy of Keith's orders for Napoleon's removal, plus a list of the other exiles. The collection of the arms began, but on Las Cases' return from the *Tonnant* Maitland received Keith's letter respecting Napoleon's sword and so did not ask for it. Down to the gun room, however, went a number of swords and pistols, several braces of which were marked with a large silver "N" on their butt ends. Three of the swords, the English were informed, belonged to Napoleon, and two were pointed out as those he had worn at Marengo and Austerlitz.

Breakfast on the *Bellerophon* was a hurried affair. Bertrand, who had been working for hours, did not sit down until everyone else had finished. His wife was waiting for him, as was Maitland, who, though he too was busy, nevertheless remained, as a mark of attention to the Grand Marshal. The hard-pressed Bertrand had scarcely begun eating when his wife again started to berate him for accompanying Napoleon to St. Helena. She pleaded with him to quit Napoleon and remain in England. Bertrand—who had been henpecked long enough to know that silence is the only way to end such scenes—squirmed, glanced apologetically at Maitland, but said nothing. At last Madame Bertrand gave up and turned to the captain. She begged him to give his opinion and to use his influence in favor of her proposal.

"Madame Bertrand," Maitland replied, looking first at her and then at her husband, "I have from the beginning endeavored to avoid meddling in the very unpleasant discussions that have been going on for some days. But as you demand my opinion, and force me to give it, I must acquaint you that I think, if your husband quits his master at such a time as the present, he will forfeit the very high character he now bears in this country." Then, without giving her a chance to recover or reply, he rose and strode out upon deck. Madame Bertrand, however, was not subdued; a few minutes later she was out on deck after him, her eyes flashing and her voice angry. "So, Captain Maitland," she said heatedly, "I hear the Emperor is not to have the whole of the after-cabin on board the *Northumberland*."

Maitland replied that he understood that Admiral Cockburn had received orders to that effect.

"They had better treat him like a dog at once," snapped Madame Bertrand, "and put him down in the hold."

Maitland could control himself no longer. The pressures the past several days had imposed on him—pressures that had in no small way been increased and rendered more irritating by this woman—at last proved too great to contain. "Madam," he said sharply, "you talk like a very foolish woman; and if you cannot speak more to the purpose or with more respect of the Government I have the honor to serve, I request you will not address yourself to me." At which he turned his back on her and walked away—angry with her for having goaded him into rudeness and with himself for having displayed it.

As he paced the deck, regaining his composure, Marchand came up and said that Napoleon wished to speak with him. Maitland found Napoleon—dressed now in a dark green coat with gold epaulettes, a white waistcoat and breeches, silk stockings and silver-buckled shoes—standing to receive him. "I have requested to see you, Captain," he said, "to return you my thanks for your kindness and attention to me while I have been on board the *Bellerophon,* and likewise to beg you will convey them to the officers and ship's company you command. My reception in England has been very different from what I expected; but it gives me much satisfaction to assure you that I feel your conduct to me throughout has been that of a gentleman and a man of honor."

This unsolicited tribute rings true; let us not suppose that it was insincere. Indeed it would be hard for anyone to dispute its sentiments. Despite his being kept persistently and dramatically in the public's eye, despite the opportunity and perhaps temptation to bolster his self-importance that his part in this affair offered, Maitland had conducted himself with dignity and with decency.

Napoleon and Maitland spoke of other matters at this meeting. Napoleon again expressed his desire to have O'Meara as his medical attendant and asked Maitland's opinion of the surgeon.

Maitland praised O'Meara highly for his skill and attention as a medical man, saying that he had made a point of having O'Meara as surgeon on his last three ships, and adding that he was convinced that O'Meara was a man of principle and integrity. They talked of Bertrand. Napoleon expressed deep affection for him and stressed his obligations to Bertrand for not deserting him at this trying time. He knew, he said, that strong attempts had been used to induce the Grand Marshal to abandon him. Maitland did not need to ask to what or whom he referred.

It may have been at this meeting that Napoleon talked of his wife and son. Turning to Marchand, he asked him to bring three miniatures to show Maitland—two of his son and one of Marie Louise. Emotion charged his voice as he spoke of them. "I feel," he confided, "the conduct of the Allied sovereigns to be more cruel and unjustifiable towards me in that respect than in any other. Why should they deprive me of the comforts of domestic society and take from me what must be the dearest objects of affection to every man—my child and the mother of that child?"

As Napoleon spoke, Maitland studied his face closely. "Tears were standing in his eyes," he wrote later, "and the whole of his countenance appeared evidently under the influence of a strong feeling of grief."

Since Cockburn's barge was approaching the ship, Maitland was needed on deck. Bowing, he left Napoleon. It was the last time that they would be alone together. At nine-thirty Cockburn, accompanied by Mr. Byng his secretary, arrived to examine Napoleon's effects. The stiffness of the rear admiral's bearing, the hard lines of his mouth and jaw, and the terseness with which he acknowledged Maitland's greeting revealed his distaste for the duty he had come to perform and his desire to accomplish it as quickly and quietly as possible. He, Maitland, and Byng went directly to the anteroom, where Napoleon's baggage had been collected. Bertrand was summoned. His order, Cockburn reminded the Grand Marshal, directed that the examination be made in the presence of a member of Napoleon's suite. Would Bertrand witness the procedure?

His voice vibrant with indignation, Bertrand refused. Furthermore, he would not direct any other member of the suite to super-
intend the examination—he considered the search a deliberate
insult. No French officer would sanction by his presence an action
that was clearly intended to place the Emperor on the footing of
a felon. Strain thickened the atmosphere of the cabin. Cockburn
repeated his instructions; and Bertrand obstinately refused to cooperate. Only after some delay was it arranged that Marchand
would be present during the search.

Byng conducted the examination—as cursory a one as Cockburn could direct without violating the letter of his orders. The
secretary unpacked nothing; he merely opened the covers of the
trunks, glanced at the contents, and passed his hand down the
sides of the trunks. Trunks containing clothing, services of plate,
a field library, toilet articles, and other personal belongings were
examined in this fashion, Byng working quickly and dexterously,
Cockburn, Maitland, and Marchand silently watching. Once or
twice the door of the after-cabin opened, and Napoleon, glancing
out and observing Byng's examination, bowed in acknowledge-
ment of the delicacy with which it was being conducted.

Finally, Byng came to two boxes containing the money. Marchand asked permission to remove such a sum as would be necessary for paying the wages of the servants who were to be left behind and for clearing up other expenses. Cockburn nodded. The
second box was placed in Maitland's charge, and Marchand
signed it over to him: "On the 7th of August, I have left on
board the *Bellerophon,* in charge of Captain Maitland, the sum
of eighty thousand francs, in four thousand gold Napoleons." In
return he received Maitland's receipt for it: "I acknowledge to
have received a box with four paper packages, *said* to contain four
thousand gold Napoleons, the property of Napoleon Buonaparte."

Shortly before eleven o'clock Byng finished. Cockburn, Maitland, and he left the cabin. After the somber tensions that had
suffused the room during the search, the sunlight, sea-view, and
breeze were refreshing. They watched as a party of seamen car-

ried the trunks, boxes, and bags from the cabin onto the deck and lowered them into the boats waiting to take them to the *North-umberland*. Already the children and nine of the servants bound for St. Helena had been ferried to that frigate. Cockburn and Maitland waited for Keith to arrive from the *Tonnant*. Behind them on the quarterdeck, a captain's guard of marines, with a drummer beside them, stood ranked at ease. The officers and mid-shipmen were also ranged about the quarterdeck, while in the waist and forecastle were drawn up as many of the ship's com-pany as could be accommodated there. The breeze carried the murmur of their voices; the sun heightened the sharp colors of their dress uniforms and gleamed from the rims of their var-nished caps.

It was nearing eleven-thirty when Keith's barge was at last seen leaving the *Tonnant*'s side. It came toward the *Bellerophon* —Keith's ensign snapping from its staff, spray puffing up from its bow, its clean-lined oars rising and falling in rhythm. Domi-nating all was the erectly seated figure of Admiral Lord Keith, attired in the blues and whites and golds of a full-dress uniform emblazoned with the decorations of his order. The barge neared, then was lost to view as it came alongside and was secured. Com-mands sounded smartly; the men on the frigate's decks snapped to attention; the bosun's pipe shrilled; and then Admiral Keith came up the gangway to receive the salutes of the assembled crew.

As soon as Keith came on board, Bertrand went to Napoleon's cabin to announce his arrival. Long minutes passed, and neither of them appeared. Keith spent the time talking with Cockburn about the examination of Napoleon's effects, checking the cap-tain's guard of marines, and informing Maitland that when Na-poleon came out he was to be accorded the usual salute given to a general officer. He also acquainted the captain with the asser-tions made against him by Las Cases that morning.

More time passed, and still the door of the outer cabin re-mained closed. Cockburn, anxious to return to the *Northumber-*

land, impatiently remarked to Keith that Napole<
put in mind of their waiting upon him. "No, no," ʲ
equably. "Much greater men than either you or]
longer for him before now. Let him take his time; let him take
his time." At length, Bertrand rejoined them. The Emperor, he
said, would receive Admiral Keith now. After giving Cockburn
leave to return to his ship, Keith followed Bertrand to the after-
cabin.

Alone together, Napoleon and Keith conversed easily and
civilly. Their mutual respect, which had grown during this affair,
lent a freeness and intimacy to the meeting that neither depre-
ciated. Not that Napoleon had, at this hour, become reconciled to
his fate. He remained anxious and indignant about it; he repeated his former protestations to Keith; he asked the admiral's
advice about the law and opportunities for appeal to it. Again,
he voiced his displeasure at being styled "General." "If not Emperor, I am First Consul," he insisted. "You made treaties with
me as such."

"Yes, Sir," Keith answered readily, "but when you crushed
the Commonwealth, you sank that title in Emperor."

Frowning, Napoleon declared that he would not quit England
alive. Keith's reply was unexpected: he laughed. Napoleon's eyebrows arched in surprise. "Would you go to St. Helena, Admiral?" he asked. "Oh, no. It will be death. I do not voluntarily
go either from this ship, or from England. It is your admiral who
takes me. I will not leave this ship; you must take me by force."

Keith shook his head in disapproval. "I surely hope, Sir," he
said, "that you will not reduce an officer like me to do so disagreeable an act as to use force towards your person."

"Oh, no!" Napoleon assured him. "But you shall order me."

Keith bowed, but said nothing. Together, they walked to the
door of the cabin. "Admiral," Napoleon said, "I have given you
my solemn protest in writing. I now repeat: I will not go out of
this ship but by force."

Keith nodded. "My barge is ready for your reception," he said, "and if you choose to go in her, please to warn them [Napoleon's suite] and the ladies. It depends on you, and," he finished, his hand on the doorknob, "I order you to go."

"Let us go."

"I shall attend you at your convenience in my barge," Keith informed him, "and I beg not to hurry you."

Napoleon thanked him, then said that he wished to speak to Bertrand. Bowing, Keith left the cabin. Another protracted spell of waiting ensued. Napoleon and Bertrand remained closeted, talking and going over last-minute correspondence. Most of the members of the suite were gathered in the outer cabin, from time to time casting anxious glances at the closed door of the inner cabin. Some busied themselves writing letters; some just sat quietly. On the whole, those accompanying Napoleon appeared calmer than those who were remaining behind. Savary and Lallemand, in particular, were agitated; they stood tensely or paced the cabin, speaking tersely and making impatient gestures.

Keith and Maitland stayed outside on the quarterdeck, looking in on the Frenchmen from time to time. At one point Las Cases and Maitland engaged in earnest conversation on the quarterdeck. Keith, who was standing near by, caught part of their talk, which concerned Las Cases' charges with regard to Maitland's role in the negotiations at Rochefort. From what the admiral overheard, it appeared to him that Las Cases "by no means established the truth of the assertions which he had made."

Madame Bertrand was called into Napoleon's cabin. She remained with Napoleon and her husband for some time; and when she came out, she looked comparatively composed and serene. Whatever the interview had encompassed, it apparently had assured that she would indulge in no more emotional scenes that day. Montholon was then summoned by Napoleon. When he emerged from the after-cabin, he sought out Maitland on the quarterdeck. "I am directed by the Emperor," he announced, "to return you his thanks for the manner in which you have conducted yourself throughout the whole of this affair; and he desires me to say that the greatest cause of disappointment he feels in not being admitted to an interview with the Prince Regent is that he had intended to ask as a favor from his Royal Highness that you should be promoted to the rank of Rear Admiral."

Maitland acknowledged the compliment with a nod. "Although the request could not have been complied with under any circumstances, as it is contrary to the regulations of our naval service," he said, "yet I do not the less feel the kindness of the intention."

"He meant also," Montholon continued, "to have presented you with a box containing his portrait, but he understands you are determined not to accept it."

"In the situation I am placed in," Maitland said, "it is quite impossible I can receive any present from him."

"He is perfectly aware of the delicacy of your situation," Montholon said, "and approves of your conduct."

The matter of his conduct, and the serious charges brought against him by Las Cases that morning, had troubled Maitland no little since Keith had informed him of them. Now he said, "I feel much hurt that Count Las Cases should have stated to Lord Keith that I had promised Buonaparte should be well received in England, or indeed made promises of any sort. I have endeavored to conduct myself with integrity and honor throughout the whole of this transaction, and therefore cannot allow such an assertion to go uncontradicted."

Montholon waved his hand placatingly. "Oh," he explained, "Las Cases negotiated this business. It has turned out very differently from what he and all of us expected. He attributes the Emperor's situation to himself, and is therefore desirous of giving it the best countenance he can. But I can assure you," he added earnestly, "the Emperor is convinced your conduct has been most honorable—and that is my opinion also," he finished, taking Maitland's hand.

At last the door of the inner cabin was opened by Bertrand. He stepped aside, to reveal Napoleon standing at the threshold, his little cocked hat set firmly on his head, his face stern but composed. The assembled suite rose as one, bowing, as Napoleon stepped into the room. He was ready to leave. With a sob, Savary burst from the group and threw himself at Napoleon's feet. Bending, Napoleon raised him to his feet and embraced him. Next, he embraced Lallemand; and then, one by one, he bade farewell to those who were being left behind. Some, as they knelt to kiss his hand, shed tears; but Napoleon's eyes remained dry and his face expressionless. "Be happy, my friends," he told them. "We shall never see each other again, but my thoughts will never leave you nor any of those who have served me. Tell France that I pray for her."

Las Cases, who was standing near Keith by the outer doorway, turned to the admiral and remarked, "You see, my Lord, that the only persons who shed tears are those who remain."

At Napoleon's appearance on deck, silence fell over the ship. The assembled men, standing at attention, strained to catch a last glimpse of him. Five days had passed since they had last seen him on deck. They noted now that his face was unshaved, pale, and haggard, his small smile forced. His melancholy look and manner awed them and stirred them to pity. "Had his execution been about to take place," one of them reminisced later, "there could not have prevailed a more dead silence—so much so, that had a pin fallen from one of the tops to the deck, I am convinced it would have been heard; and to anyone who has known the general buzz of one of our seventy-fours [74-gun frigates], even at the quietest hour, it is a proof how deeply the attention of every man on board must have been riveted."

With a steady, firm step, Napoleon crossed the quarterdeck while the guard of marines presented arms and the drummer beat out three ruffles. He raised his hat to the guard in recognition of their salute, smiled at the officers of the *Bellerophon* as he passed through their ranks to where Maitland waited by the gangway. He stopped in front of Maitland, took off his hat again, and said, "Captain Maitland, I take this last opportunity of once more returning you my thanks for the manner in which you treated me while on board the *Bellerophon*; and also that you will convey them to the officers and ship's company you command." Then, turning to the officers standing by Maitland, he added, "Gentlemen, I have requested your captain to express my gratitude to you for your attention to me and to those who have followed my fortunes."

He walked to the head of the gangway; but, before descending it, he paused again and, turning, removed his hat once more and bowed two or three times to the ship's company assembled in the waist and on the forecastle. Then, grasping the manropes, he walked down the gangway and into the waiting barge.

The Bertrands, the Montholons, Gourgaud, and Las Cases then approached the gangway, preparatory to joining Napoleon in the boat. Just before Madame Bertrand descended, she turned aside and went up to Maitland. "Captain Maitland," she said, her voice soft and friendly, "you called me a very foolish woman this morning, but I should be sorry to part with you on bad terms. Have you any objection to shaking hands with me? As God knows if we shall ever meet again."

Maitland bowed. "Very far from it," he said. "I should be extremely sorry if you left the ship without receiving my good wishes for your happiness and prosperity; and if, in the warmth of my temper and under the harassing circumstances of my situation, I have said anything unpleasant, I most sincerely beg your pardon, and hope you will forgive and forget it."

They shook hands. Keith saw her and the others into their places in the barge, then boarded it himself. Napoleon looked up at him inquiringly. "What!" he said. "Do you take the trouble to come in the boat too? I am obliged to you, Admiral. Sit by me," he invited, "and we shall chat."

At Keith's word, the barge shoved off. When it had pulled clear of the *Bellerophon* by about thirty yards, Napoleon turned to look back at the frigate. He saw the railings and ports crowded with the officers and men of the ship's company, all gazing silently

›d, and pulling off his hat, he bowed
...d to the men. Then he resumed his
...Keith.

...e barge widened the gap between it-
...yes on Napoleon. Neither he nor his
...heir association with Napoleon. He
...ed along the railings and at the ports
...hat prevailed among them. Beckoning
his ... ...e gestured toward the departing barge
and then toward the men in the ship's waist and on the forecastle.
"What do the people say of him?" he asked.

"Why, Sir," his servant replied, "I heard several of them conversing together about him this morning; when one of them observed, 'Well, they may abuse that man as much as they please;
but if the people of England knew him as well as we do, they
would not hurt a hair of his head'; in which the others agreed."

An extraordinary reaction, Maitland thought, for Napoleon
had gone through the ship's company only once, and that immediately after he had come on board. Even then he had not spoken
to any of the men, but merely had returned their salutes by removing his hat. For nearly a month now his presence on board
had meant privation for the crew: they had not been allowed to
see their wives or friends, had not been permitted to go ashore,
had been required to keep watch while in port, and had been so
crowded by the addition of the Frenchmen that many were hard
pressed to find space in which to sling their hammocks. Nor had
their attitude toward Napoleon been influenced by any material
reward from him. When Napoleon left the ship, Maitland knew,
he had distributed only twenty Napoleons to Maitland's steward,
fifteen to one of the underservants, and ten to the cook; so no one
could assert that he had purchased the goodwill of the crew.

And yet, Maitland could understand the feelings of his men
toward their captive. In a way, they were like his own. "It may
appear surprising," he stated later,

that a possibility could exist of a British officer, being prejudiced in favour of one who had caused so many calamities to his country; but to such an extent did he possess the power of pleasing, that there are few people who could have sat at the same table with him for nearly a month, as I did, without feeling a sensation of pity, allied perhaps to regret, that a man possessed of so many fascinating qualities, and who had held so high a station in life, should be reduced to the situation in which I saw him.

As the barge made way toward the *Northumberland,* Napoleon seemed relaxed and in good humor. The solemn scene on the *Bellerophon* and that to come on the *Northumberland* appeared to have been put out of his mind. He laughed at Mesdames Bertrand and Montholon and joked with them about being seasick; and he and Keith carried on a lively conversation. They talked of Egypt and St. Helena. Pointing to Keith's ship, Napoleon asked if that was the *Tonnant* of Aboukir? If the *Bellerophon* was old? Why Keith had changed his name from Elphinstone, by which Napoleon had known him ever since Toulon?

But he turned grave again when the barge reached the *Northumberland's* side. The other passengers fell silent; while from the ship utter silence greeted them. The men on the frigate strained for their first glimpse of Napoleon. Cockburn, solemn and anxious, stood at the gangway. Behind him, the quarterdeck was crowded with officers; a guard of marines occupied the front of the poop; and the ship's company was drawn up at quarters in the waist and on the forecastle.

Bertrand ascended first, bowed to Cockburn, announced Napoleon's arrival, and then stepped aside. Slowly, Napoleon mounted the gangway, and reaching the quarterdeck, raised his hat in greeting to Cockburn and the officers, all of whom had bared their heads. The guard presented arms and the drum rolled out its salute. Then the rest of the suite quickly came aboard. "Lord Keith was the last who quitted the barge," wrote William Warden, the *Northumberland's* surgeon, "and I cannot give you a more compleat idea of the wrapped attention of all on board to the figure of Napoleon, than that his Lordship, high as he is in naval character, Admiral also of the Channel Fleet, to which we belonged, and arrayed in the full uniform of his rank, emblazoned with the decorations of his order, did not seem to be noticed, nor scarcely even to be seen, among the group which was subject to him."

Napoleon's appearance, however, rudely shocked many of those on board who, believing the myths that had grown about him the past twenty years, had drawn idealized portraits of him. "I felt very much disappointed," wrote Captain Charles Ross of the *Northumberland*,

> as I believe everybody else did, in his appearance, as I have never seen a picture of him that conveys any likeness to what he really is. He appears by no means that active man he is said to be. He is fat, rather what we call pot-bellied, and altho' his leg is well-shaped, it is rather clumsy, and his walk appears rather affected, something between a waddle and a swagger—but probably not being used to the motion of the ship might have given him that appearance. He is very sallow and [has] quite light *grey Eyes*, rather thin, greasy-looking brown hair, and altogether a very nasty, priestlike-looking fellow.

And Colonel George Bingham, commander of the 53d Regiment, found "his hair out of powder and rather greasy, his person corpulent, his neck short, and his *tout ensemble* not at all giving an idea that he had been so great or was so extraordinary a man."

These unflattering descriptions, so at variance with those of the officers and men of the *Bellerophon*, are not really to be wondered at. For the men of the *Bellerophon*, the aura of the Emperor had always clung to Napoleon. But to the men of the *Northumberland* he was "General" Bonaparte, a prisoner under sentence, whose presence on board their ship meant not glory and public attention but rather the unwelcome duty of a long, monotonous voyage. And this short, paunchy, sallow-faced fellow did not impress them.

Napoleon spoke briefly to Cockburn and requested an introduction to the ship's captain. He, Cockburn, and Keith walked toward the after-cabin, pausing a number of times while Napoleon was introduced to some of the men on the quarterdeck: Colonel Bingham; an officer of the artillery; Captain Beattie of the marines; and Lord William Lowther and Mr. William Lyttelton, two members of Parliament whom Cockburn had invited on board to witness the event. Napoleon chatted amiably with them for a short while, then continued on into the cabin, where Cockburn presented Captain Ross to him.

With 1,080 men on board, space on the *Northumberland* was at a premium; the addition of Napoleon and his attendants would congest the quarters still more. Cockburn had allocated to them what space he could, giving them the area abaft the mizzenmast. Las Cases described it:

The space ... contained two public and two private cabins; the first was a dining-room about ten feet broad, and extending the whole width of the ship, lighted by a port-hole at each end, and a sky-light above. The drawing room was composed of all the remaining space, diminished by two symmetrical cabins on the right and left, each having an entry from the dining or mess-room, and another from the drawing-room. The Emperor occupied that on the left, in which his camp-bedstead had been put up; that on the right was appropriated to the Admiral.

More rigid in his interpretation of orders than either Keith or Maitland was, Cockburn had determined that Napoleon would be granted no concessions beyond the privileges that protocol accorded to a general officer. On this ship, restrictions in keeping with Napoleon's status as a state prisoner would be observed closely, a prominent one being a limit on the amount of living space to be given him. Accordingly, Cockburn had designated the drawing room as a public room rather than a private cabin for Napoleon and his suite. Thus, as soon as he had introduced Ross to Napoleon, he invited Lord Lowther, Mr. Lyttelton, and Colonel Bingham into the room. Napoleon—who no doubt did not miss the implications of the invitation—received them standing. Next, the ship's lieutenants were brought in and introduced; but as they spoke no French they merely bowed and retired. Napoleon conversed with the others for a time—particularly with Lyttelton, who spoke French fluently. Then, as the visitors prepared to retire, Napoleon turned to Keith and said, "Let us look at the cabin."

They inspected it, and Napoleon nodded approval. "This is very good, better than the *Bellerophon*," he pronounced, "for my little green bed is in it."

They went out onto the deck, where Keith took his final leave of Napoleon. They did not linger over their farewells. Before Keith left the ship to return to the *Tonnant*, he ascertained that Cockburn had clearly explained to those accompanying Napoleon the nature of the restraints under which they would live on St. Helena. At the same time he received from Bertrand a number of personal letters. The first was from the Grand Marshal himself:

MILORD,

I am leaving with the Emperor for the island of St. Helena, but I do not wish to stay there, desiring to return to Europe with my family at the end of the year. I beg you to obtain the necessary authorisation of your Government to this request.

A second letter from him contained a similar request on behalf of Marchand and two other domestics, Pierron and Le Page. More surprising in view of what had happened that morning on the *Bellerophon* was this letter from Gourgaud:

MILORD,

Honour having prevented me from quitting the Emperor Napoleon in his misfortune, I am accompanying him to St. Helena, but my feelings for my family and my attachment to my country make me foresee a time when it will be impossible to resist the need to see once more my infirm and aged mother. I therefore beg your Lordship to make my position known to the ministers of His Royal Highness the Prince Regent and to obtain for me permission to return to Europe the day when I shall inform the Governor of St. Helena that I no longer wish to serve the Emperor Napoleon.

Madame Montholon had written in the same vein on behalf of herself and her husband and child. A last letter, written by the Polish captain Piontkowski, who was on the *Eurotas*, was in striking contrast to the others. He wrote:

MILORD,

It is your humanity and magnanimity which I implore, and it is to your heart that I speak in order to obtain permission to accompany my unfortunate sovereign. I have lost my entire fortune and my sentiments do not allow me to serve any other sovereign without betraying him. There is no interest which guides me and I should be very happy to serve as one of the least of the domestic staff. Being without any honest means of livelihood my only alternative is death, and I beg you to confer a favour on me to prevent the crime that sorrow and despair might compel me to commit. Be so good my lord as to save an unhappy man by agreeing to my humble request, and use your interest to have me included among the twelve domestic servants. I shall never cease to regard you as the author of my happiness.*

We do not know if Napoleon was aware of these letters. If he was, we do not know whether he approved or disapproved of them. It may even be that he had directed them to be written, hoping that in some way the requests they contained would result in a mitigation of his sentence. But one can easily judge which letter Keith found most impressive.

After Keith had left him, Napoleon turned his attention to Lord Lowther and Mr. Lyttelton, with whom he talked for well over an hour on many subjects: his opinions of the British infantry, of Louis XVIII, of Tsar Alexander, and of the Prince Regent; the motives behind his invasion of Spain; the suicide of Mr. Samuel Whitbread, an outspoken supporter in Parliament of the legitimacy of Napoleon's rule in France; and the return from Elba. Primarily, however, Napoleon stressed his shock and in-

---

* Regarding Piontkowski's request, Melville wrote to Keith on August 14: "Partly out of compassion to the poor Pole, who is at least faithful to Bonaparte, and partly because he seems to be a person who will be less mischievous at St. Helena than in his own country, we have determined to send him out with Sir Hudson Lowe."

dignation at being sent to St. Helena. In confining him there, he charged, England was acting like a petty aristocratic power and not like a great free people. He had been mistaken in relying upon English generosity. "I would have given my word of honor to have remained quiet and to have held no political correspondence in England," he said. "I would have pledged myself not to quit the place assigned me, but to live as a simple individual."

"That seems next to impossible," Lyttelton answered; "for though you have had great reverse, you could never so far forget what you had been as to conceive yourself to be, or conduct yourself as, a simple individual."

"But why not let me remain in England upon my pledge of honor?" Napoleon insisted.

"You forget," Lyttelton reminded him, "that some hundreds of French officers violated their pledge of honor, and that you not only did not express any indignation against them, but received them with particular distinction—Lefebvre Desnouettes,* for instance."

To this Napoleon made no reply; and soon after, the conversation ended, the two Englishmen prepared to go ashore, and Napoleon retired to the cabin. After a while he was visited by Savary and Lallemand, whom Maitland had brought on board for a last farewell. The three talked for a considerable time, and at length Maitland entered the cabin to inform Savary and Lallemand that it was time to return to the *Bellerophon.* Once again Napoleon embraced them affectionately, putting his arms around them and touching their cheeks with his. Watching, Maitland noted that "Napoleon was firm and collected; but, in turning from him, the tears were streaming from their eyes."†

As evening drew on, activity quickened on the vessels under Admiral Keith's command; and at six o'clock the *Tonnant,* the *Bellerophon,* the *Eurotas,* the *Myrmidon,* and the express schoo-

---

* A marshal of France who served Louis XVIII after Napoleon's first abdication, but sided with Napoleon during the Hundred Days.

† Savary and Lallemand were deported to Malta and interned there. They were freed in April 1816.

ner weighed, made sail, and stood to the south and west, bound back to Plymouth. Cockburn sent off a dispatch to the Admiralty giving notice that Napoleon was aboard the *Northumberland*. The *Northumberland*, the *Bucephalus*, the *Ceylon*, and the *Nimble* remained off Berry Head to await the ships being outfitted in Plymouth; as soon as the new ships arrived, the two-month-long voyage would begin.

It was hazy, and a fine rain began sifting down after dinner while the *Northumberland* prepared to get under weigh. The cutter *Nimble*, left behind by Keith to act as courier for any messages from Cockburn, was patrolling the waters around the frigate, where, despite the late hour, the onset of the drizzle, and the distance that the ships lay offshore, a number of boats from the vicinity of Tor Bay lingered. Suddenly, as one of these boats, laden with a party of eight or nine persons from Torquay, rounded the bow of the *Northumberland*, it was met head-on by the *Nimble*. Smashed and overturned, the small boat sank at once, its passengers and crew flung into the water. Two of the young women in the boat—a Miss Edwards and a Miss Allin—were drowned. The first lieutenant of the *Northumberland*, who had witnessed the collision, leaped into the sea and succeeded in rescuing the wife and child of one of the other passengers; and the cutter's crew saved the remaining members of the shore party. The bodies of Miss Edwards and Miss Allin were not recovered. When at half-past seven the *Northumberland* weighed and made sail to the southward, the stain of death still lay over the darkening waters.

It now remained only for the other vessels assigned to Cockburn's squadron to join the *Northumberland*. When daybreak on August 8 revealed only the brig *Zenobia* coming out to rendezvous with her, Cockburn impatiently edged the ships westward, closer to the longitude of Plymouth Sound. It was a gray morning; low clouds flung down curtains of rain, obscuring the horizon, and a stiff breeze and lively seas buffeted the ships' heads and made the going heavy. At eleven o'clock the frigate *Havannah* joined the company, and early in the afternoon the brig *Peruvian* came up. But although the weather cleared and turned fine during the afternoon, no more ships reported. The squadron lay to off the Eddystone Light, a few leagues out from the entrance to the Sound. There, in order to relieve the congestion on his ship, Cockburn sent part of the 53d Regiment on board the *Havannah*. Napoleon did not appear on deck that day, nor did many of his companions. The inclement weather, seasickness, and perhaps their somber thoughts kept them to their quarters.

At dawn on August 9, the remaining ships of the squadron came into sight. The *Zephyr*, the *Ferret*, the *Redpole*, the *Icarus* —all but the storeship *Weymouth* joined. Cockburn decided to sail at once and leave the *Weymouth* to follow when she could. Signals flew between the ships; and at nine o'clock the *Northumberland* came to the wind on the starboard tack and made all possible sail, with the escort ships falling into position around her. They bore westward as they stood out of the Channel, bound for St. Helena. Moderate breezes and clear, sunny weather saw them on their way.

Napoleon left his cabin at eleven o'clock for half an hour's walk on the quarterdeck. He strolled back and forth, talking with Cockburn and Bingham about Waterloo, and the reasons for his defeat there. He was talkative and appeared healthy and in good spirits. He spent the rest of the day in his cabin. At eight o'clock in the evening, Lizard Point rose into view five and a half leagues west by north, and Pendennis Castle reared its towers five leagues to the northwest in Falmouth. When dawn came, England would be out of sight.

For a time, the rival-party newspapers battled on about the justice or injustice of Napoleon's fate. Capel Lofft addressed another long letter to the *Morning Chronicle*, decrying the Ministry's action. The *Chronicle* revealed that it had received over a hundred letters on the affair from different parts of England and that Lofft's letters had "evidently made a strong sensation." It predicted that the ministers would apply for an Act of Parliament "to indemnify them (as well as to authorize his Majesty to detain Bonaparte during pleasure), as it is evidently against the law."

What an inestimable proof of the superiority of our Constitution, if it had been shewn that the moment Bonaparte touched the sacred soil of Britain he would have been entitled to a fair trial according to the laws of the land. If our Ministers had consulted the true honour of the Sovereign and the glory of the country, they would have said to the sovereigns of Europe, "By your declaration of the 13th of March, you filed a Bill of Indictment against this *brother* Sovereign (as you had all acknowledged him to be), you accused him of violating a treaty which you concluded with him in that character. All his former acts were by that treaty laid asleep. Here he is a prisoner. Bring him to trial. He stands on his defence. No man can come within the jurisdiction of England without being entitled to his trial." This ought to have been the language of the British Government; and if they had done this, a new and curious case would have occurred in the public law of nations.

The Courier bade a different farewell to the man whose presence off the shores of England had filled so many columns of print during the preceding fortnight:

Thus departs for ever from the scene of European politics and from political life (at least let us trust that it is so decreed), one of the most extraordinary characters that has ever appeared. Whether we regard his elevation or his fall—the talents he possessed and the talents he abased—the crimes he committed, countless, enormous and unnecessary—the difficulties he had to overcome—the means by which he overcame them—the great skill with which he built up the fabric of a colossal power, and the still greater skill with which he destroyed it.— To no one tyrant that ever lived can he be very closely compared. Yet, perhaps, we shall find in him some feature, some resemblance to each. If pity were a discriminating feeling, we should be more surprised than we are at the sympathy some have expressed for him in his humiliation and fall. But we would request those who are disposed to yield to this feeling not entirely to forget upon whom they are disposed to bestow it. We would desire them to remember that when they look at him (thank God! Europe is destined to look at him no more), they behold the cause of the death of hundreds of thousands of human beings, not cut off in the fight for independence or for freedom, but cut off for the gratification of his own personal ambition and pride; that they behold in him the assassin of some of the noblest of human creatures; of the Duke D'Enghien, whose whole life had been a life of honour; of that confiding but virtuous black, Toussaint L'Ouverture; of Pichegru, who refused to execute the orders of the Jacobin butchers to give no quarter to the English and Hanoverians; of our own brave countryman, Captain Wright; of that noble Tyrolean, Hofer; of many others whose names are known only to that Being who will not suffer their blood to be shed in vain; that when they survey him they view a tyrant who had threatened to make this great and glorious land a territory unfit for the residence of human beings; that to pity his fall is to be sorry that cruelty is deprived of the power of torturing the human race, that tyranny is shorn of its strength, and that he who poured out the blood of man like water is unable longer to spill any blood but his own; it is to repine at the merciful dispensations of Providence; and to question that goodness which has at last delivered us from a visitation more awful and terrible in its effects than plague, pestilence, and famine.

APPENDIXES

Appendix I

Persons Composing Napoleon's Suite

On the Bellerophon

GENERALS. Lieutenant General Count Bertrand, Grand Marshal. Lieutenant General the Duke of Rovigo. Lieutenant General Baron Lallemand, His Majesty's aide-de-camp. Brigadier General Count de Montholon, His Majesty's aide-de-camp. Count de Las Cases, Councillor of State.

LADIES. Countess Bertrand. Countess de Montholon.

CHILDREN. Three children of Countess Bertrand. One child of Countess de Montholon.

OFFICERS. M. de Planat, Lieutenant Colonel. M. Maingaut, His Majesty's surgeon. M. Las Cases, page.

SERVICE OF THE CHAMBER. Marchand, head valet. Gilli, valet. St. Denis, valet. Novarra, valet. Denis, chamber boy.

LIVERY. Archambaud, head footman. Gaudron, footman. Gentilini, footman.

FOOD SERVICE. Fontain, maître d'hôtel. Pieron, butler. La Fosse, cook. Le Page, cook.

SERVANTS OF THE PERSONS ACCOMPANYING HIS MAJESTY. Two lady's maids of Countess Bertrand. One lady's maid of Countess de Montholon. One valet of the Duke of Rovigo. One valet of Count Bertrand. One valet of Count de Montholon. One footman of Count Bertrand.

On the Myrmidon

OFFICERS. Lieutenant Colonel Resigni. Lieutenant Colonel Schultz. Captain Autrie. Captain Mesener. Captain Piontkowski. Lieutenant Rivière. Second Lieutenant Ste.-Catherine.

MEMBERS OF HIS MAJESTY'S HOUSEHOLD. Cipriani, steward. Santini, usher. Chauvin, usher. Rousseau, lamplighter. Archambaud, footman. Joseph, footman. Le Charron, footman. Lisiaux, pantry man. Ortini, footman. Fumeau, footman.

Appendix II

Mackenrot's Writ

George the Third by the Grace of God of the United Kingdom of Great Britain and Ireland King, Defender of the Faith, to Napoleon Bonaparte, Admiral Willaumez and Jerome Bonaparte greeting; We command you and every of you that all other things set aside and every of you appearing in your proper person before our right truly and well beloved Edward, Lord Ellenborough, our Chief Justice assigned to hold pleas in our court before us on Friday the tenth of November by nine of the clock in the forenoon of the same day to testify the truth according to your knowledge in a certain action now in our Court before us in our said Court depending between Sir Alexander Forrester Cochrane, Knight, plaintiff, and Anthony Mackenrot, defendant of a plea of trespass on the part of the defendant, and at the aforesaid day by a jury of the country between the parties aforesaid of the place aforesaid to be tried; and this you nor any of you shall in no wise omit under penalty of every of you of £100. Witness Edward, Lord Ellenborough of Westminster the fourteenth day of June in the fifty-fifth year of our reign.

LAW AND MARKHAM.

INDEX

Index